Chordal Approach to Learning Piano/Keys for Worship

Worship the Lord with gladness; come before Him with joyful songs. Psalms 100:2 NIV

Written by Susan Hall - Inspired by the Holy Spirit

Table of Contents

Introduction

This method of learning how to play chords on the keyboard is intended for those who wish to play with their church worship team. I was blessed to have started studying piano at the age of five. I became an accomplished pianist and could read most types of classical written musical notation by the time I entered college. I attended Berklee College of Music in Boston Massachusetts where, for the first time was asked to read "chord changes". I was confused as I had never been asked to do that before. At Berklee, I learned about a variety of chords not taught within the typical classical music course of study. Eventually, I was able to read from chord charts without any musical notation. Years later, I began playing with a worship team where notes were never provided. While there is immense value in learning to read musical notation, for those who want to play with their church worship team, it is not a necessary skill to have and often, especially for adults, becomes an obstacle for learning as written notation can be overwhelming to some when first learning to play.

I have met many people who comment about how they wish to be able to play keys on the worship team. I believe that God is leading me to help others understand the composition and basic technique of playing chords for worship on the keyboard. Worship music is usually a very simple style of music to play. My passion is to teach this skill to others who have a passion for worship music. With the Lord as my guide, I believe He will work through me to create a method that is understandable to those who possess a strong desire play. Practice will be necessary as anything worthwhile requires work, however with a regular practice routine of at least 25 minutes, 4-5 times per week, I have faith that the Lord will provide the results coming from the learner's desire to play.

The first part of this method will focus on the most basic chords used in worship music. Only the right hand will be used initially. The left hand will be added after a basic understanding of simple chords is reached.

"Let the message of Christ dwell among you richly as you teach and admonish one another with all wisdom through psalms, hymns, and songs from the Spirit, singing to God with gratitude in your hearts." Colossians 3:16 NIV

How this Method is Designed

Book 1 of NoNotes presents 33 common worship songs in the key of C major and A minor. Subsequent books will add additional keys progressing in complexity. After an explanation of the musical concepts, well-known worship songs are presented in two ways. The first way the song will be displayed is with the chord charts that a keyboard player would typically be presented by the worship team leader for a church service. The second way the song will be presented is by images of the keyboard with the proper keys for the chords highlighted in yellow. The worship songs in this book can all be played with knowing only six chords. Also included in this book are common variations of those six chords, but are optional in most cases. The goal is to become familiar enough with the six chords used in this book that the player would no longer need keyboard images to remember how to play the chords. How the chords are displayed in the keyboard images is only one common way that the chords can be played. After the player knows and understands the chords as shown, the ability to change the way the chords are played will come with practice and experience playing with a worship team. The initial form displayed in this book will sound appropriate and would be universally accepted by worship teams. Most of the keyboard images will only show one verse, one chorus, and one bridge as the chords will be the same in subsequent sections. The chord chart will have a common version of the song in its entirety. When possible, "Play Along!" links are added to allow the learner to play along with the song from a YouTube video in the same key.

Video Library (VL)

Each new concept and song will be explained and demonstrated through videos that have been uploaded to the NoNotes Worship YouTube channel.

NoNotesWorship - http://www.youtube.com/@NoNotes.Worship

Google Classroom

You are also invited to join the NoNotes Worship Google Classroom where you can ask questions and provide feedback. The goal of NoNotes is to make playing worship keys possible for anybody who has a desire and commitment to learn. Your suggestions will be welcomed and appreciated.

https://classroom.google.com/c/NjMxMTUzNjk3OTMx?cjc=kkqt4yb

The Direction of Sound on the Keyboard

When referring to how high or how low a pitch (sound) is on the keyboard, the pitch becomes higher as the keys move to the right, and the pitch becomes lower as the keys move to the left. Therefore, when notes are referred to as going up or down, this means moving to the right or left on the keyboard.

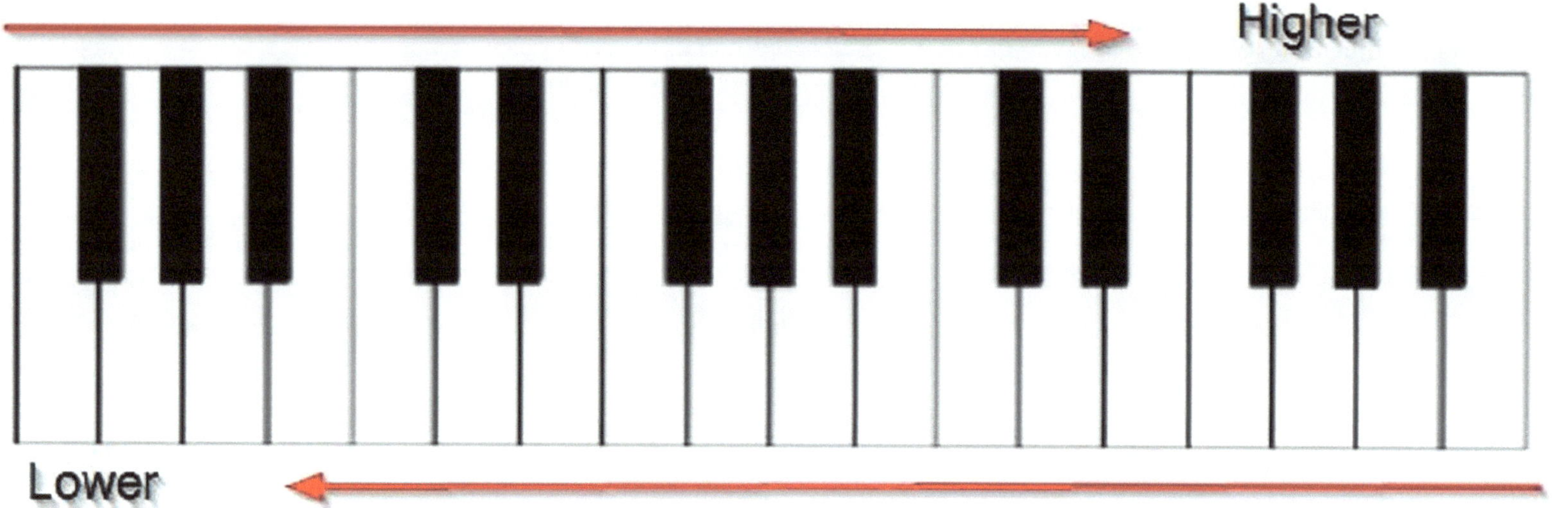

VL-1

Steps

The keys on the keyboard are separated by steps. The distance between to key REGARDLESS OF THE COLOR is a half-step. Two half steps equal a whole step.

Major and Minor Triads

The sound of major triads is oftentimes described as "bright" or "happy" while the sound of a minor triad is described as "dark" or "sad". The only difference between the two types of triads is the lowering of the third by one-half step.

Time

When time is referenced, think of it as the "beat" of the music. Most worship music has beats grouped in "threes" or "fours". There is an emphasis on the first beat of each group.

Notice how the piano keyboard only has 7 different letters. Then the pattern repeats.

Most worship chords can be played using three keys. For a C major chord, we use C, E, and G to make a C major **TRIAD**. A triad means three keys on the keyboard that "skip" over the next key. When we talk about triads, we call the name of the chord the **ROOT.** The next key (highlighted) is called the **"THIRD"** and the last (highlighted) is called the **"FIFTH"**.

Major and Minor Triads

The sound of major triads is oftentimes described as "bright" or "happy" while the sound of a minor triad is described as "dark" or "sad". The only difference between the two types of triads is the lowering of the third by one-half step.

C MAJOR TRIAD

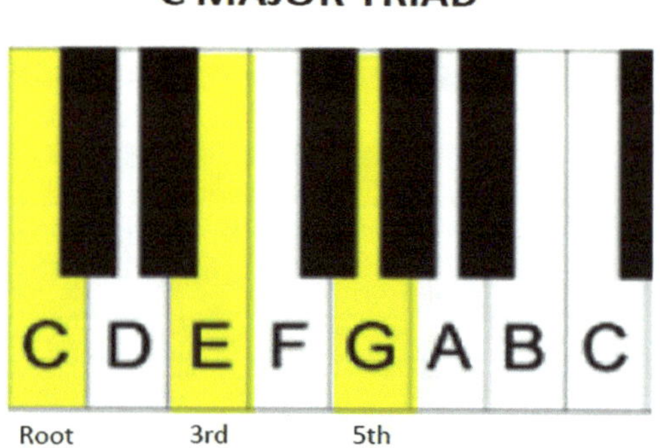

Next, we will see a triad in F major. The same concept applies. We are going to start on F and "skip" keys. An F major triad uses F, A, and C.

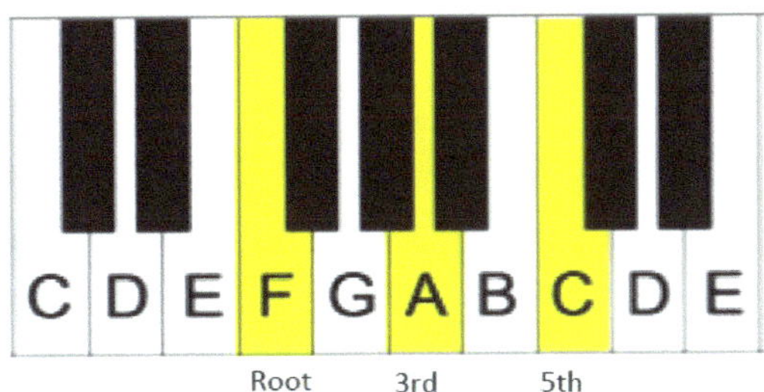

The last chord in this lesson will be a G major triad. Let's start with G and "skip" keys. The G major triad uses G, B, and D.

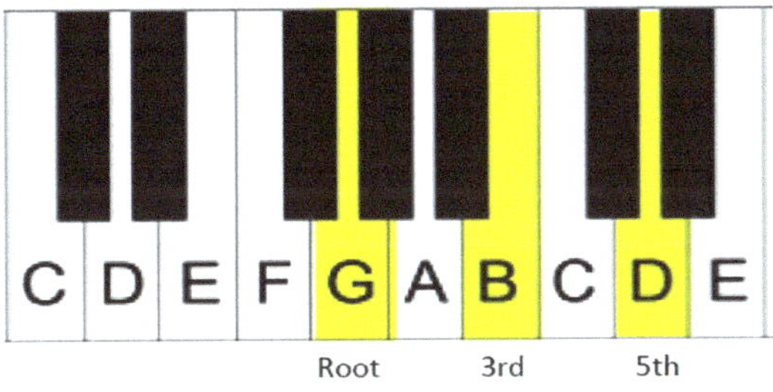

The Key of a Song

The word "key" is used in two ways. There are the "keys" on the keyboard, and then there is the "key" of a song.

The key of a **SONG** is referring to its **TONAL CENTER**. This is a crucial concept to understand, as there are a wide variety of vocal ranges in which singers can comfortably sing. The key of a song can frequently be determined by the last chord of the song. This is when the sounds of the chord movement feel as though it has reached "home".

The **MELODY** is the primary voice of the song. The melody is supported by the **HARMONY.** Most often the role of the worship keyboard is to support the melody and harmony sung by the worship singers using chords within their key of comfort.

Chord Progression

A chord progression is a series of chords that make up the foundation of a piece of music. The more different chords within a song, the more complex the chord progression.

The key of C is considered the easiest key for most keyboard players as it does not require the use of any of the black keys on the keyboard.

Fingers should be rounded when playing the keyboard. They should NOT be flat, as that will negatively impact dexterity. The numbers on the highlighted keys are for the recommended fingerings.

VL-2

Typical Chord Charts: The chords are indicated above the lyrics. When the word is sung with the chord symbol above it the specified chord is played. When sections are repeated exactly, this will be shown by either seeing a number followed by an **"X" (2X= 2 times)** or by diagonal lines at the beginning and the end of the repeated section - **//play section two times//, ///play section 3 times///**

Amazing Grace (Traditional)

```
      C                 F       C
Amazing grace, how sweet the sound!

                        G
That saved a wretch like me

      C                 F       C
I once was lost, but now I am found,

      C       G   C
Was blind, but now I see
```

How Great Thou Art (Traditional)

```
                        C
O Lord my God,

                        F
When I in awesome wonder,

                 C    G              C
Consider all, the worlds Thy hands have made

             C           F
I see the stars, I hear the rolling thunder,

                 C        G        C
Thy power throughout, the universe displayed

                   C        F        C
Then sings my soul, my Savior God to Thee,

                 G              C
How great Thou art, how great Thou art!

                   C        F        C
Then sings my soul, my Savior God to Thee,

                 G                C
How great Thou art, how great Thou art!
```

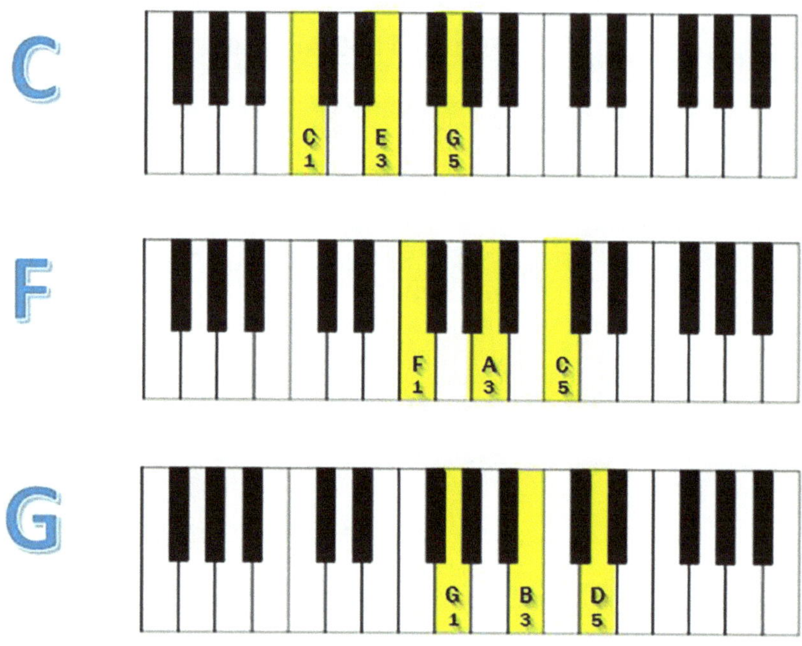

The keyboard player has flexibility in the manner that the chords are played in reference to "time". While the pulse must remain with the set time of the song, how the player articulates that time can vary. In the examples below, the dashes represent the beat where a chord is not played. The chord is not played on the dashes, but the beat continues.

Time = 3
Progression:
C-- C-- F-- C-- C-- C-- G-----
C-- C-- F-- C-- C-- G-- C-----

Another Option:
C-CC-CF-FC-CC-CC-CG-----
C-CC-CF-FC-CC-CG-GC-----

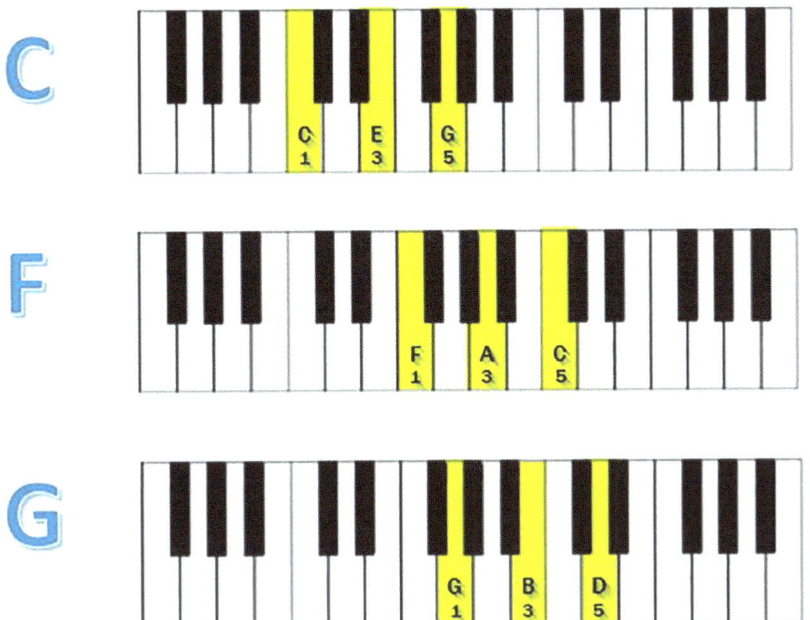

Time: 4
Progression:
Verse
C---F---C-G-C---
C---F---C-G-C---
Chorus
C-F-C---G---C---
C-F-C---G---C---

Another chord duration option: Playing the chord on each beat:

CCCCFFFFCCGGCCCC
CCCCFFFFCCGGCCCC
CCFFCCCCGGGGCCCC
CCFFCCCCGGGGCCCC

Major Triad INVERSIONS

Triads can be played in three different forms since they contain three keys (root, third, and fifth) The keys do not need to stay in order with the root at the bottom, the third in the middle, and the fifth on top. For a C major triad, **the root will always be C**, but C does not have to be placed as the lowest key. As we have seen previously, this is a C major triad in **ROOT POSITION**:

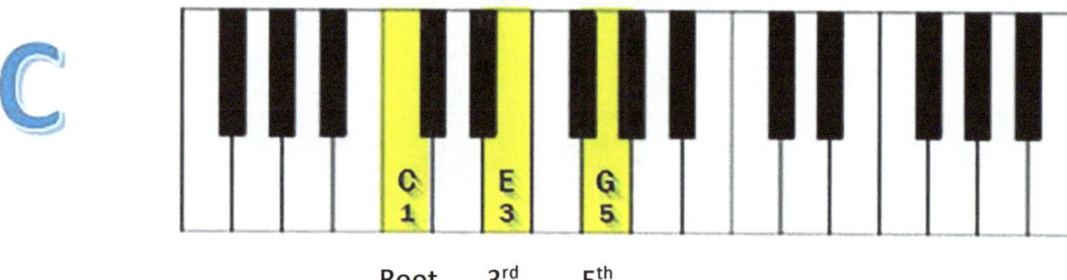

Recommended finger numbers will be the number *on* the key in the keyboard images. Using recommended fingers will allow for smother transition between chords.

To create the **FIRST INVERSION,** take the C from the bottom and move it to the next C *above.*

Finger Numbers

To create the **SECOND INVERSION,** take the E from the bottom and move it to the next E *above.*

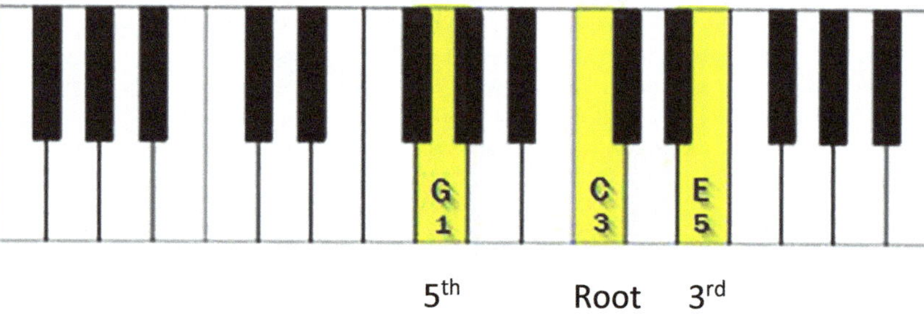

F Major Triads

Inversions function the same way for all triads.

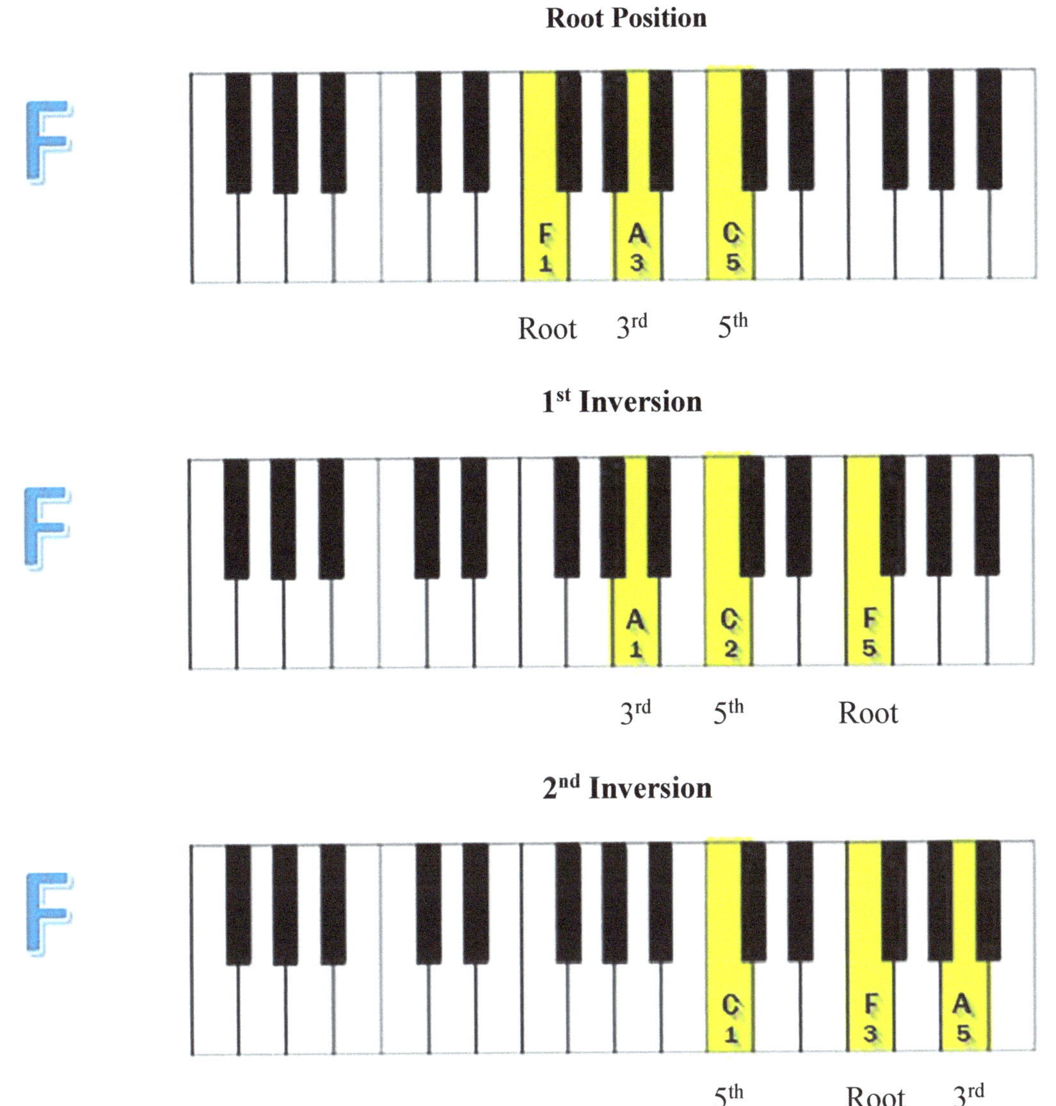

G Major Triads

Root Position

G

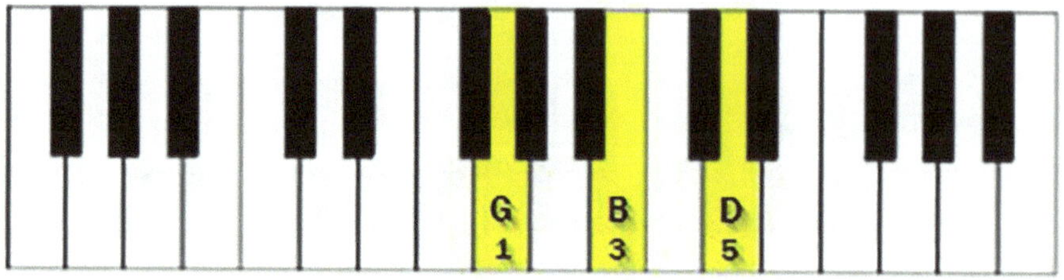

G
1

B
3

D
5

Root   3rd   5th

1st Inversion

G

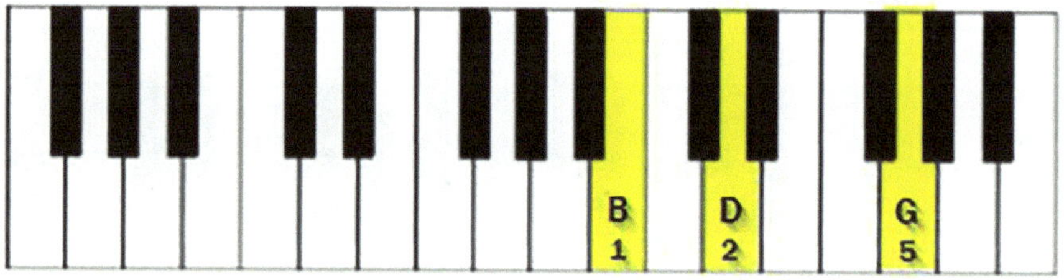

B
1

D
2

G
5

3rd   5th   Root

2nd Inversion

G

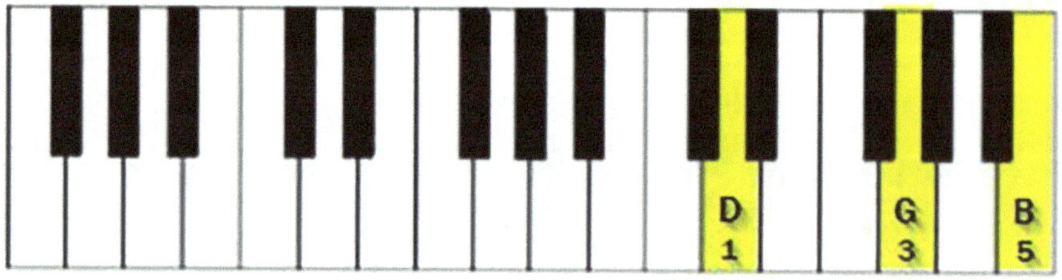

D
1

G
3

B
5

5th   Root   3rd

The Importance of Practicing Triad Inversions

It is crucial to practice inversions until they become recognizable by sight and by sound. To transition between chords smoothly and quickly, inversions must be used. To accomplish this, drill the inversions in the following ways:

1. **Block** – Playing all three keys of the triad at the same time beginning on the root of the chord, moving from the left end (lowest chord) of the keyboard, using each inversion, all the way to the right end (highest) of the keyboard. Then practice each inversion from the right end of the keyboard, all the way down to the left end of the keyboard finishing the triad in root position.

2. **Broken** – Play each key of the triad beginning with the root of the chord one at a time moving from the left end of the keyboard and progressing to the right end of the keyboard. Then do the same moving from the right end of the keyboard to the left end finishing the triad in root position.

3. **Finger Drills with Inversions** – In all three positions (Root, 1st inversion, and 2nd inversion) drill using broken chords with the following fingering:

Fingers to use for Root and 2nd inversion: 1,3,5,3,1 and 1,5,3,5,1

Fingers to use for 1st inversion: 1,2,5,2,1 and 1,5,2,5,1

Practice these with eyes open and closed when able to. When eyes are closed, the ability for the ear to pick up sounds strengthens.

Recognizing Patterns:

Nithin, (one of my students) shared with me that he was able to remember the keys for the inversion by recognizing patterns. One pattern he noticed was that there was always a larger space between keys in the first and second inversion than in the chord when in root position. Recognizing patterns is a useful tool for most learners.

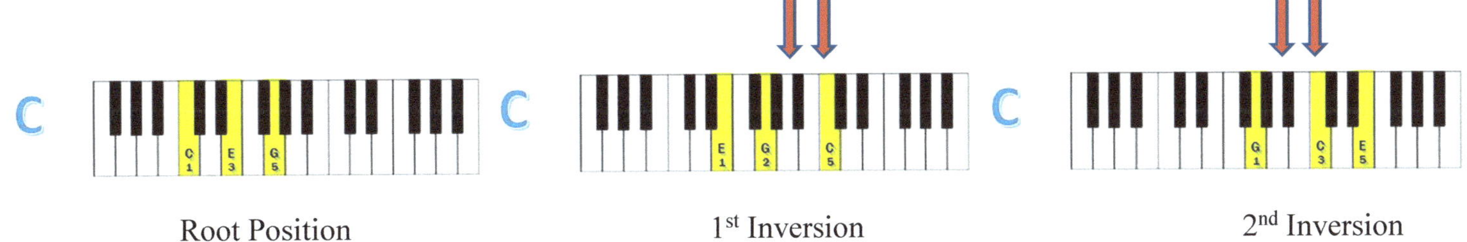

| Root Position | 1st Inversion | 2nd Inversion |

Amazing Grace Using Inversions

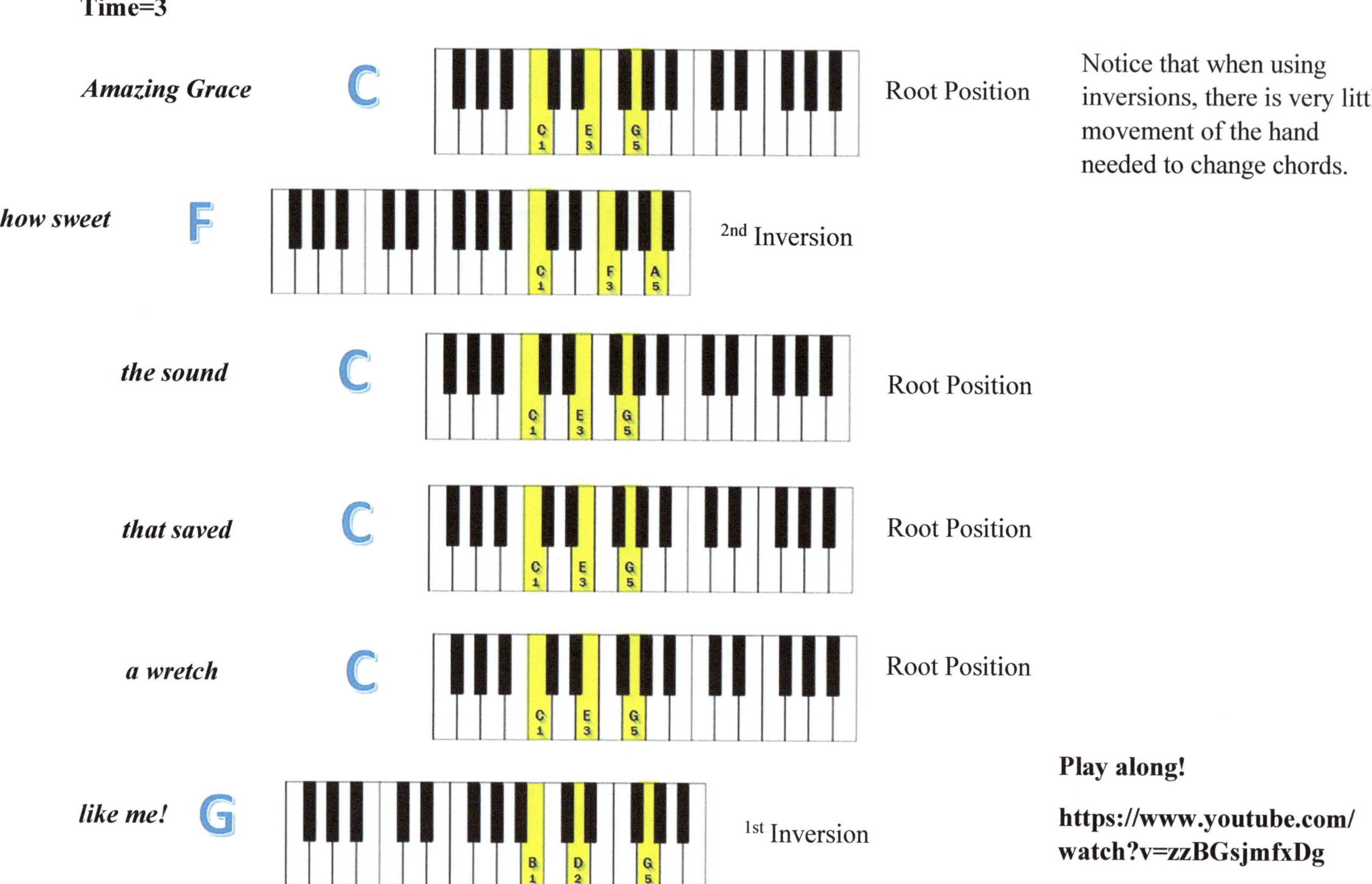

Notice that when using inversions, there is very little movement of the hand needed to change chords.

Play along!

https://www.youtube.com/watch?v=zzBGsjmfxDg

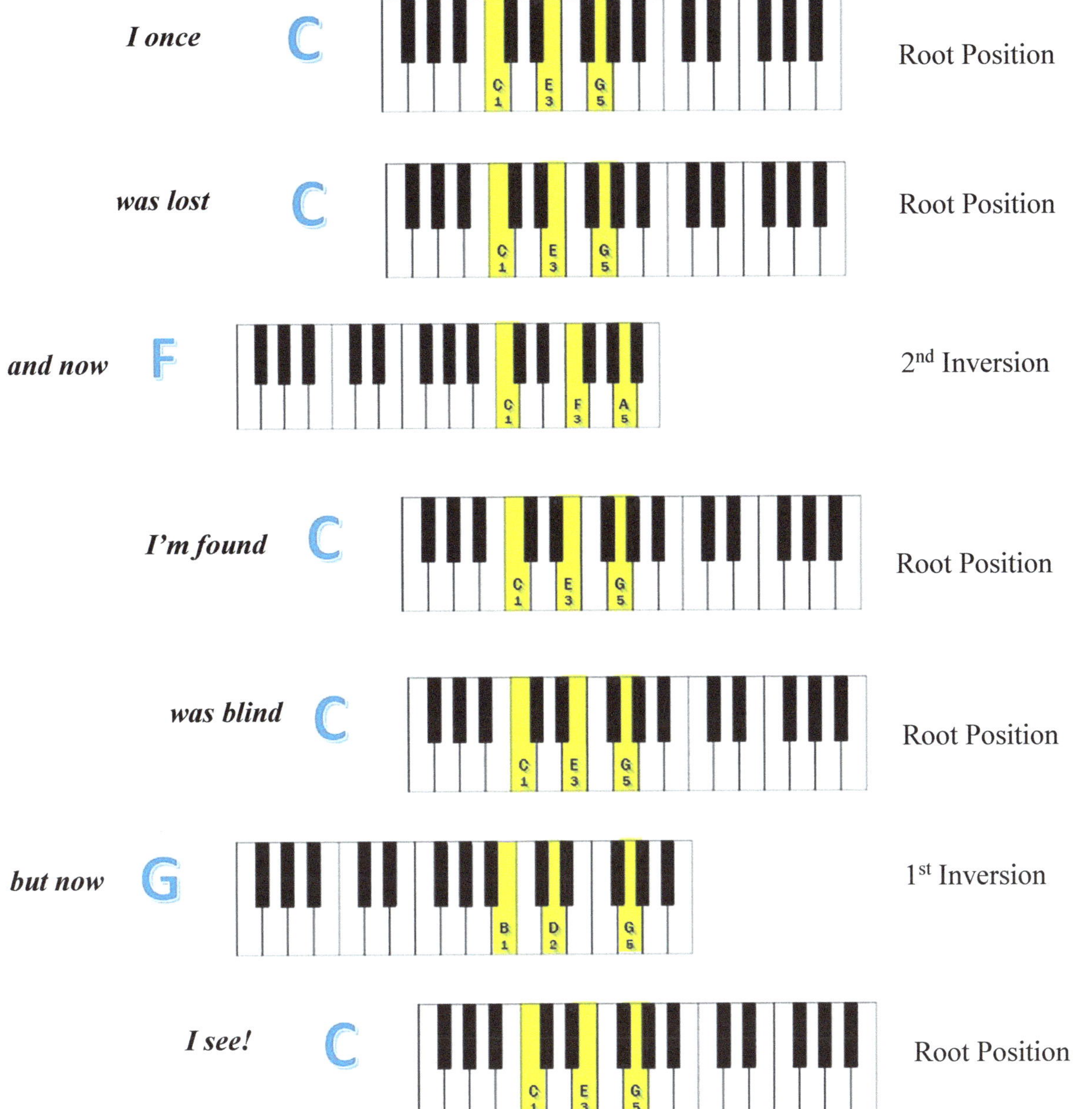

I once
C
C
1
E
3
G
5
Root Position

was lost
C
C
1
E
3
G
5
Root Position

and now
F
C
1
F
3
A
5
2nd Inversion

I'm found
C
C
1
E
3
G
5
Root Position

was blind
C
C
1
E
3
G
5
Root Position

but now
G
B
1
D
2
G
5
1st Inversion

I see!
C
C
1
E
3
G
5
Root Position

How Great Thou Art Using Inversions

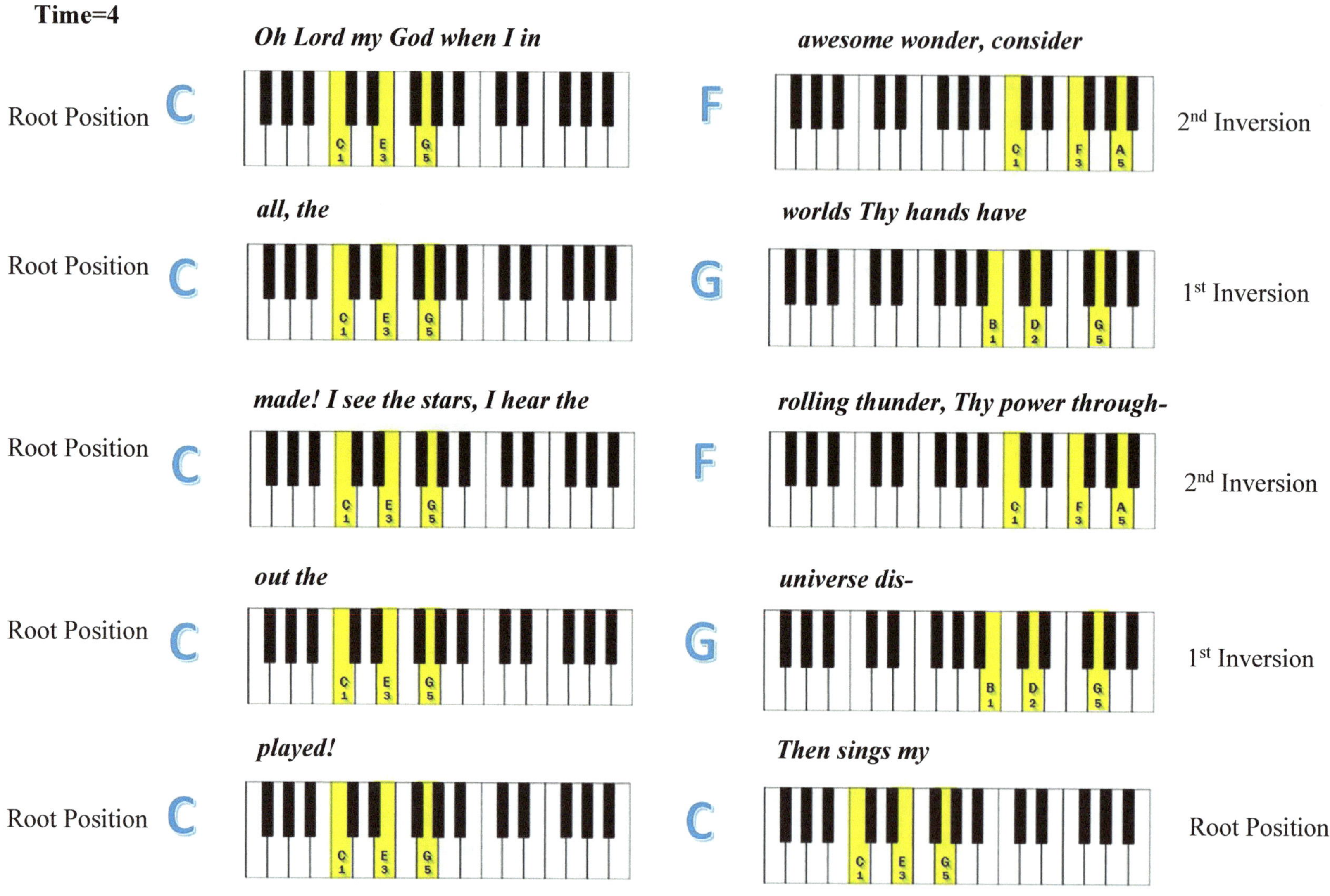

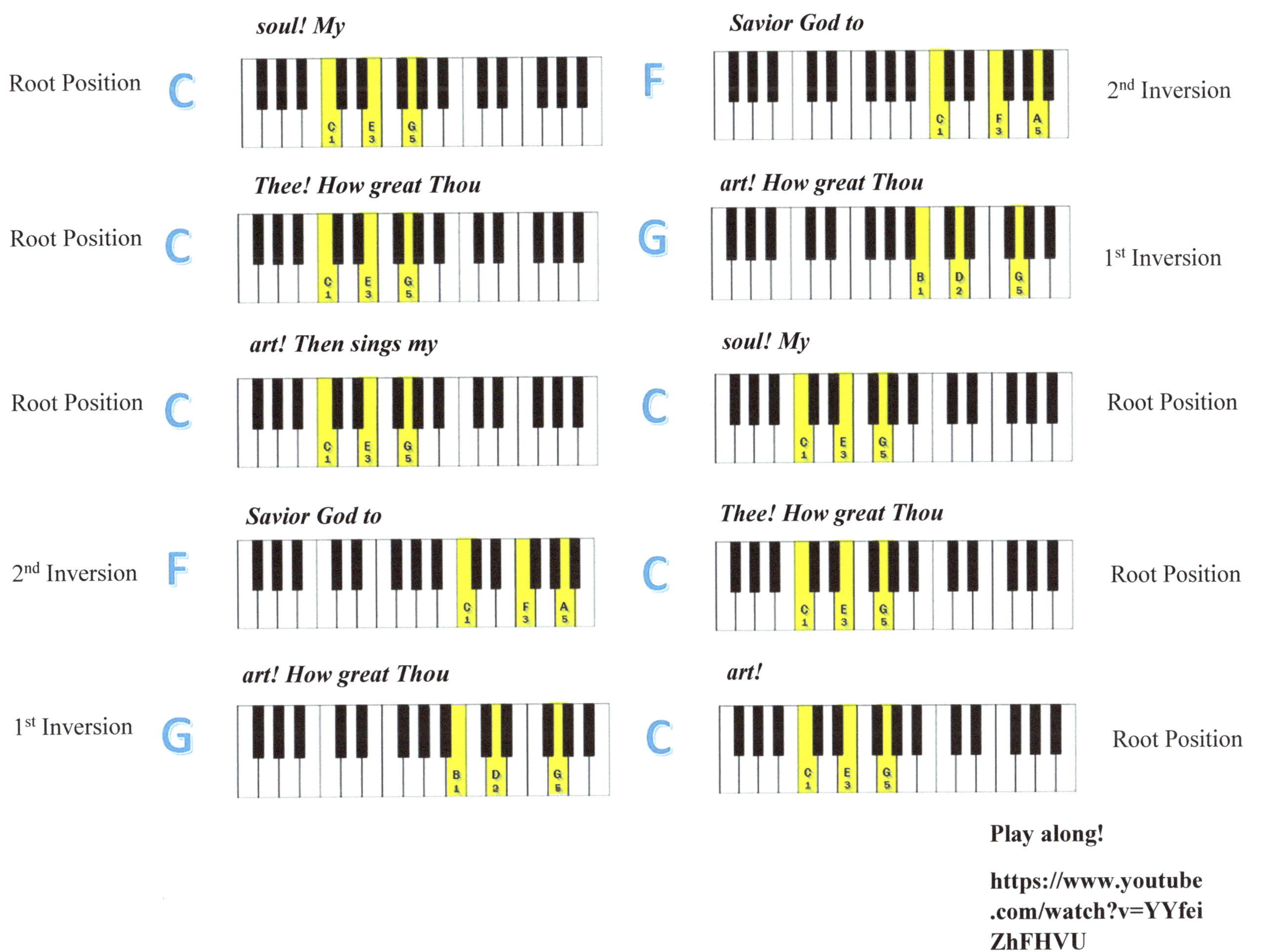

Play along!

https://www.youtube .com/watch?v=YYfei ZhFHVU

Time=4

C   F   G   C

I exalt Thee, I exalt Thee, I exalt Thee, O Lord!

I exalt Thee   C
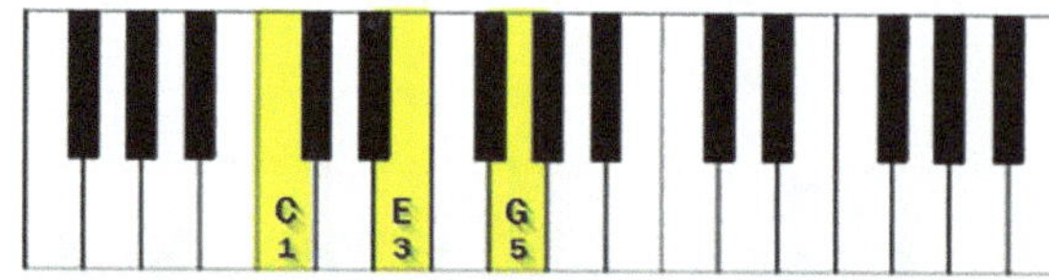

Root Position

I exalt Thee   F
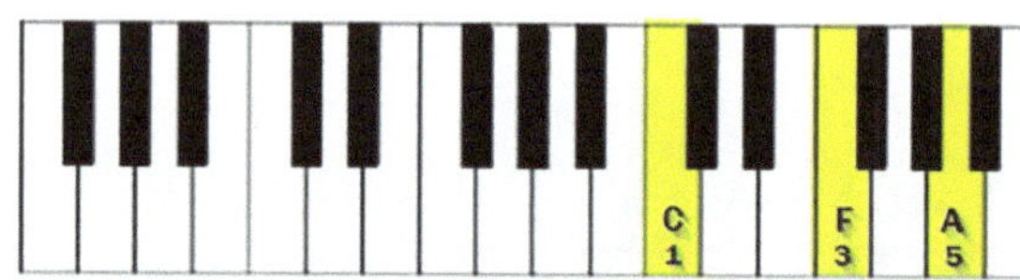

2nd Inversion

I exalt Thee   G
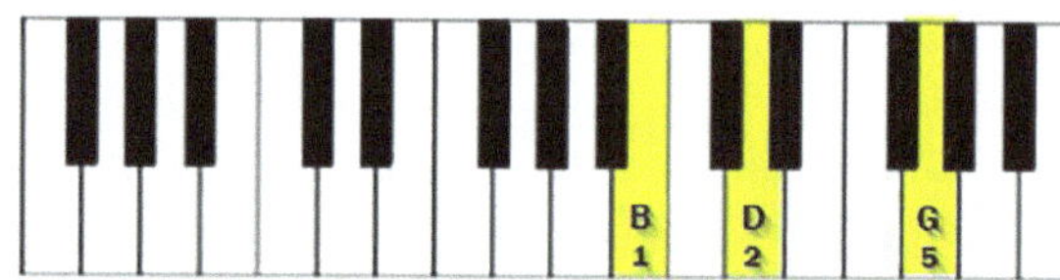

1st Inversion

O Lord!   C
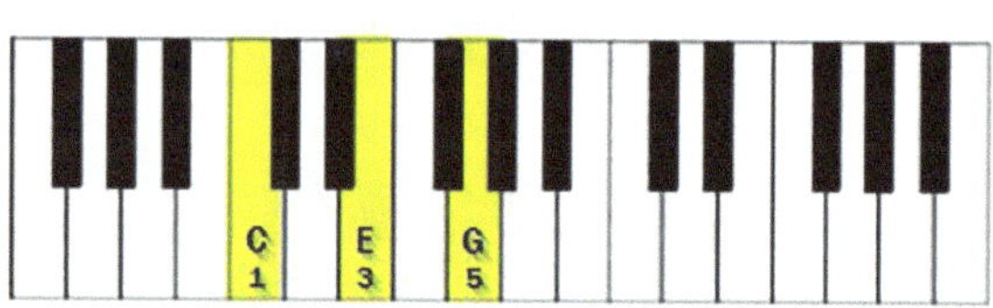

Root Position

VL-5

Chord Numbering

One system for numbering chords uses Roman numerals. When in the key of C, C is the "I" chord, F is the "IV" chord and G is the "V" chord. Looking at the keyboard, this aligns with their place on the keyboard when in the key of C. Chord numbering makes transferring chord progressions to different keys easier to communicate to other musicians. The jazz community uses Roman numerals. There is another numbering system used by many worship teams called the "Nashville Numbering System" which is very similar. The primary difference is that the Nashville system uses the Arabic (123…) numbers. I prefer the Roman numerals because the chord quality can be determined by the upper- and lower-case numerals.

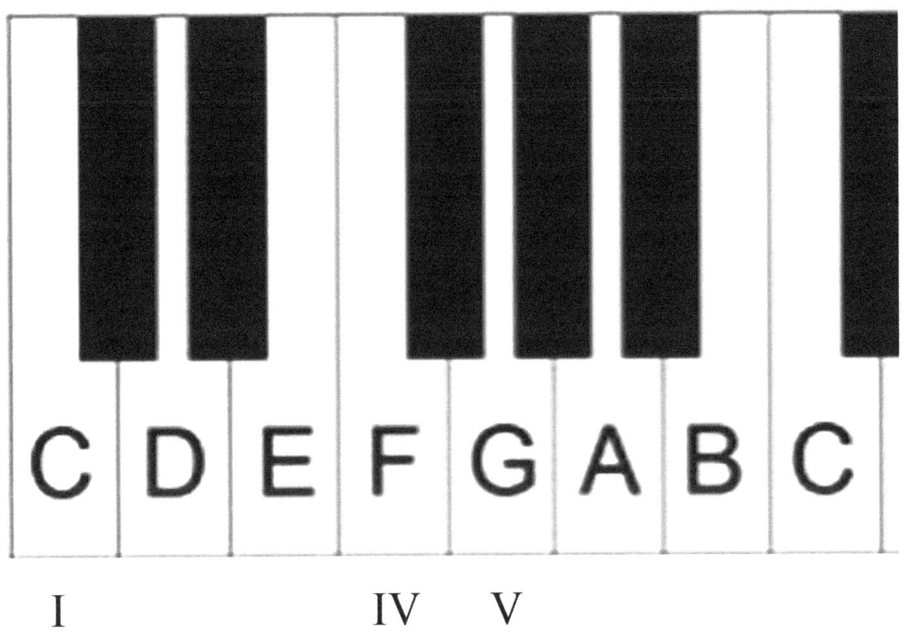

The I, IV and V triads in major keys are major chords. As mentioned earlier, major chords have a "bright" or "happy" sound and the only difference between a major triad and a minor triad is that the third of the chord is lowered by ½ step. We will now add our first minor chord to our repertoire.

D Minor

The Roman numeral for minor chords is always a lower-case numeral. In the key of C, the D chord is the "ii" chord. The ii chord in major keys is *always minor*.

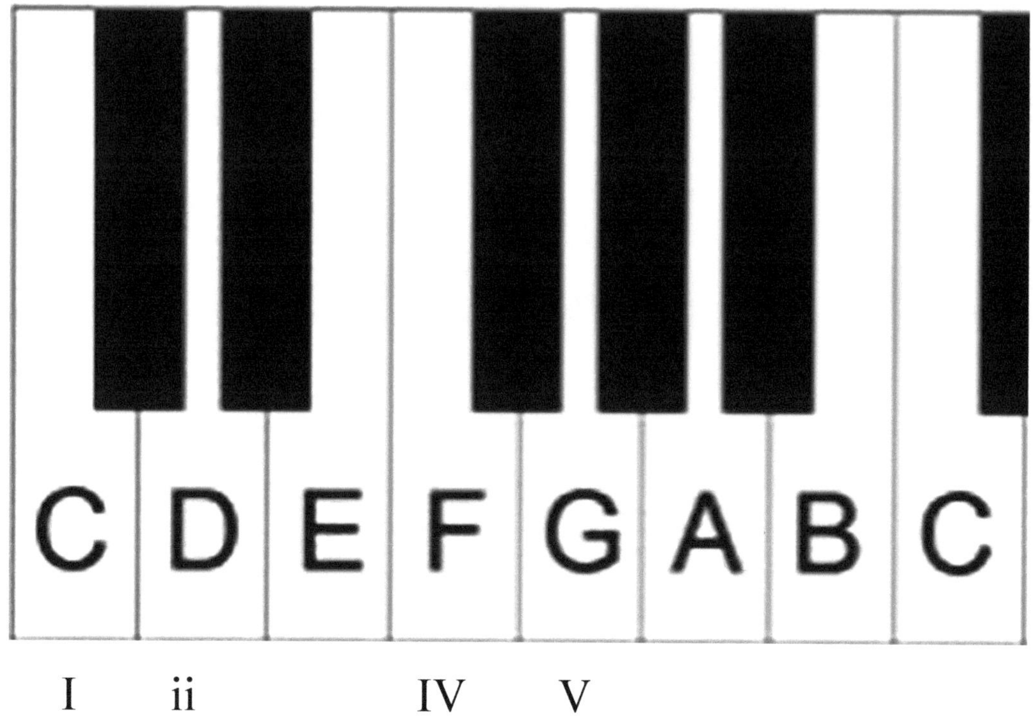

A minor chord is most often seen with a lower case "m" following the letter of the chord (Dm). If nothing follows the letter, the chord is major.

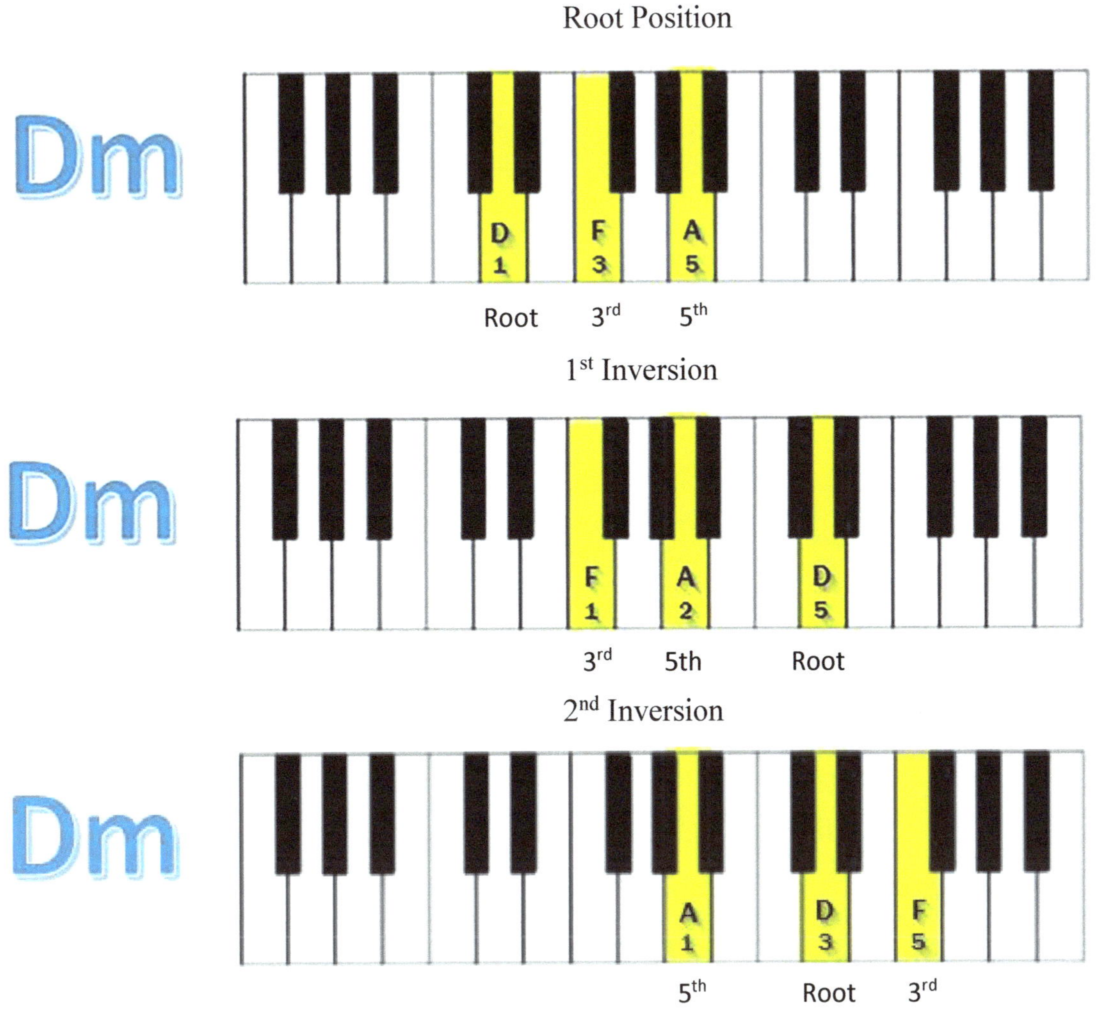

Count the half steps between the root and the third of each chord. Remember, the distance between every key is 1/2 step, regardless of the color.

Steps

(4) C

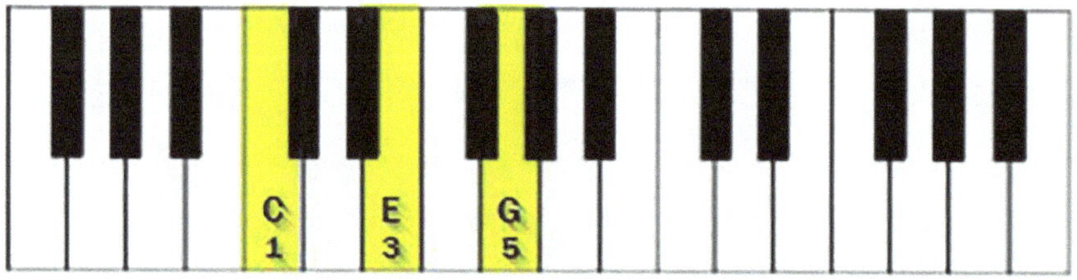

(4) F

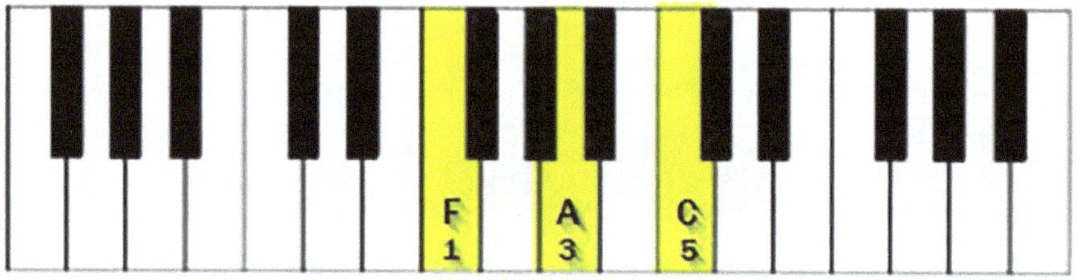

(4) G

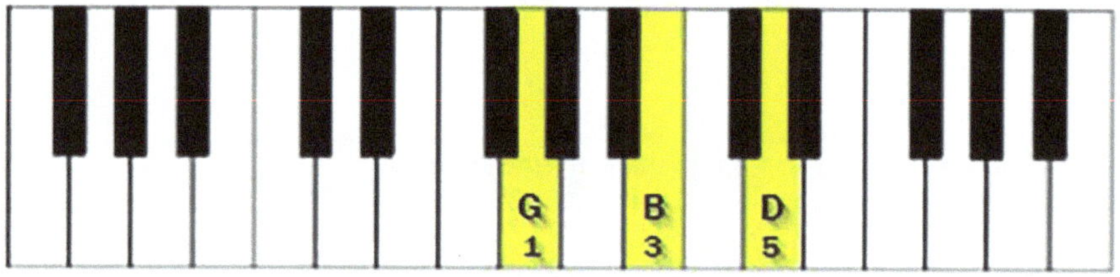

(3½) Dm

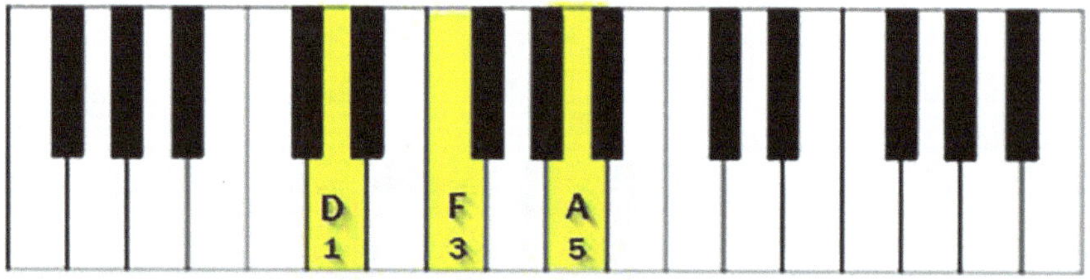

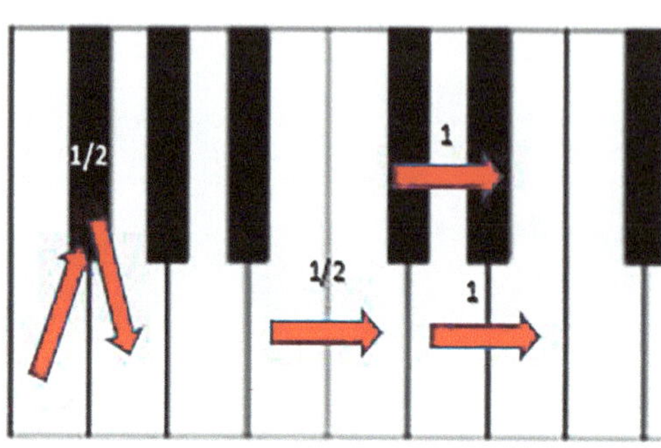

Notice how the D minor triad has only 3 half-steps between the root and the third. The major triads have 4. Minor triads have a ***LOWERED THIRD.***

A Minor (Am)

Am is the "vi" chord in the key of C Major. The vi chord is ***always minor*** when playing in a major key.

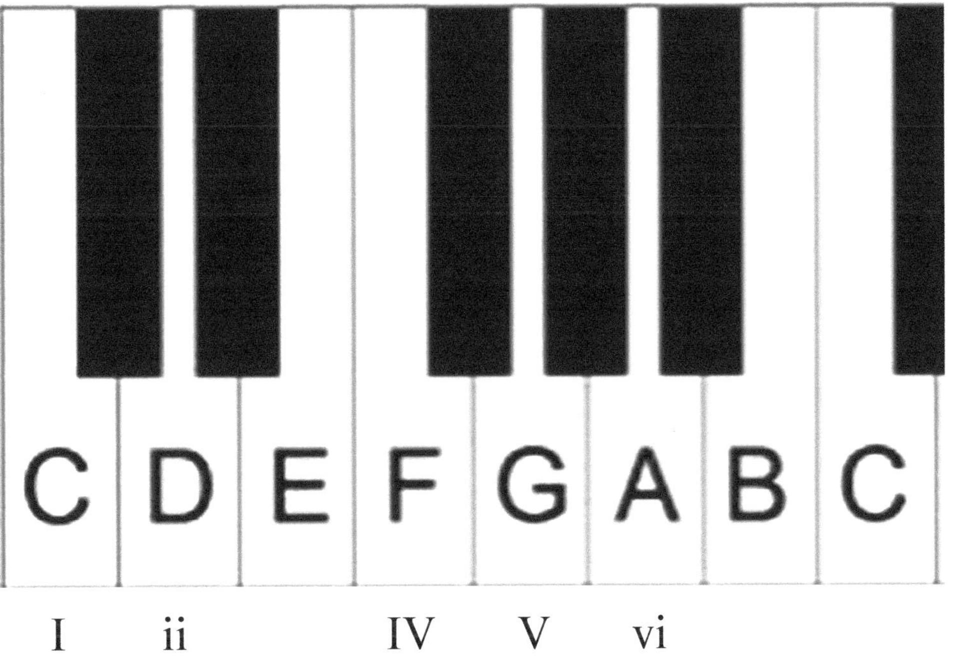

In this example, the Am chord is showed two times. This is to remind you that the keyboard is a pattern that repeats. Both are Am triads. One is one OCTAVE lower than the other. An octave is a span of eight notes and when the pattern of the keyboard repeats.

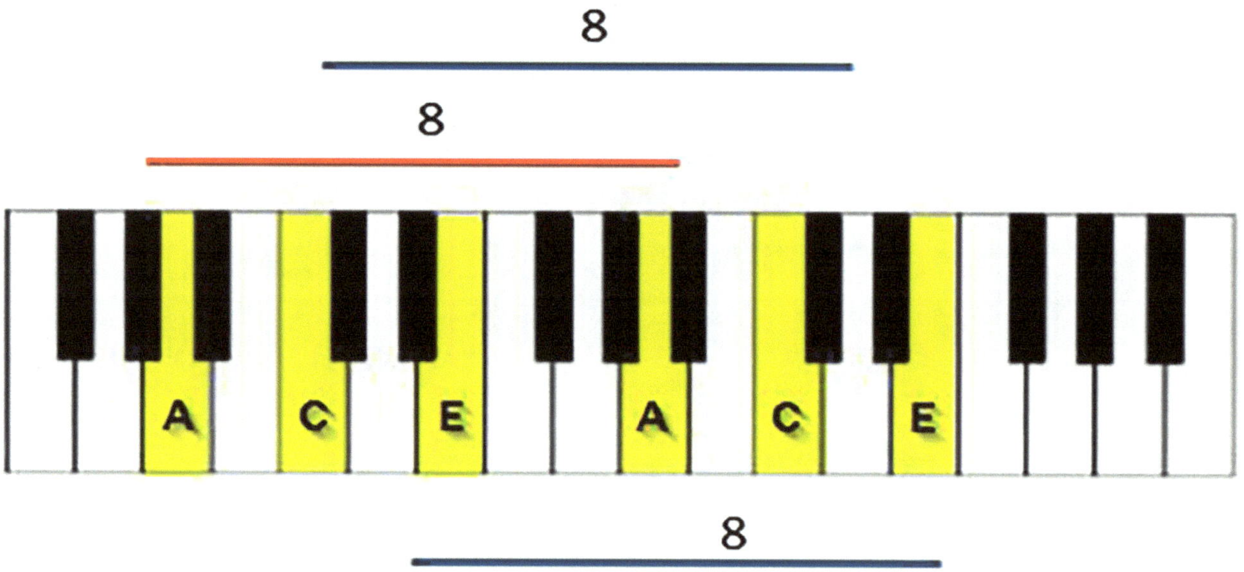

A Minor Triad Inversions

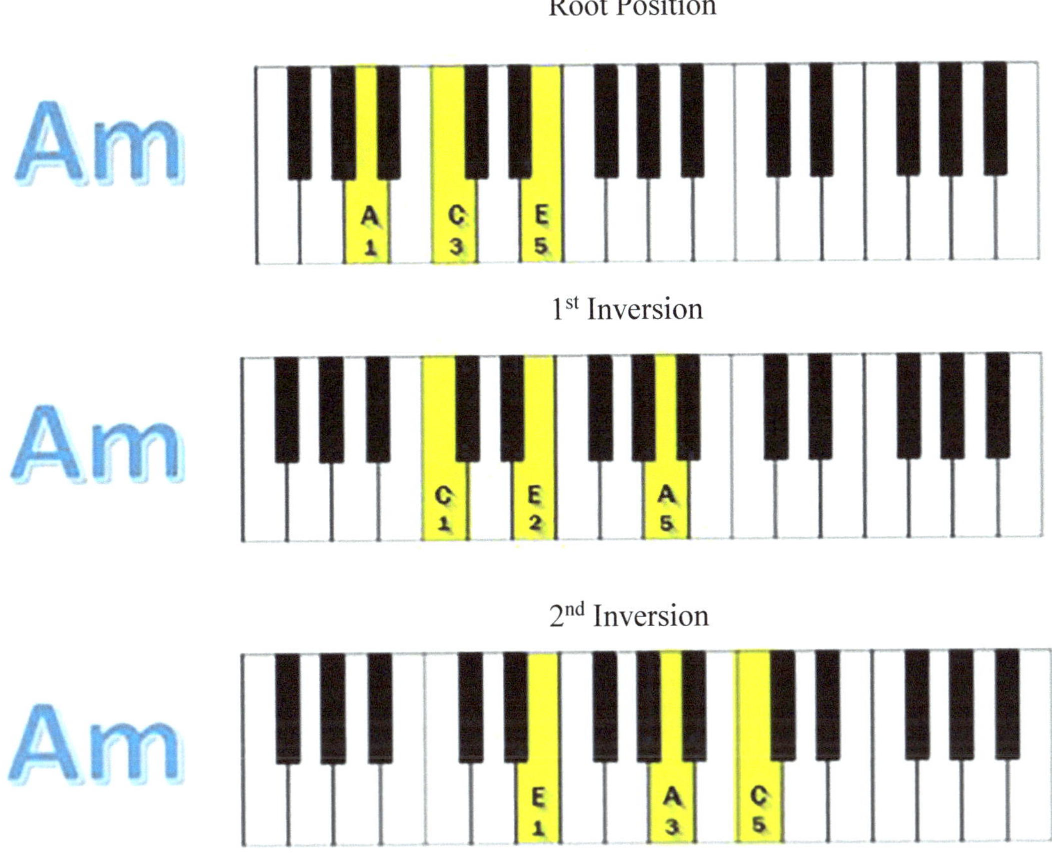

How to Practice

1. LISTEN to the song multiple times.

2. Purchase or download a metronome or metronome app. A metronome is a device that keeps a steady beat with a sound, usually a beep or a tick. Practicing with a metronome will develop the player's sense of time which is crucial when playing with a group. A metronome replaces a drummer for practice purposes.

3. Include drills with each practice section to build finger strength as well as musical vocabulary.

4. When playing with both hands, practice hands separately before putting them together.

5. Begin practicing slowly but in time. The chords should be held out the same relative duration as if it was being played up to tempo.

6. Practice the song in sections. For example, practice the chords of the verse first. Do not move to another section until the verse chords are played without hesitation. Practice any chord transitions slowly and repeatedly until smooth, steady movement is achieved. Once one section of the song is accomplished, move to another section such as the chorus, and repeat the method described above. When the chorus can be played smoothly, then practice the verse and the chorus consecutively. Follow the same pattern of practice with the bridge. Do not play the song from beginning to end until each section can be played well independently.

7. Even if you are not a singer, sing or hum the melody as you are practicing.

8. If possible, find a recording of the song in the same key and play along with recording. YouTube will have many songs in various keys.

9. Develop a regular practice routine. 25 minutes 4-5 times a week is recommended and will yield noticeable progress.

VL-8

The Blessing

Kari Jobe

Time=4

[Intro]

C F C G Am F C G C

[Verse]

   C   F   C   G   Am

// The Lord bless you and keep you make His face shine upon you and be gracious to you

                       F   C   G   C

The Lord turn His face toward you and give you peace.//

Chorus

C   F   C   G Am   F   C   G

A----------men, A---------men, A---------men, A----------men, A---------men, A---------men,

Play along!

https://www.youtube.com/watch?v=T2ngUlNoHzA0

[Bridge 1]

       Am   F   C   G

May His favor be upon you and a thousand generations and your family and your children and their children and their children

       Am   F   C   G

May His favor be upon you and a thousand generations and your family and your children and their children and their children

       Am   F   C   G

May His favor be upon you and a thousand generations and your family and your children and their children and their children

       Am   F   C   G

May His favor be upon you and a thousand generations and your family and your children and their children and their children

[Bridge 2]

       Am   F   C   G

May His presence go before you and behind you and beside you all around you and within you He is with you, He is with you

       Am   F   C   G

In the morning, in the evening in your coming and your going in your weeping and rejoicing He is for you, He is for you

[Tag]

       Am   F   C   G   VL-9

He is for you He is for you He is for you, He is for you, He is for you, He is for you, He is for you, He is for you!

The Blessing

Kari Jobe

Chords Used: C(I) F(IV) G(V) Am(vi)

Verse

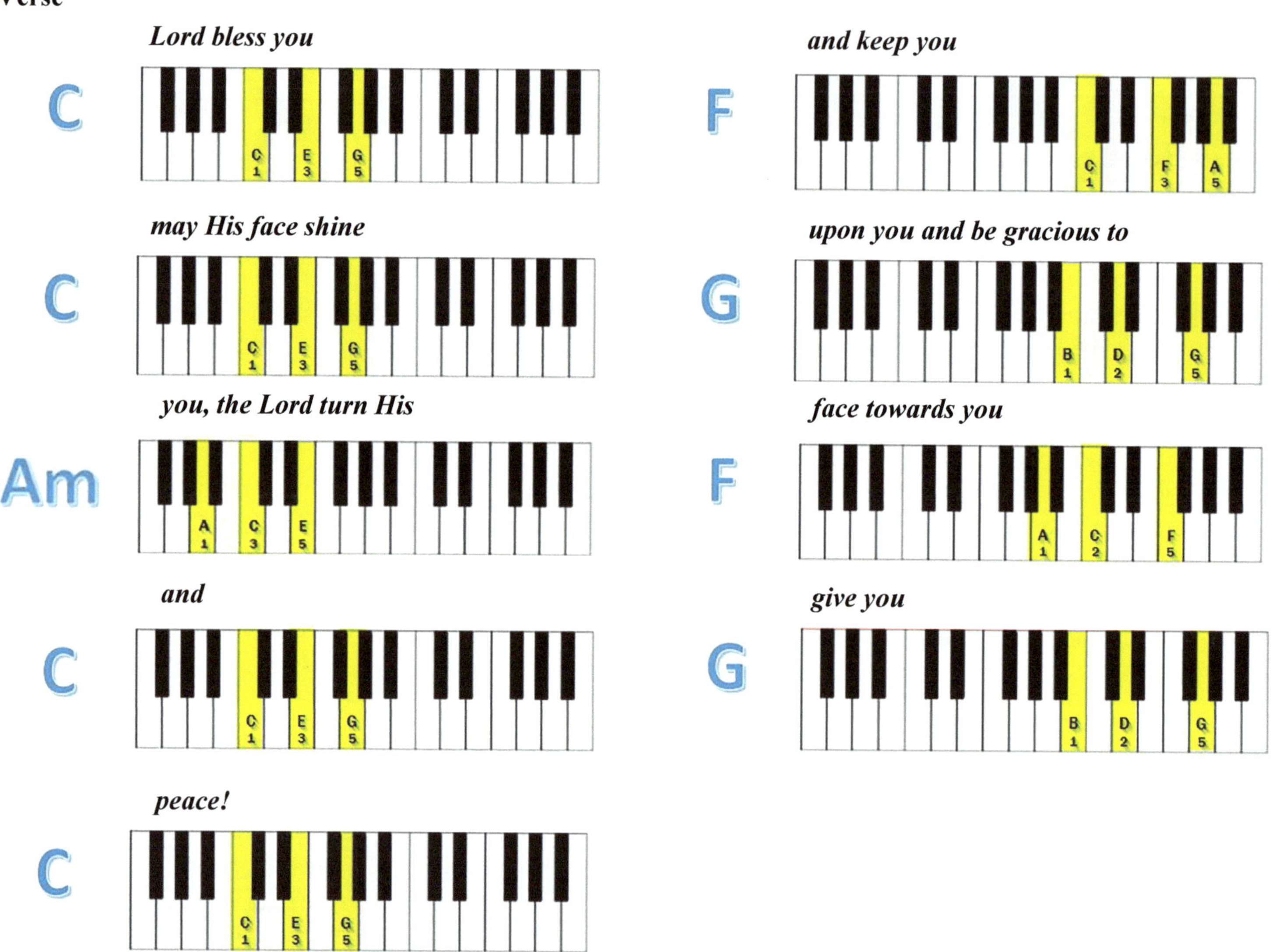

Chorus

A--men, A----------
C
C1 E3 G5
F
C1 F3 A5
men, A--men
C
C1 E3 G5
G
B1 D2 G5
A--men, A----------
Am
A1 C3 E5
F
A1 C2 F5
men, A--men
C
C1 E3 G5
G
B1 D2 G5

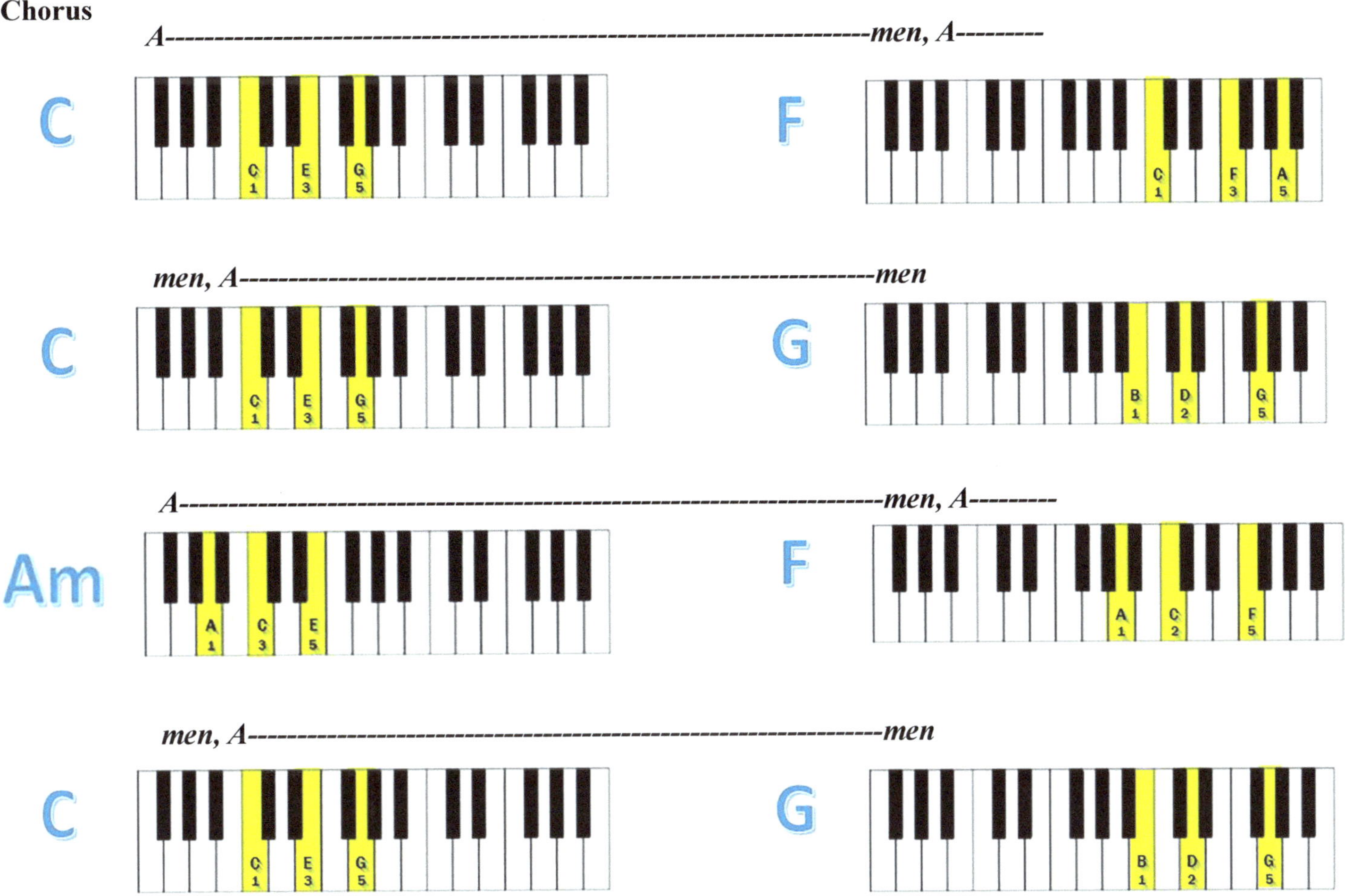

May His favor be upon you and a
May His presence go before you and

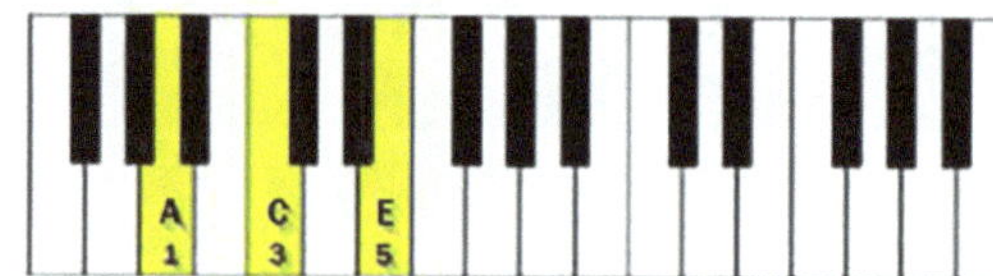

thousand generations and your
behind you and beside you all around

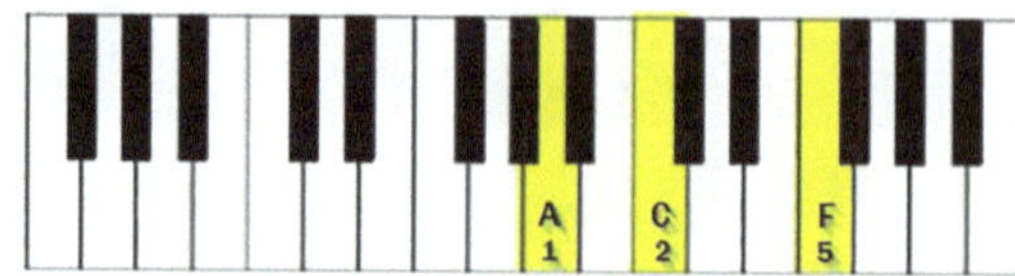

family and your children and their
you and within you He is

children, and their children!
with you, He is with you!

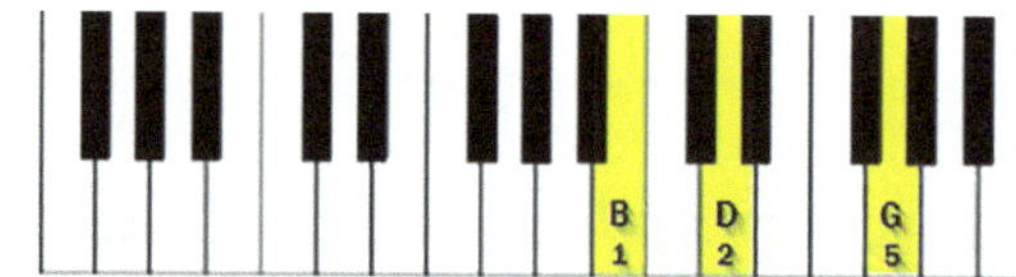

May His favor be upon you and a
In the morning, in the evening in your

thousand generations and your
coming and your going in your

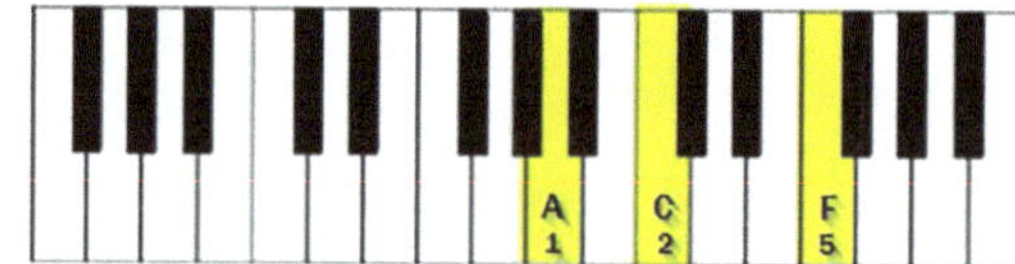

family and your children and their
weeping and rejoicing He is

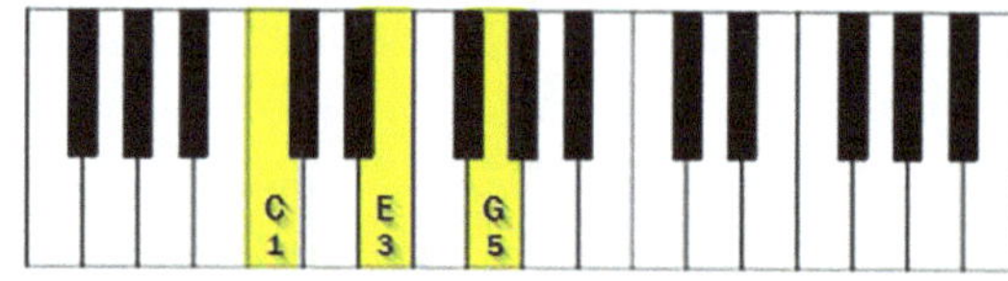

children, and their children!
for you, He is for you!

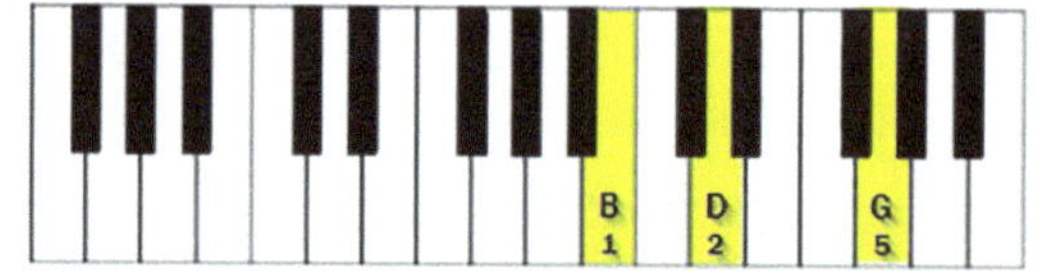

Holy Spirit

Francesca Battistelli

Time=4

[Verse 1]
```
C                                                    F
 There's nothing worth more, that will ever come close
                                  C
Nothing can compare, You're our living hope
            F
Your Presence Lord
```
[Verse 2]
```
C                                        F
I've tasted and seen, of the sweetest of loves
                                              C
Where my heart becomes free, and my shame is undone
            F
Your Presence Lord
```

Chorus]
```
C
Holy Spirit You are welcome here
        F                     Dm
Come flood this place and fill the atmosphere
        C
Your Glory God is what our hearts long for
        F          Dm      C
To be overcome by Your Presence Lord
```

[Verse 3]
```
C                                                    F
 There's nothing worth more, that will ever come close
                                  C
Nothing can compare, You're our living hope
            F
Your Presence Lord
```

[Verse 4]
```
C                                        F
I've tasted and seen, of the sweetest of loves
                                              C
Where my heart becomes free, and my shame is undone
            F
Your presence Lord
```

[Chorus]
```
C
Holy Spirit You are welcome here
        F                     Dm
Come flood this place and fill the atmosphere
        C
Your Glory God is what our hearts long for
        F          Dm      C
To be overcome by Your Presence Lord
```

[Bridge]
```
F      C       Dm          C
Let us become more aware of Your Presence
F      C       Dm          C
Let us experience the Glory of Your Goodness
F      C       Dm          C
Let us become more aware of Your Presence
F      C       Dm          C
Let us experience the Glory of Your Goodness
F      C       Dm          C
Let us become more aware of Your Presence
F      C       Dm          C
Let us experience the Glory of Your Goodness
```

VL-10

Holy Spirit

Francesca Battistelli

Chords Used: C(I) Dm(ii) F(IV)

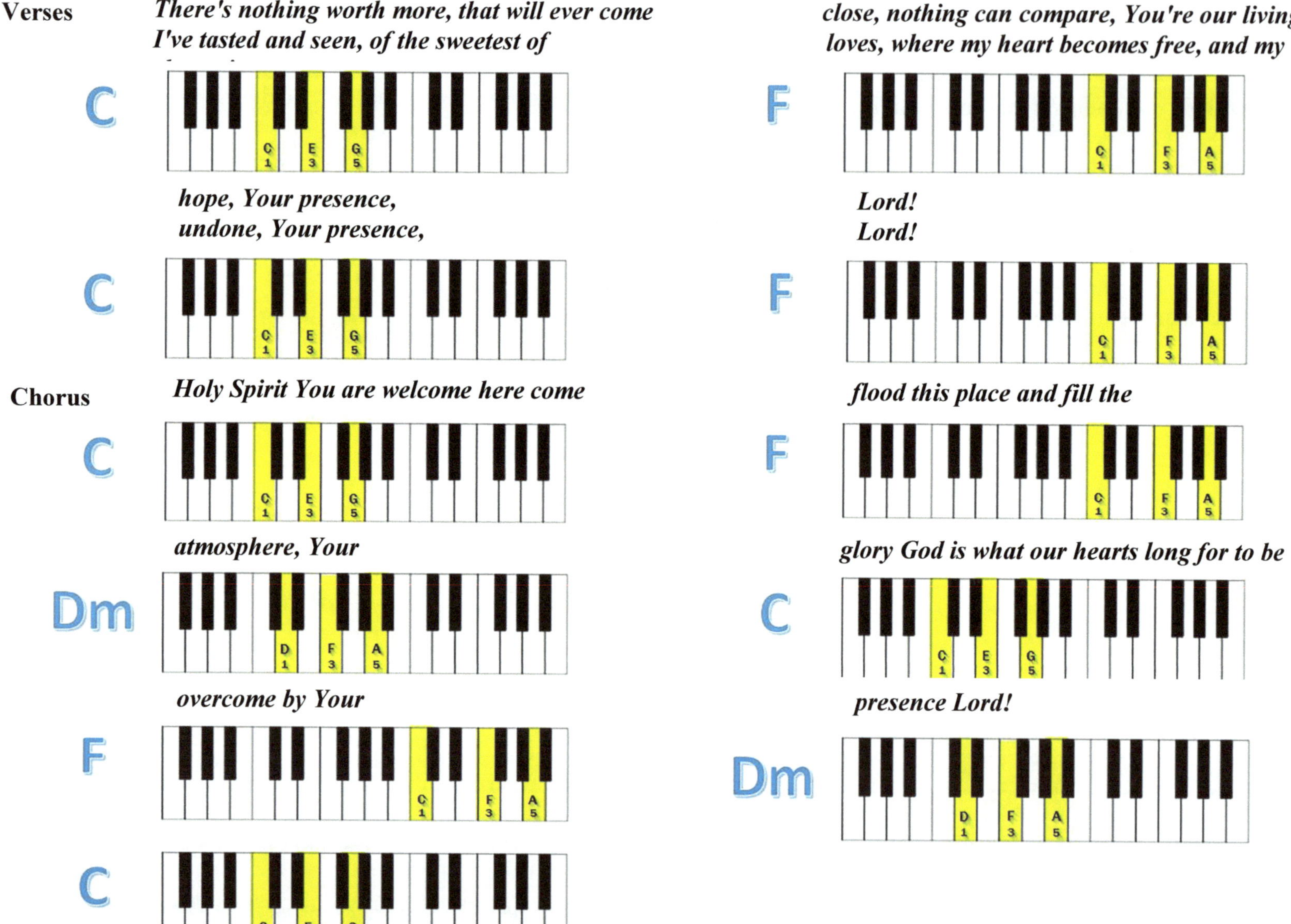

Bridge

Let us be-

 F
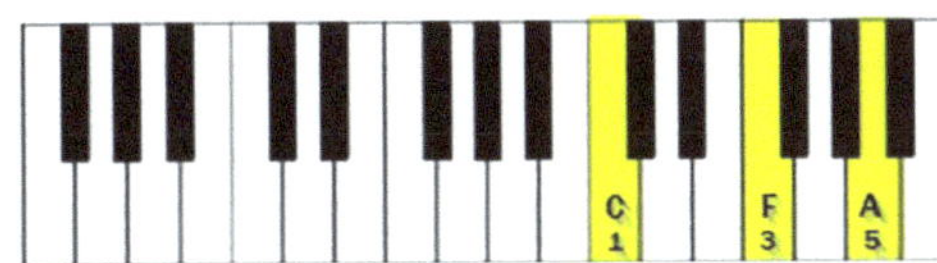

aware of Your

Dm
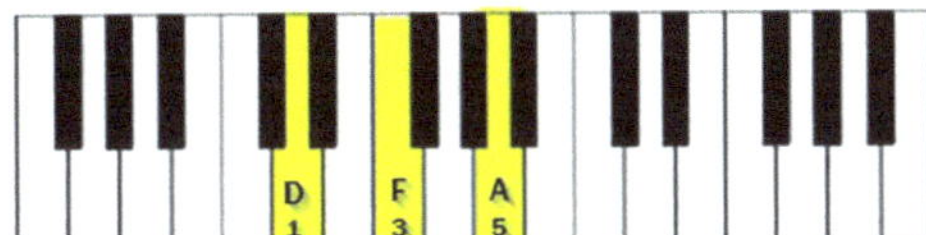

Let us

F
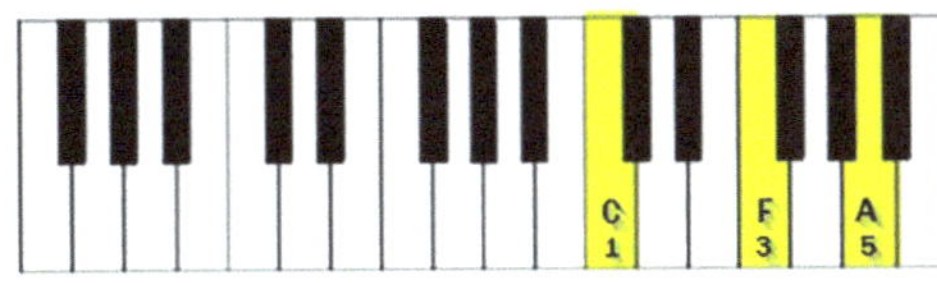

glory of Your

Dm
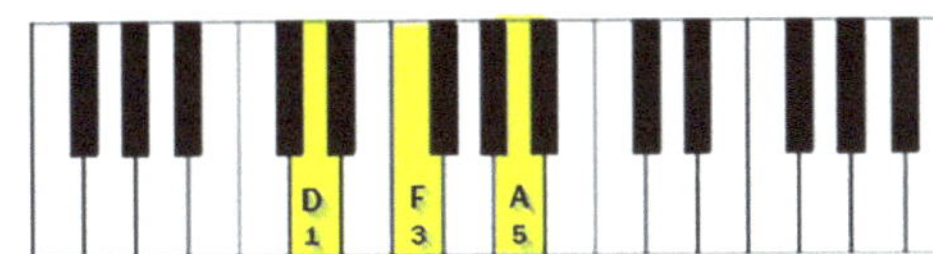

come more

C
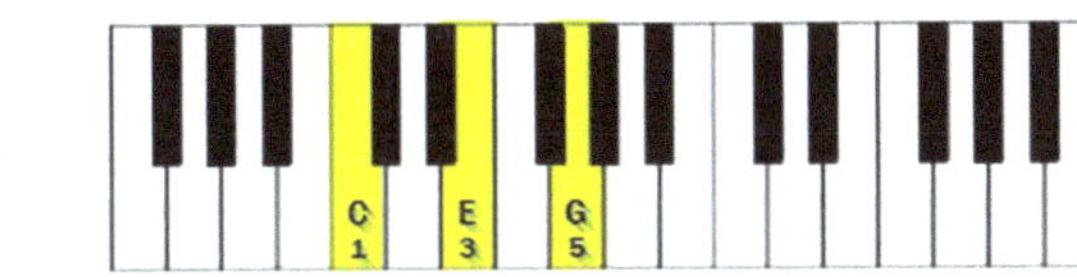

presence!

C
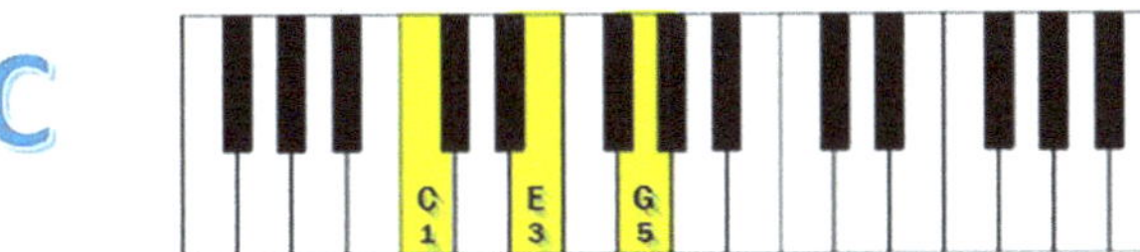

experience the

C
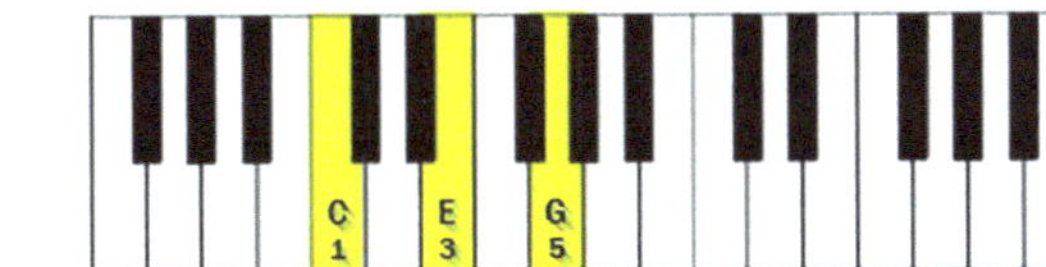

goodness!

C
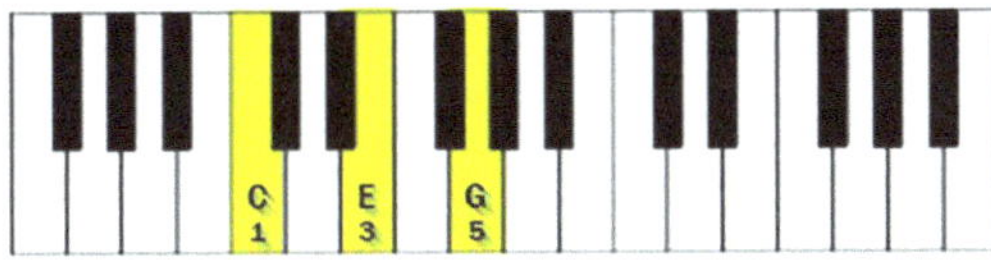

Adding the Left Hand

While the left hand in worship music frequently plays the root of the chord functioning as the bass, triad drills should also be practiced This will enable the player to play rhythmic patterns or embellish the accompaniment with the left hand. Triad drills should be played in the same manner with the left hand as with the right. The fingering suggested is as follows:

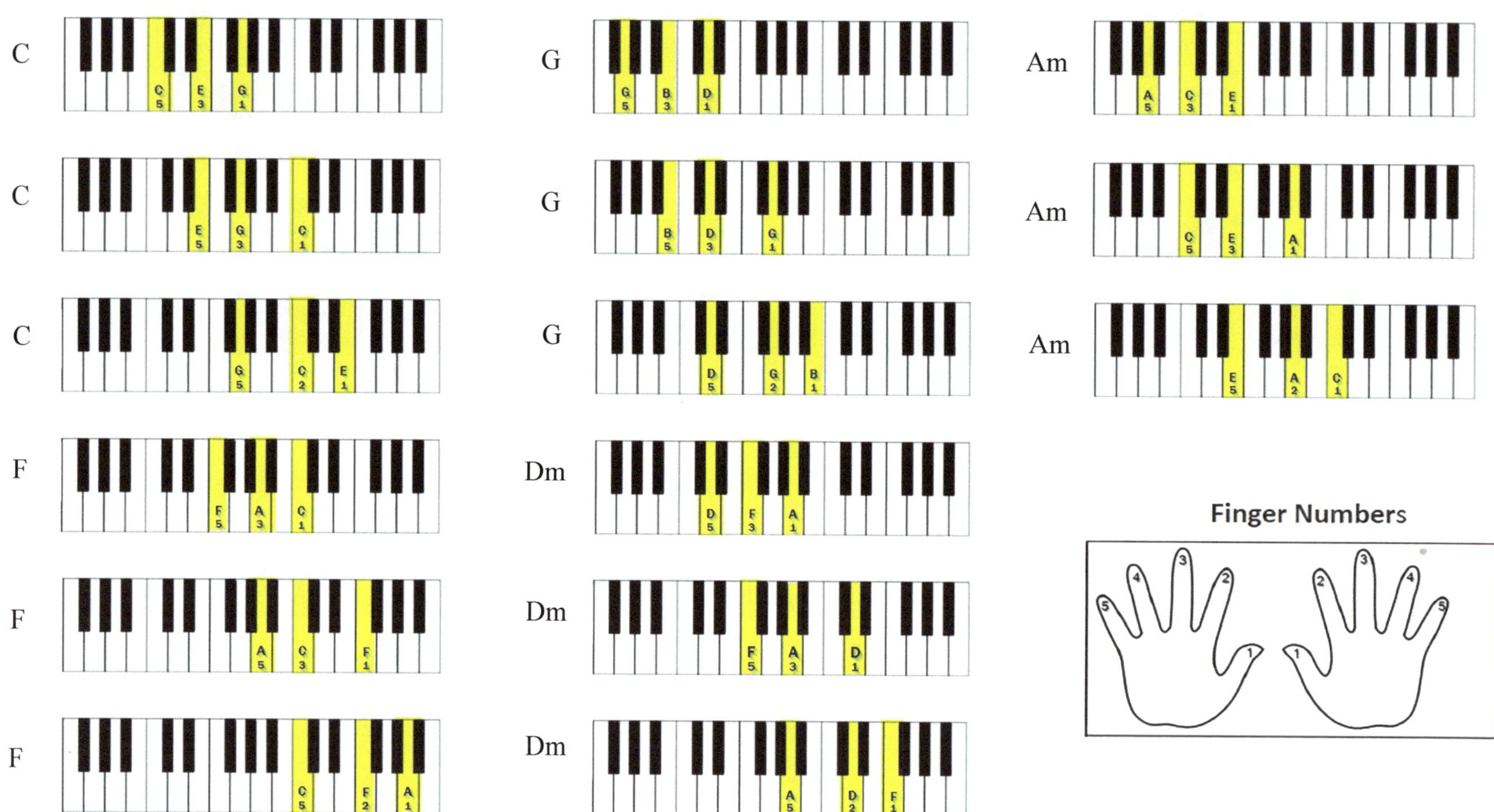

Playing the Root as the Bass - Left Hand

In worship music, the left hand frequently serves as the bass. If there is a bass player in the group, the keyboard player will have more flexibility to use the left hand for rhythmic or melodic embellishments. We will first begin as if there is no bass player, using the left hand as the primary bass sound for the group. When adding the left hand, there is a coordination element that will take time to develop. The left hand will be playing the root for each of the chords, played at the moment when the chord changes. Begin practicing the left hand without using the right hand in time to the chord changes. Initially, we will begin with the 5th finger playing the root. Both hands should be able to play the song in time separately and smoothly before putting them together.

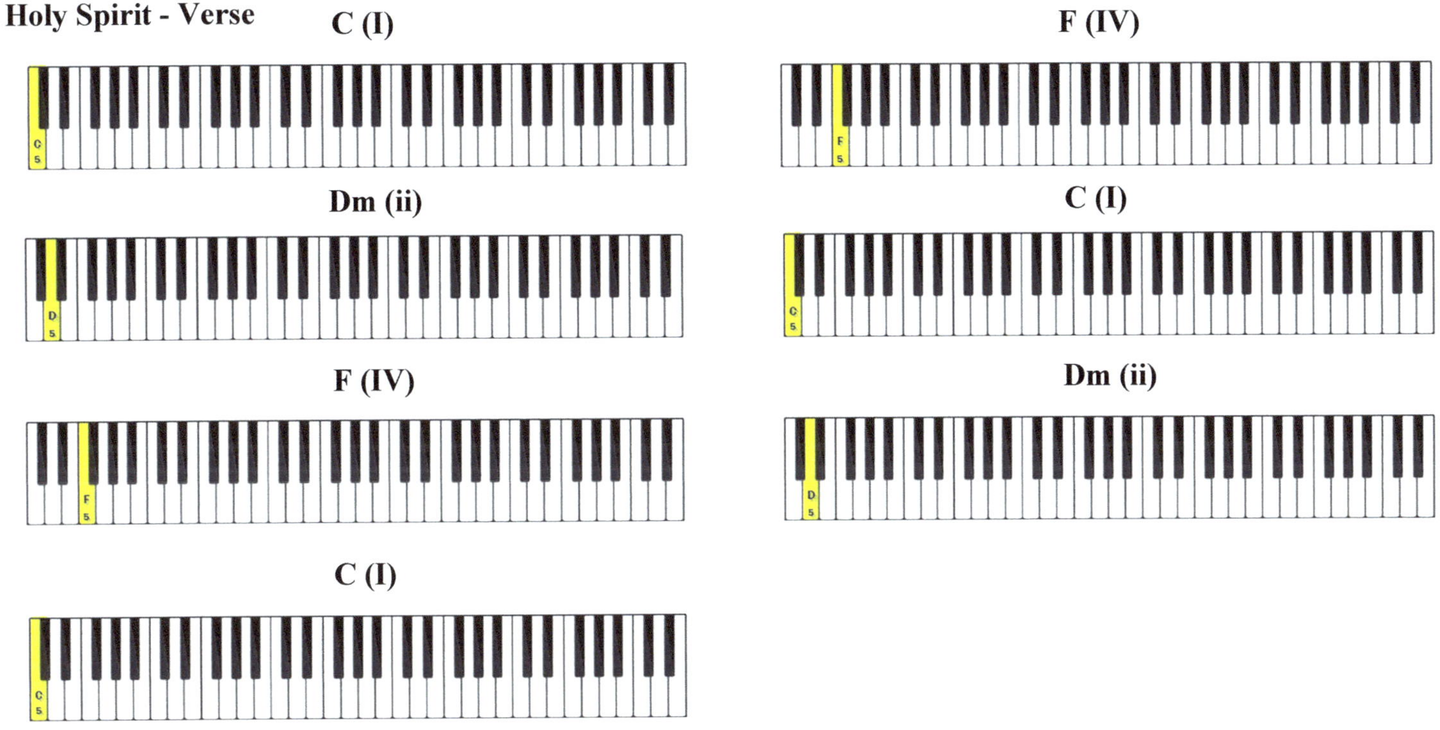

Playing the Left Hand Root in Octaves

Playing octaves in the left hand is a way to strengthen the bass sound. This is recommended when no bass player is present.

Holy Spirit - Chorus

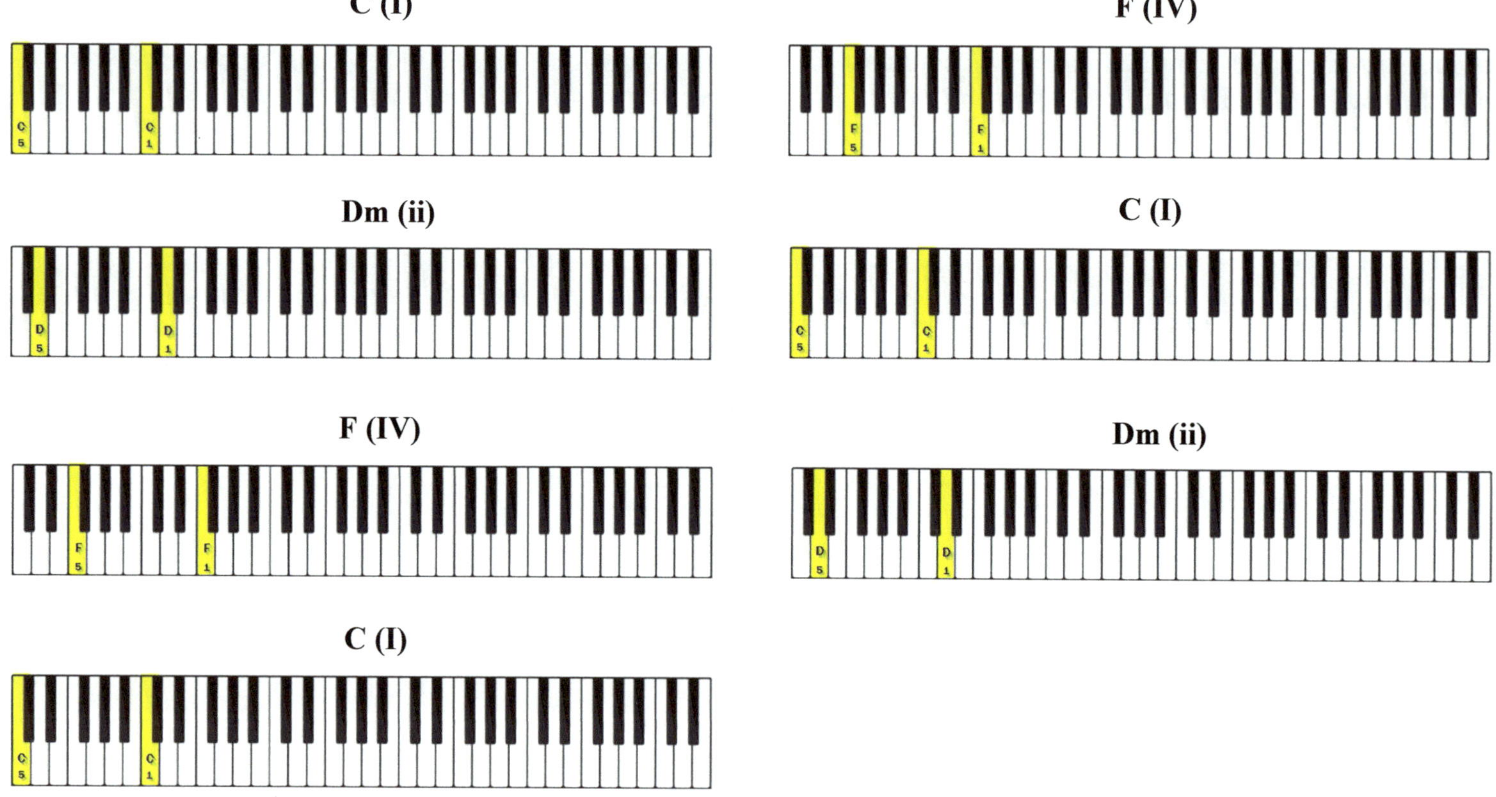

Putting Hands Together

When both hands can be played smoothly and in time (not necessarily up to tempo), hands can be put together. This should first be done at a slow tempo. The player should be able to play slowly in time before the desired tempo is attempted.

Holy Spirit – Chorus

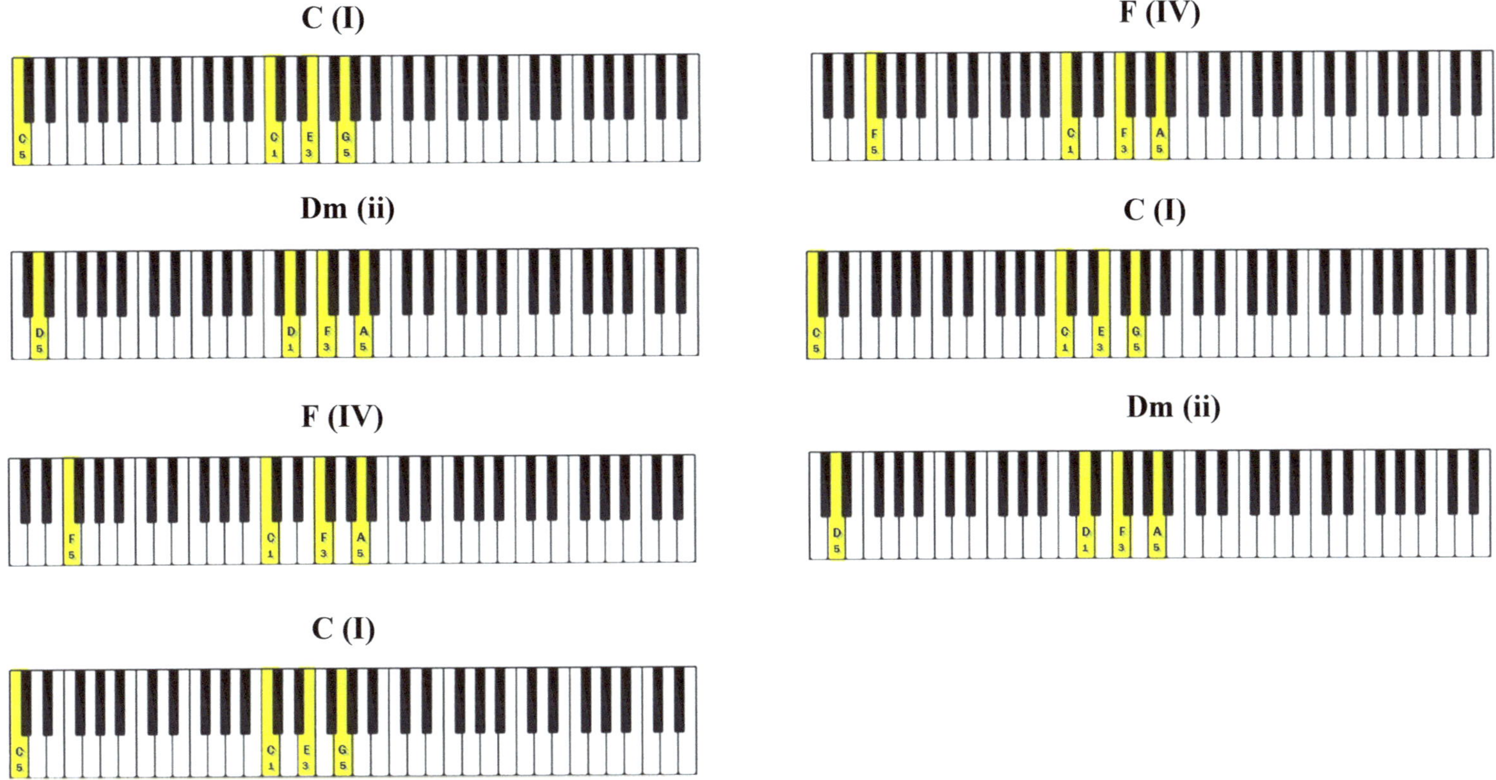

The iii Chord and the vii Chord

The iii chord in the key of C is E minor. The vii chord in the key of C is B *diminished*. A diminished chord is a minor chord with the fifth lowered by 1/2 step. It has a darker sound than the minor chord. While the iii chord is used occasionally in worship music, the vii chord is rarely used.

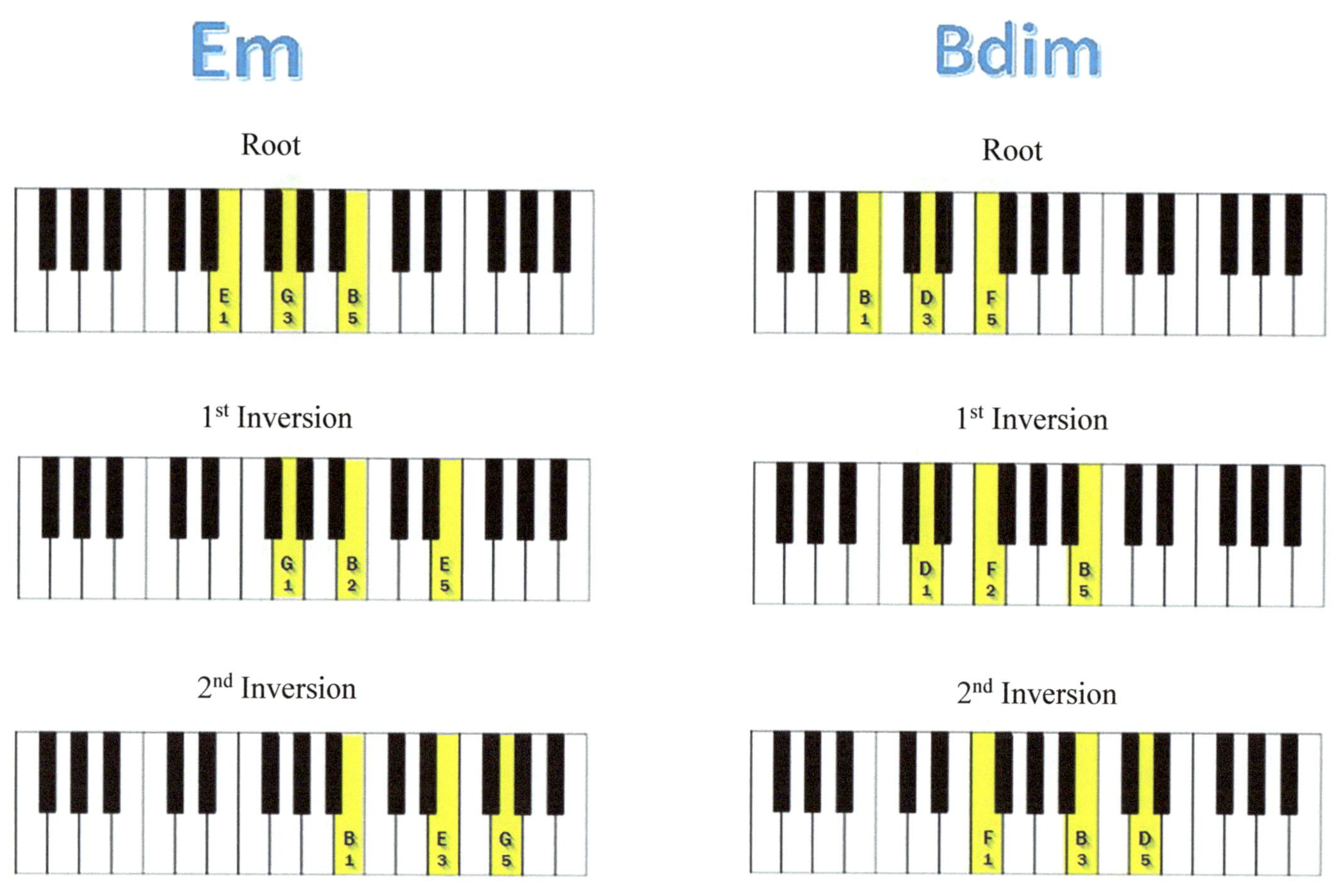

These are the chord numbers
for all **triads** in the key
of C major. In major keys, the
following is always true:

I chord is major
ii chord is minor
iii chord is minor
IV chord is major
V chord is major
vi chord is minor
vii chord is diminished
(minor with a lowered fifth).

The quality of the chord is
determined by the number of
steps between the root and
the third, and the third and
the fifth.

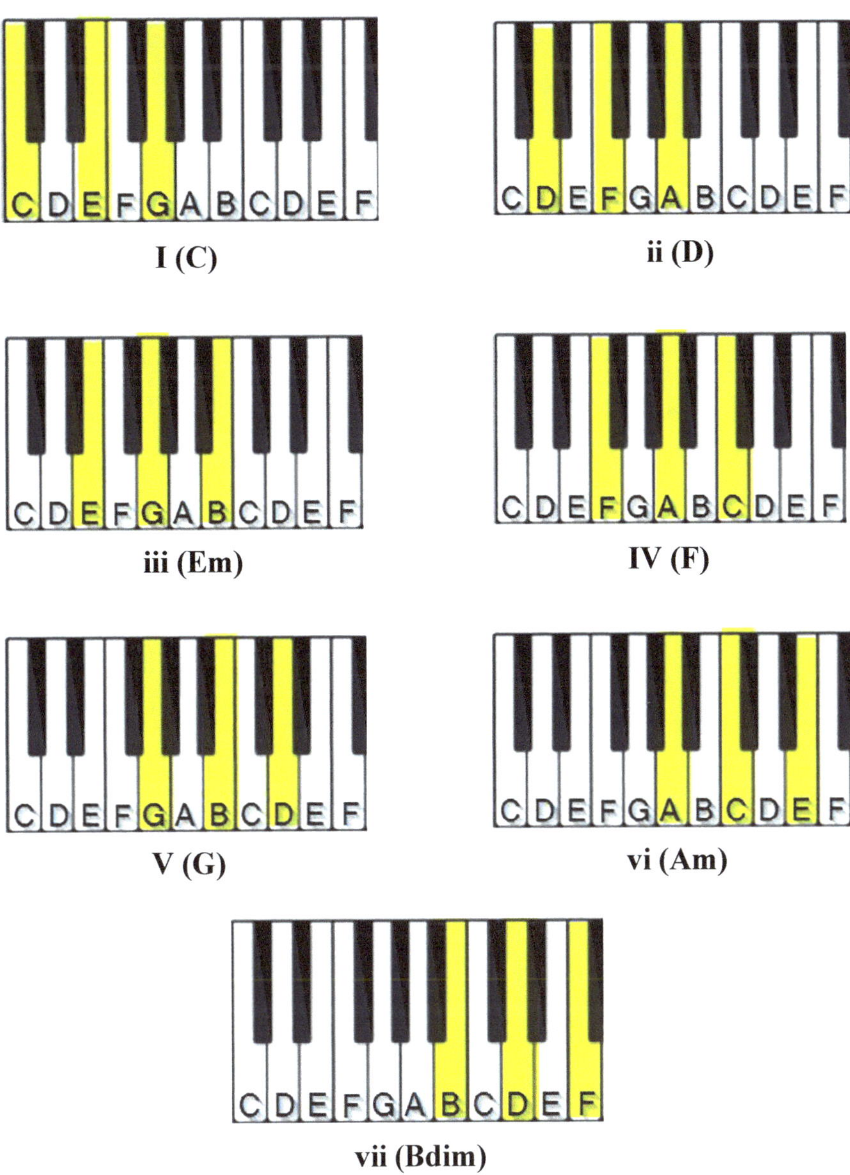

Recommended Finger Drills for Left and Right Hand

Arpeggios

As recommended earlier, practicing triad inversions in both the left and right hand is essential to become fluent in transitioning between chords. In addition to practicing triad inversions which contain the root, 3rd, and 5th of the chord, add the 8th note which is the root one octave above, playing the chord in a "broken" style. These are called *arpeggios*. "Arpeggio" is the formal term for broken chords. Play the arpeggios moving from low to high and back down. Begin practicing these in root position. Once fluent in root position, these should also be practiced in inversions.

Left Hand   Right Hand

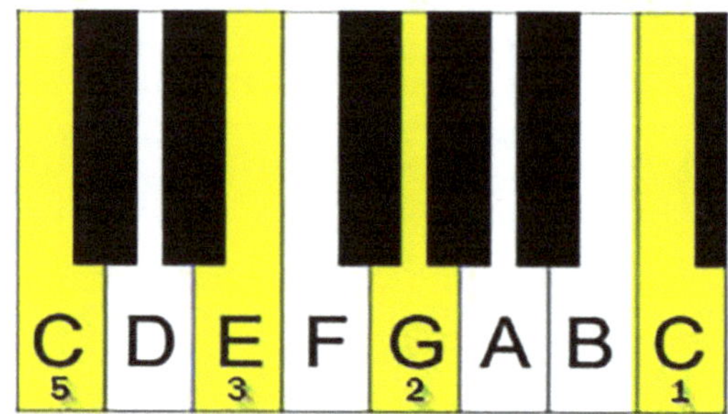

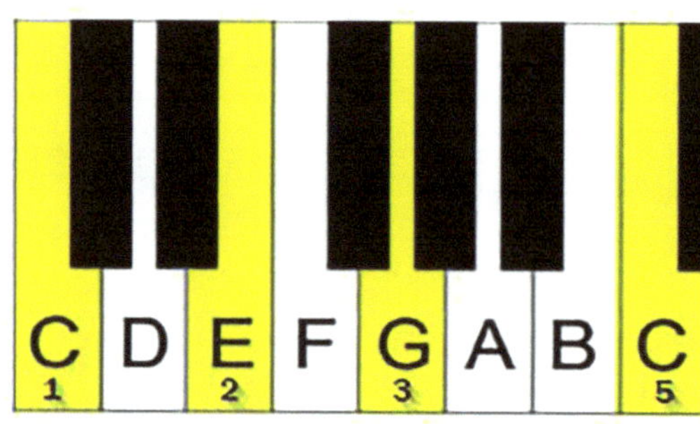

Triad Patterns

As introduced earlier, practicing triad inversions using patterns will not only strengthen fingers, but will further develop fluency in playing triads.

Left Hand Patterns:	Right Hand Patterns:
5-3-1-3-5	1-3-5-3-1
5-1-3-1-5	1-5-3-5-1

VL-15

Using the Sustain Pedal

The sustain pedal is the pedal farthest right on a traditional piano. Keyboards frequently only have one. The purpose of the sustain pedal is to connect chords smoothly without having to hold down the keys until the next chord change. It *sustains* the sound. To correctly use the sustain pedal (we will simply refer to it as the pedal), follow these steps:

1. Play the chord and then press the pedal down.
2. Lift the pedal at the same time the next chord is played.

The pedal is used in most worship music styles. It creates a smooth, connected sound between chords.

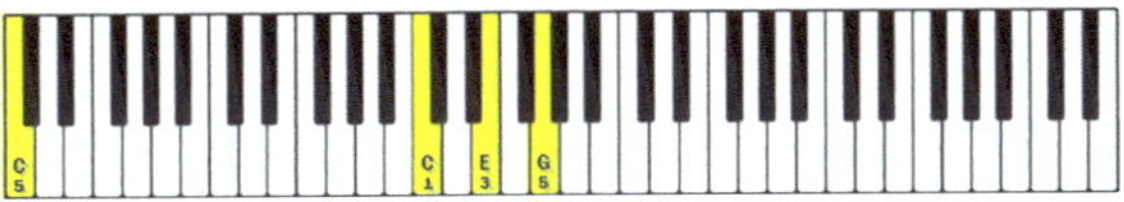
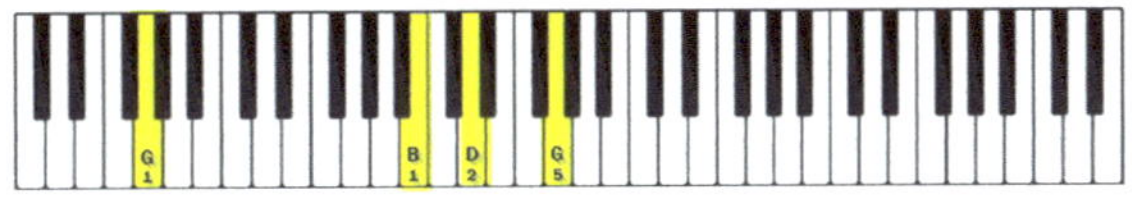
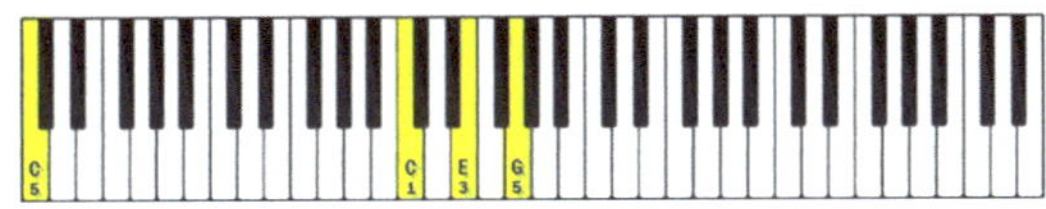

VL-16

How Great Is Our God

Chris Tomlin, Jesse Reeves and Ed Cash

Time=4

[Intro]
C Am F G

[Verse 1]
```
     C                       Am
```
The splendor of a King, clothed in majesty,
```
                       F
```
Let all the earth rejoice, all the earth rejoice.
```
     C                       Am
```
He wraps Himself in light, and darkness tries to hide,
```
                   F
```
And trembles at his voice, trembles at his voice.

[Chorus]
```
        C
```
How great is our God, sing with me,
```
     Am
```
How great is our God, and all will see,
```
     F        G          C
```
How great, how great is our God.

[Verse 2]
```
C                            Am
```
Age to age He stands, and time is in His hands,
```
                   F
```
Beginning and the end, beginning and the end.
```
       C                 Am
```
The Godhead, three in one: Father, Spirit, Son,
```
              F
```
The Lion and the Lamb, the Lion and the Lamb.

[Chorus]

[Bridge]
C
Name above all names,
Am
Worthy of all praise,
```
     F
```
My heart will sing
```
     G          C
```
How great is our God.

[Chorus]
```
        C
```
How great is our God, sing with me,
```
        Am
```
How great is our God, and all will see,
```
        F        G          C
```
How great, how great is our God.
```
        C
```
How great is our God, sing with me,
```
        Am
```
How great is our God, all will see,
```
        F        G          C
```
How great, how great is our God.

Play Along!

**https://www.youtube.com
/watch?v=hwc2d1Xt8gM**

How Great Is Our God

Chris Tomlin, Jesse Reeves and Ed Cash

Chords Used: C(I) F(IV) G(V) Am(vi)

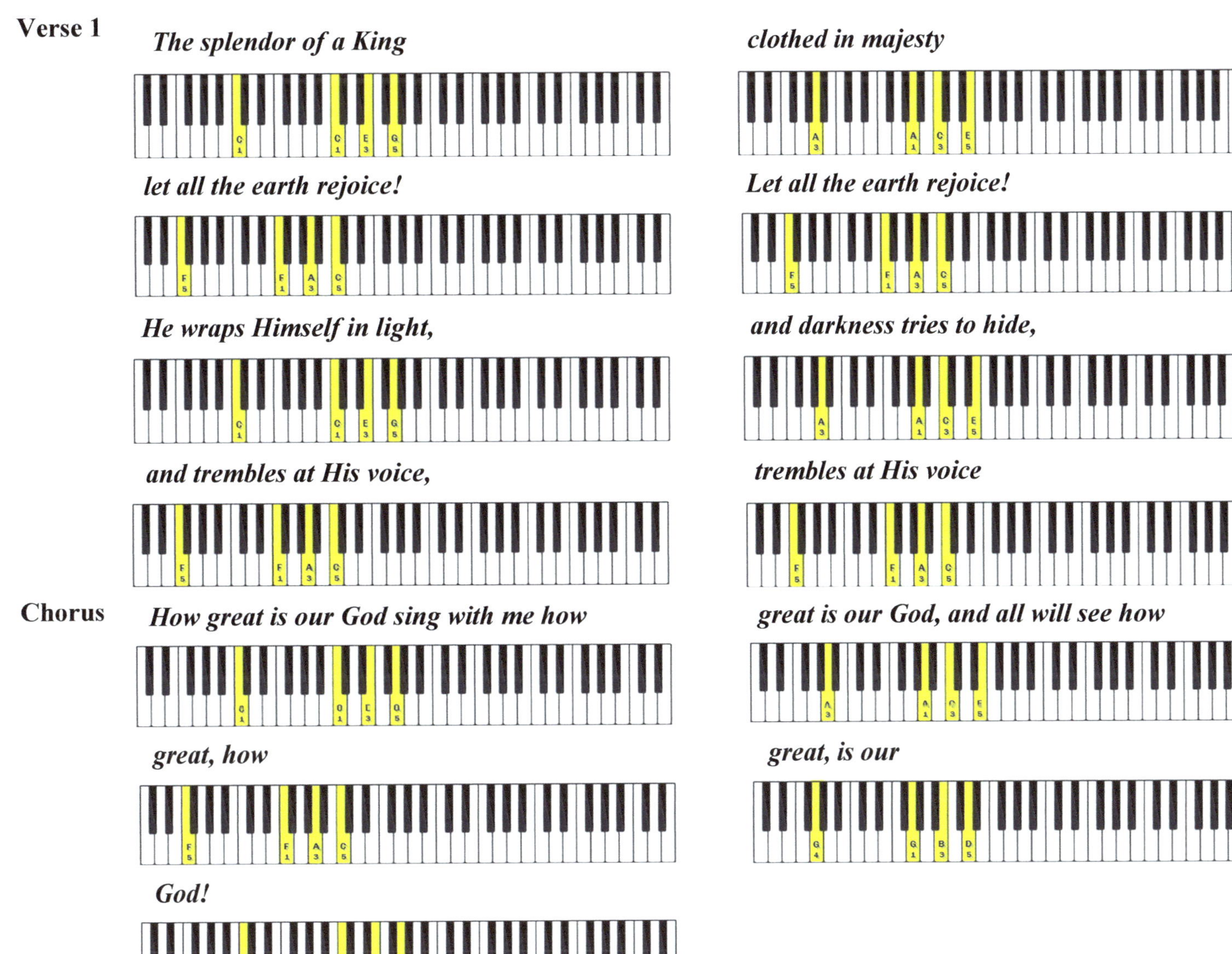

Verse 1

The splendor of a King

clothed in majesty

let all the earth rejoice!

Let all the earth rejoice!

He wraps Himself in light,

and darkness tries to hide,

and trembles at His voice,

trembles at His voice

Chorus

How great is our God sing with me how

great is our God, and all will see how

great, how

great, is our

God!

Bridge   *Name above all names!*

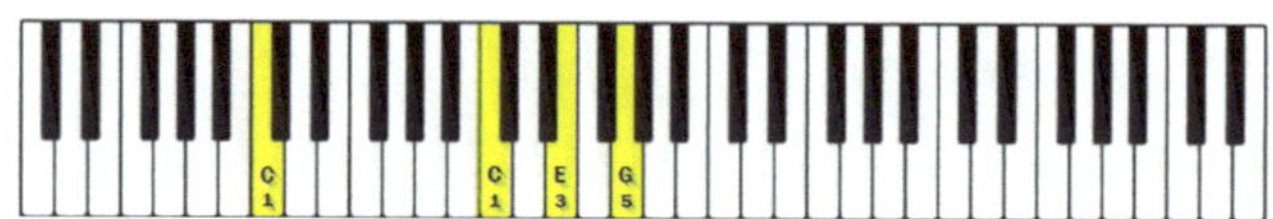

Worthy of all praise!

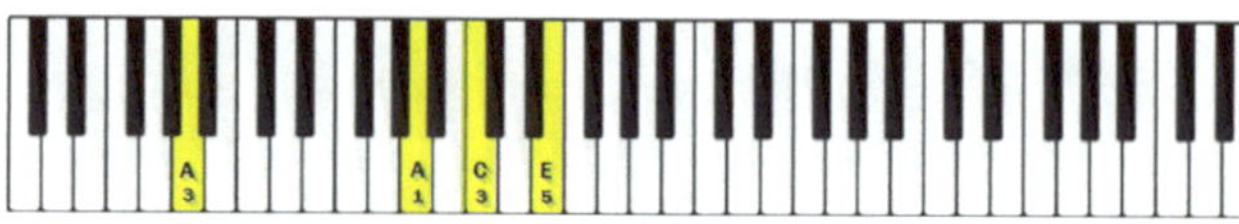

My heart will sing

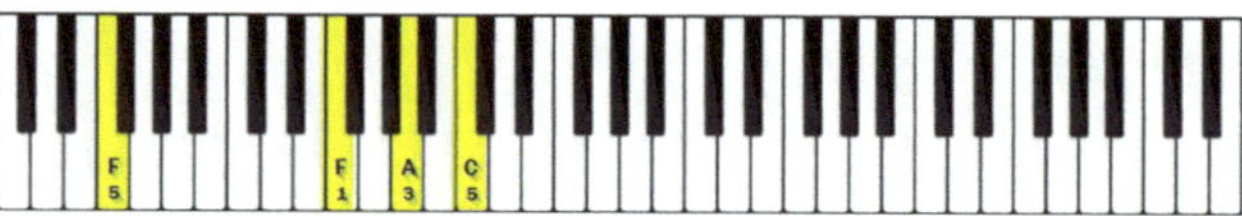

how great is our

God!

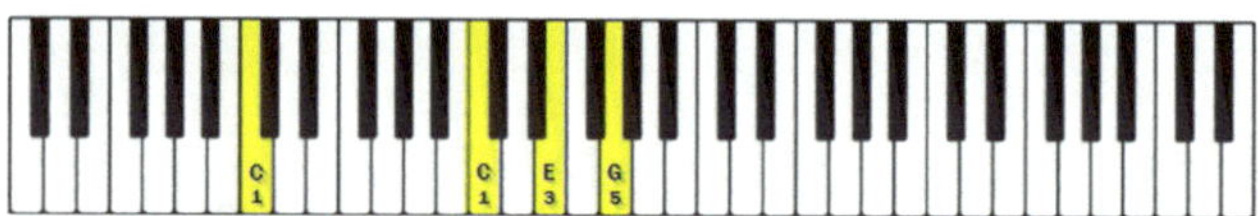

Chorus   *How great is our God sing with me how*

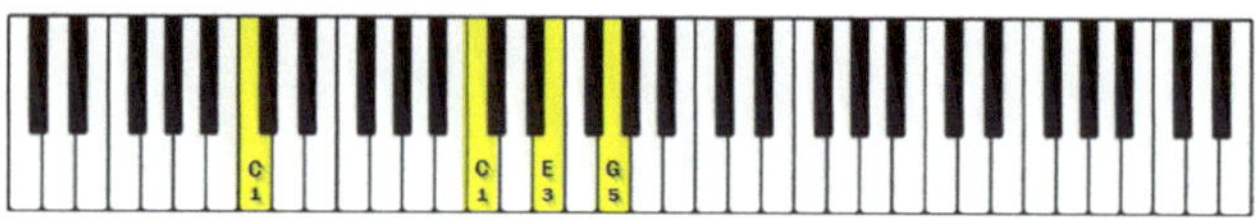

great is our God, and all will see how

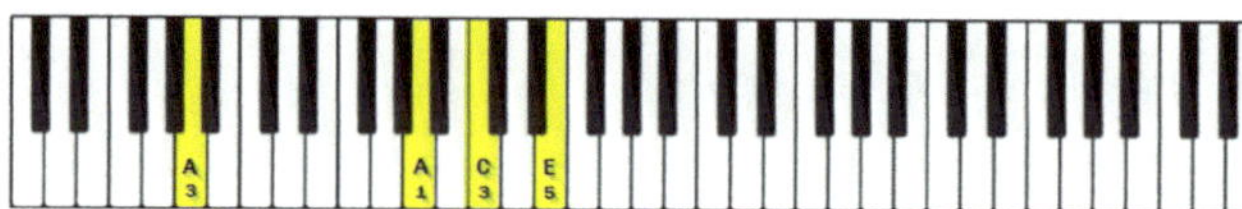

great, how

great, is our

God!

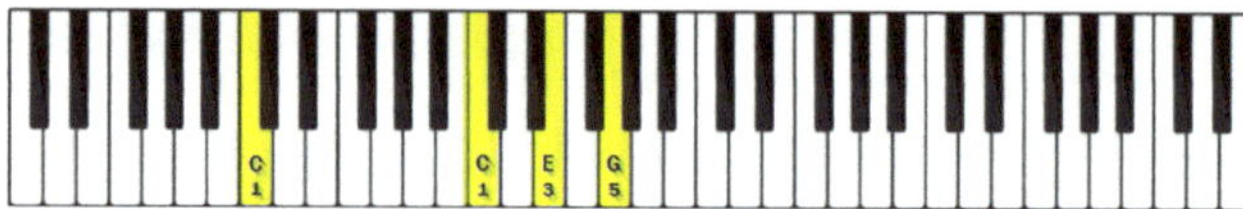

Here I Am to Worship

Tim Hughes

Time=4

[Verse 1]
```
C            G              Dm
Light of the world you stepped down into darkness
C            G         F
Opened my eyes let me see
C            G        Dm
Beauty that made this heart adore you
C            G          F
Hope of a life spent with you
```

[Chorus]
```
            C
Here I am to worship
            G
Here I am to bow down
            C                    F
Here I am to say that you're my God
            C
You're all together lovely
            G
All together worthy
            C         F
All together wonderful to me
```

[Verse 2]
```
C        G              Dm
King of all days oh so highly exalted
C          G      F
Glorious in heaven above
C            G            Dm
Humbly you came to the earth you created
C          G          F
All for love's sake became poor
```

[Chorus]
```
            C
Here I am to worship
            G
Here I am to bow down
            C                    F
Here I am to say that you're my God
            C
You're all together lovely
            G
All together worthy
            C         F
All together wonderful to me
```

[Bridge]
```
       G    C         F
And I'll never know how much it costs
    G     C   F
To see my sins upon that cross
         G    C         F
And I'll never know how much it costs
    G     C   F
To see my sins upon that cross
```

[Chorus]

Here I Am to Worship

Tim Hughes

Chords Used: C(I) Dm(ii) F(IV) G(V)

Verse 1

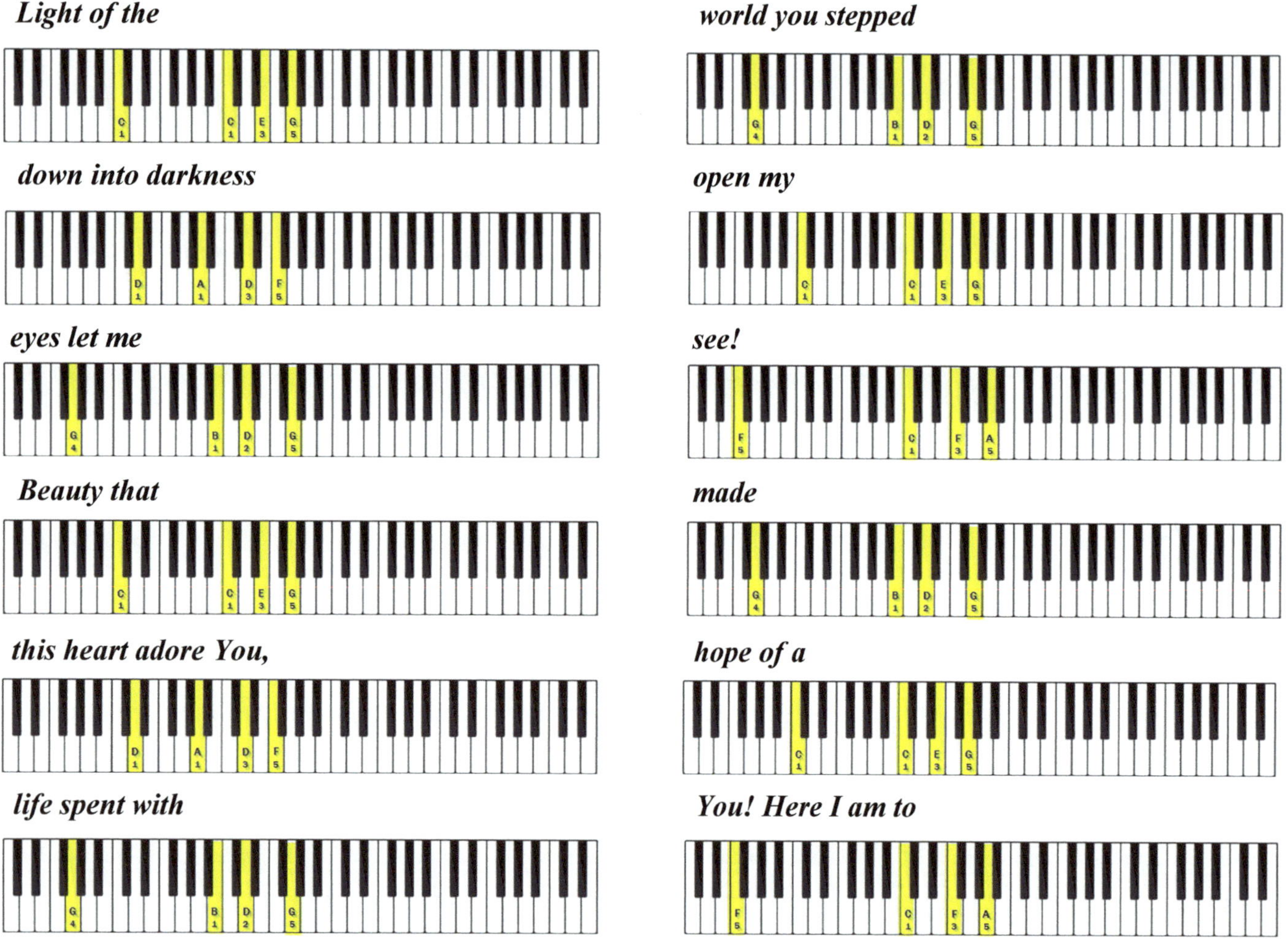

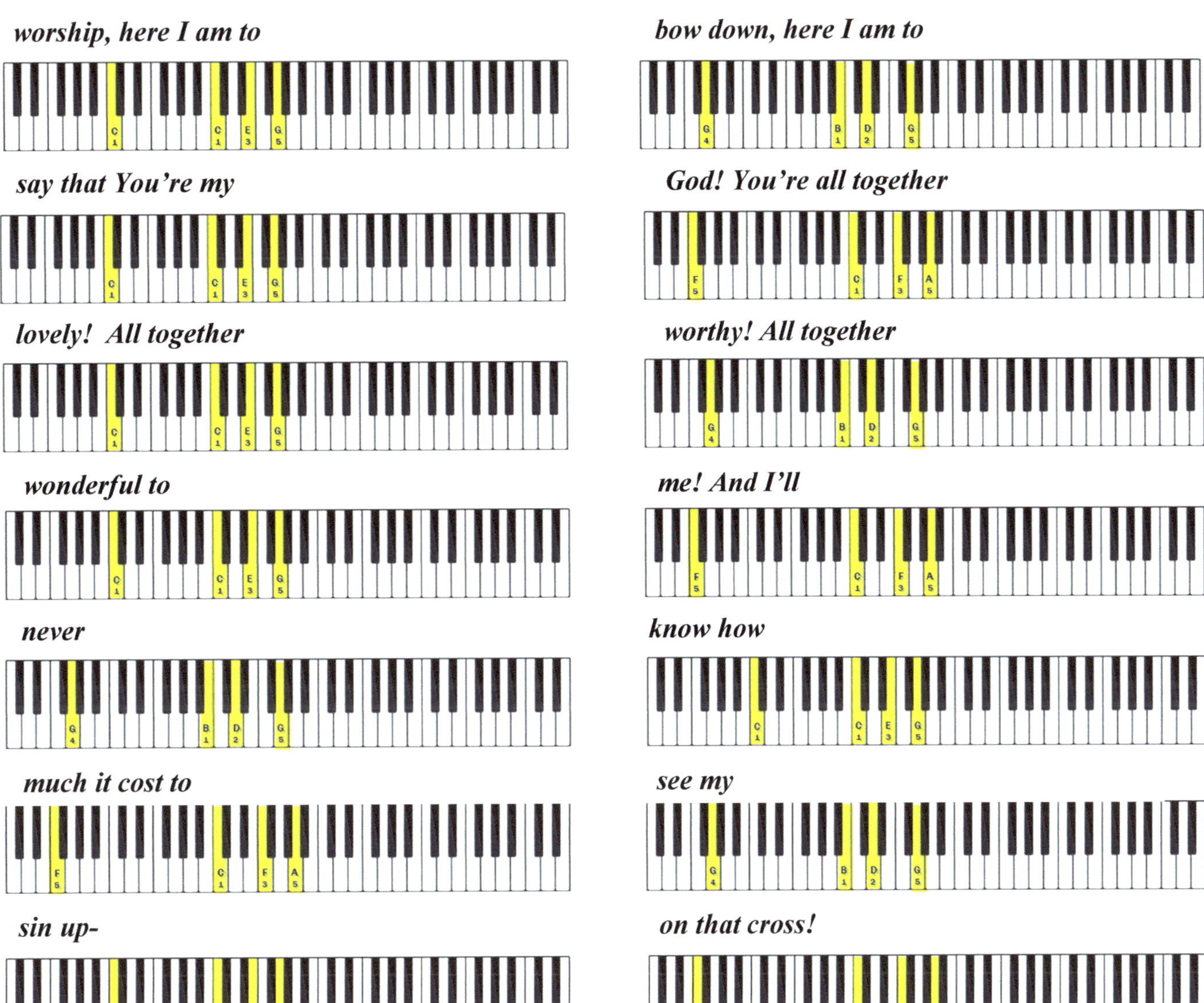
worship, here I am to
bow down, here I am to
say that You're my
God! You're all together
lovely! All together
worthy! All together
wonderful to
me! And I'll
never
know how
much it cost to
see my
sin up-
on that cross!

Bridge

Jesus Paid It All

Traditional

Time=3

[Verse 1]
```
    C
I hear the Savior say
     G              C
Thy strength indeed is small.
         C                  F
 Child of weakness watch and pray
       C    G   C
Find in me Thine all in all.
```

[Chorus]
```
C            F
Jesus paid it all.
C          G
All to Him I owe.
C            F
Sin had left a crimson stain,
      C    G      C
He washed it white as snow
```

[Verse 2]
```
      C
Lord now indeed I find
     G            C
Thy power and thine alone
        C            F
Can change the leper's spots
      C    G    C
And melt the heart of stone
```

[Chorus]
```
C            F
Jesus paid it all.
C          G
All to Him I owe.
C            F
Sin had left a crimson stain,
      C    G      C
He washed it white as snow.
```

[Verse 3]
```
        C
And when before the throne
     G            C
I stand in him complete
          C            F
Jesus died my soul to save
      C    G    C
My lips shall still repeat
```

[Chorus]
```
C            F
Jesus paid it all.
C          G
All to Him I owe.
C            F
Sin had left a crimson stain,
      C    G      C
He washed it white as snow.
```

[Bridge]
```
      C                    F
Oh praise the one who paid my debt
        C                       F
And raised this life up from the dead.
(x6)
```

[Chorus]
```
C            F
Jesus paid it all.
C          G
All to Him I owe.
C            F
Sin had left a crimson stain,
      C    G      C
He washed it white as snow.
      C    G      C
He washed it white as snow.
      C    G      C
He washed it white as snow.
```

Play along!
https://www.youtube.com/
watch?v=l1ll4K5ko7U

Jesus Paid It All

Traditional

Chords Used: C(I) F(IV) G(V)

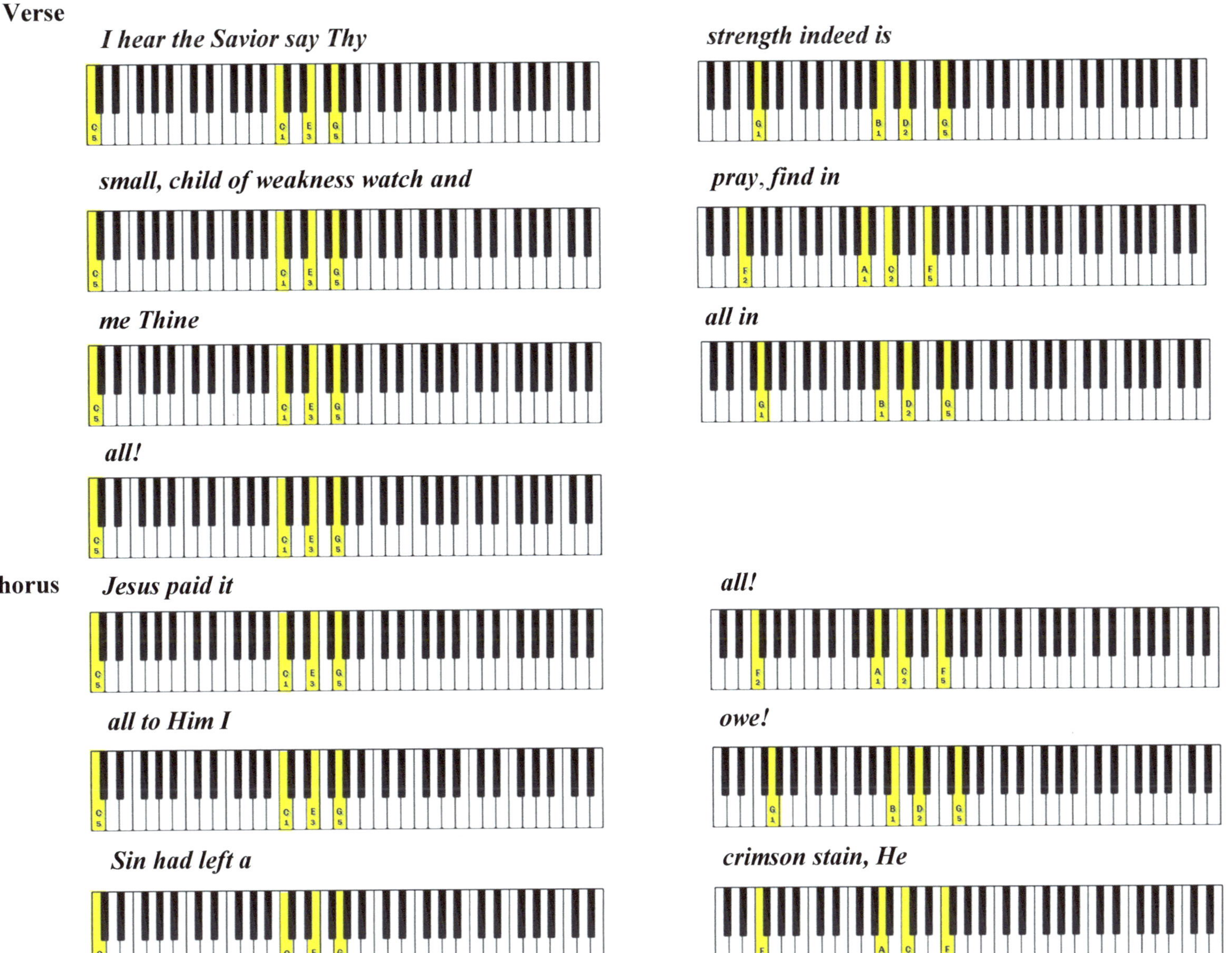

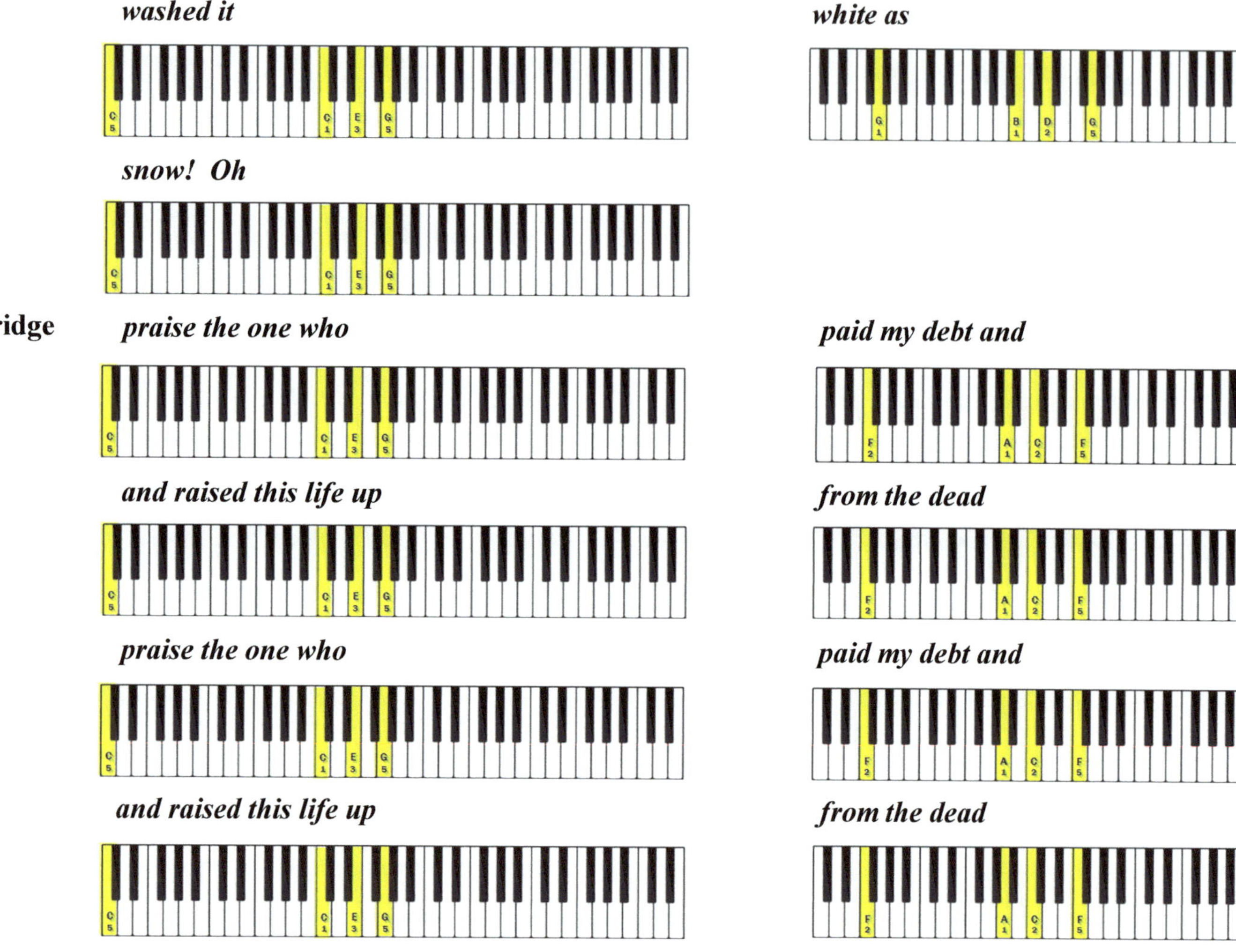

washed it
white as
snow! Oh
praise the one who
paid my debt and
and raised this life up
from the dead
praise the one who
paid my debt and
and raised this life up
from the dead

Bridge

Time=4

[Intro]

| C | C | Am | Am | F | F |

[Verse 1]

C
I just want to speak the Name of Jesus
Am
Over every heart and every mind
F
I know there is peace within Your presence
    C
I speak Jesus

[Verse 2]

C
I just want to speak the Name of Jesus
Am
'Til every dark addiction starts to break
    F
Declaring there is hope and there is freedom
    C
I speak Jesus

[Chorus]

      G
Your name is power
   C   F
Your name is healing
      C
Your name is life

      G
Break every stronghold
     C   F
Shine through the shadows
     C
Burn like a fire

[Verse 3]

C
I just want to speak the Name of Jesus
Am
Over fear and all anxiety
   F
To every soul held captive by depression
    C
I speak Jesus

[Chorus]

[Bridge] 2X

    C
Shout Jesus from the mountains
 C
And Jesus in the streets
Am
Jesus in the darkness over every enemy
F
Jesus for my family
F   C
I speak the holy name Jesus

[Chorus]

      G
Your name is power
   C   F
Your name is healing
      C
Your name is life
      G
Break every stronghold
     C   F
Shine through the shadows
     C
Burn like a fire
      G
Your name is power
   C   F
Your name is healing
      C
Your name is life
      G
Break every stronghold
     C   F
Shine through the shadows
     C
Burn like a fire

VL-20

Chords Used: C(I) F(IV) G(V) Am(vi)

My Lighthouse
Rend Collective

Time=4

[Verse 1]

```
C                   F      C
In my wrestling and in my doubts
F      C            G
In my failures You won't walk out
C                   F      C
Your great love will lead me through
F        C        G        C
You are the peace in my troubled sea
F        C        G        C
You are the peace in my troubled sea
```

[Verse 2]
```
C                   F      C
In the silence You won't let go
F      C            G
In the questions Your truth will hold
C                   F      C
Your great love will lead me through
F        C        G        C
You are the peace in my troubled sea
F        C        G        C
You are the peace in my troubled sea
```

[Chorus]

```
F  C         Am  G
My lighthouse, My lighthouse
F            C        Am          G
Shining in the darkness, I will follow You
F  C         Am       G
My lighthouse, My lighthouse
F            C        Am          G
I will trust the promise, You will carry me
        F    C    G
Safe to shore-woah-woah
        F    C    G
Safe to shore-woah-woah
        F    C    G
Safe to shore-woah-woah
        C
Safe to shore
```

[Verse 3]
```
C    F              C
I won't fear what tomorrow brings
F            C        G
With each morning I'll rise and sing
C                  F      C
My God's love will lead me through
F        C        G        C
You are the peace in my troubled sea
F        C        G        C
You are the peace in my troubled sea
```

[Chorus]

[Bridge]

```
F        C
Fire before us
Am       G
You're the brightest
F        C        Am          G
You will lead us through the storms
F        C
Fire before us
Am       G
You're the brightest
F        C        Am          G
You will lead us through the storms
F    C
Fire before us
Am       G
You're the brightest
F        C        Am          G
You will lead us through the storms
F    C
Fire before us
Am       G
You're the brightest
F        C        Am          G
You will lead us through the storms
```

Play along!

**https://www.youtube.c
om/watch?v=HA8VtU**

Chords Used: C(I) F(IV) G(V) Am(vi)

Verse 1

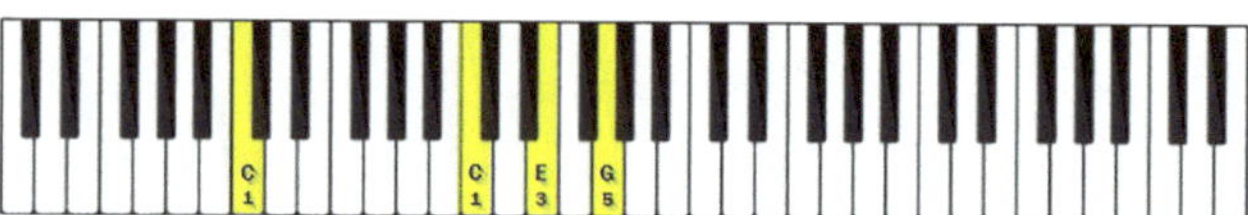

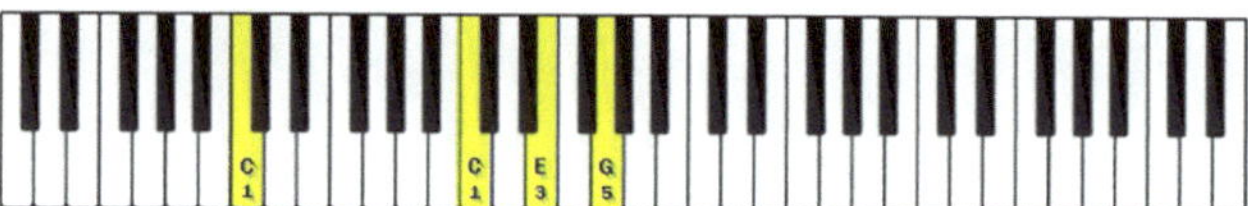

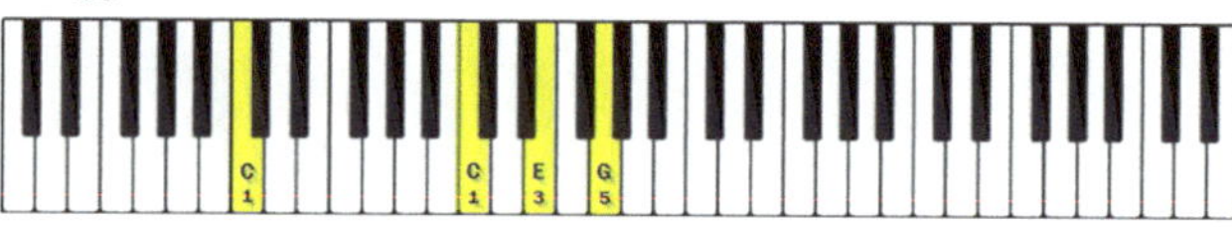

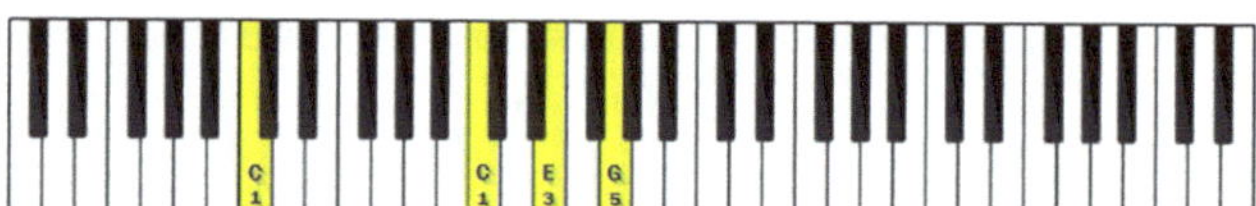

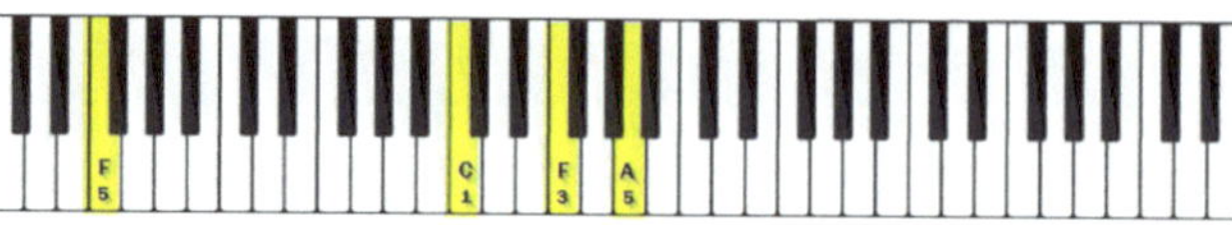

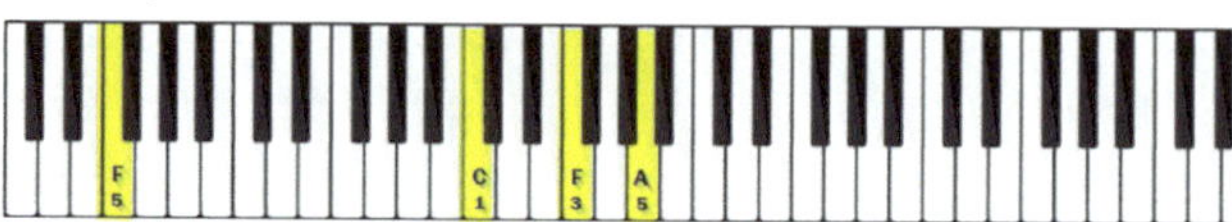

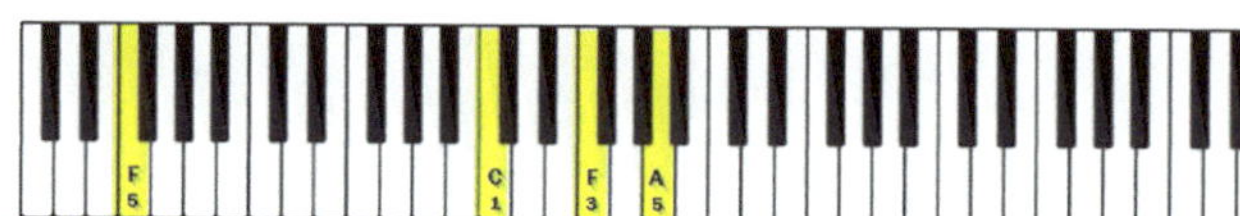

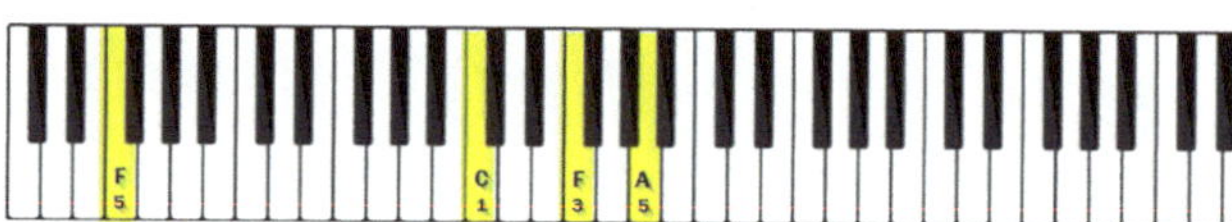

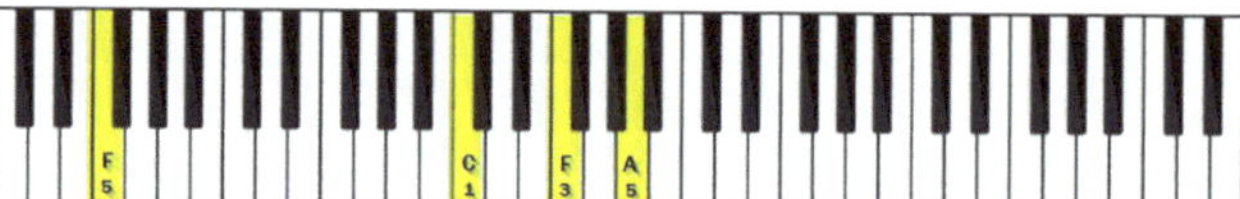

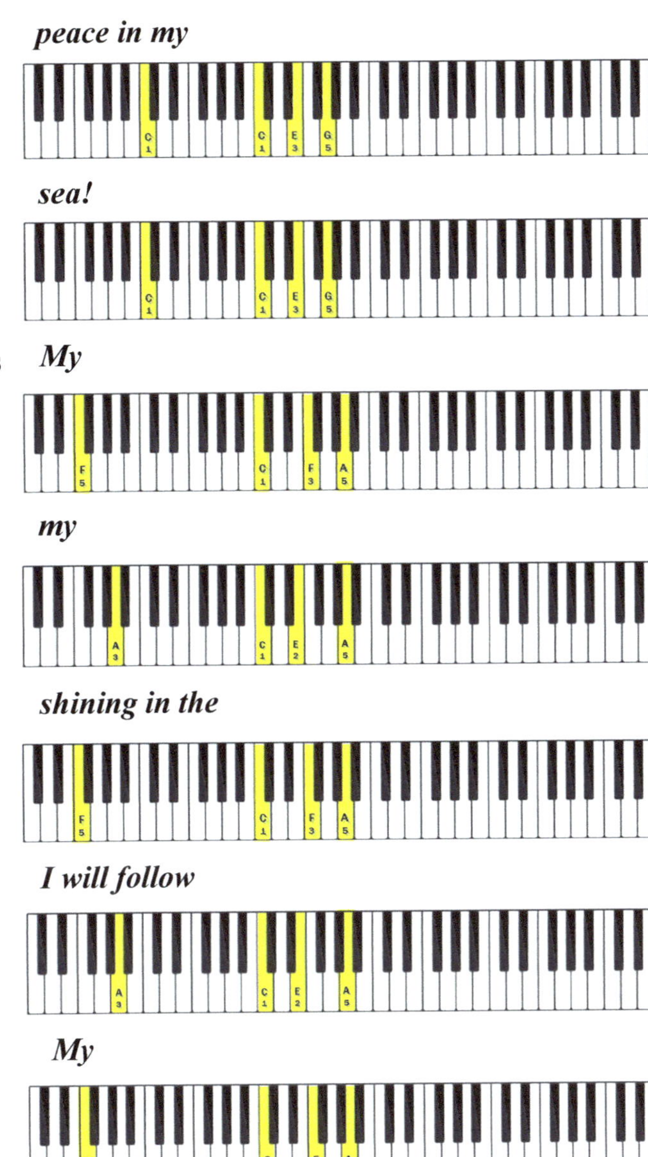

peace in my
sea!
My
my
shining in the
I will follow
My

Chorus

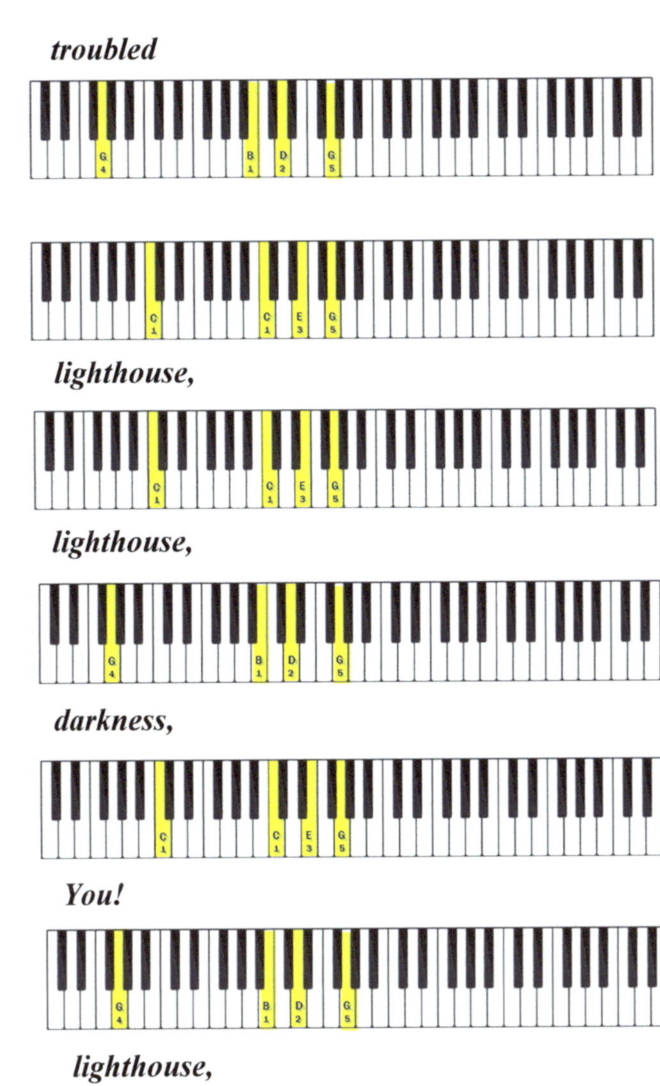

troubled
lighthouse,
lighthouse,
darkness,
You!
lighthouse,

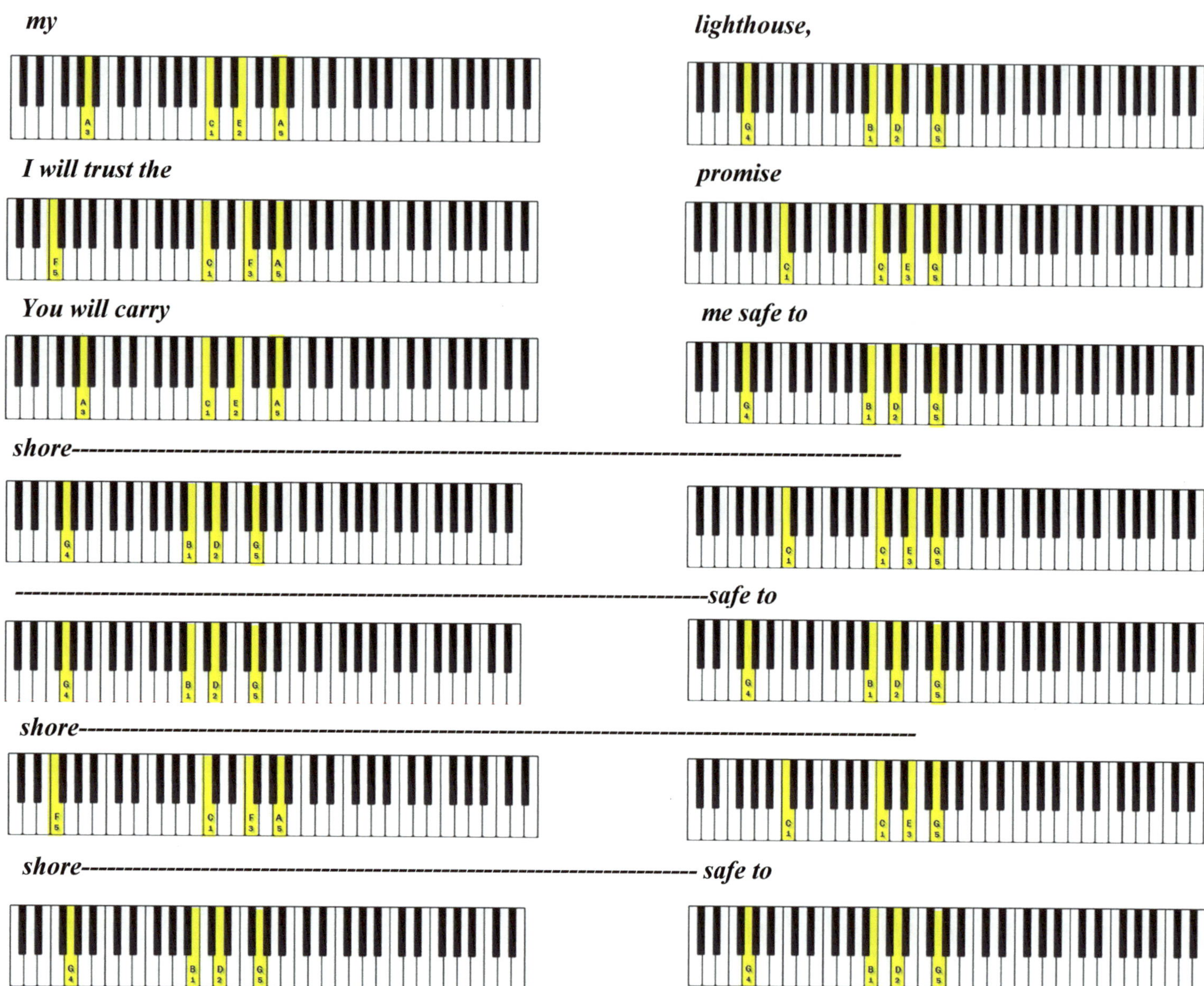

my
lighthouse,
I will trust the
promise
You will carry
me safe to
shore---
---safe to
shore---
shore-- safe to

shore---
F5 C1 F3 A5
C1 C1 E3 G5
--safe to
G4 B1 D2 G5
G4 B1 D2 G5
shore!
C1 C1 E3 G5
C1 C1 E3 G5
Fire be-
F5 C1 F3 A5
fore us
C1 C1 E3 G5
You're the
A3 C1 E2 A5
brightest
G4 B1 D2 G5
You will
F5 C1 F3 A5
lead us
C1 C1 E3 G5
through the
A3 C1 E2 A5
storm!
G4 B1 D2 G5

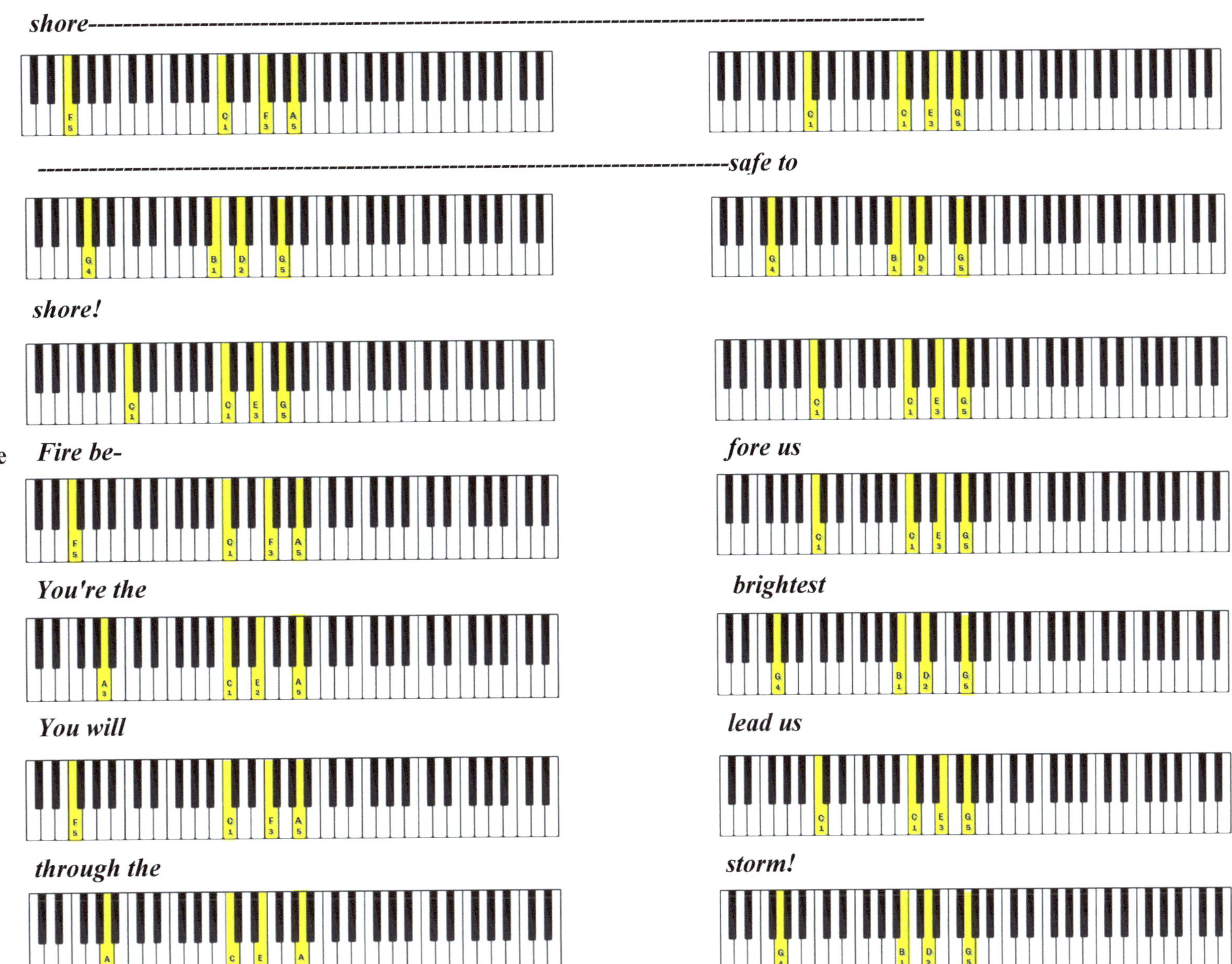

Bridge
4X

The Battle Belongs

Phil Wickham

Time=4

[Verse 1]
```
C                                        F
When all I see is the battle, You see my victory
Am                                 G         F
When all I see is the mountain, You see a mountain moved
C                                            F
And as I walk through the shadows, Your love surrounds me
Am                              G      C
There's nothing to fear now, for I am safe with You
```

[Chorus]
```
           F       C        G          Am        F
So when I fight, I'll fight on my knees, with my hands lifted high
    C            G     Am
Oh God, the battle belongs to You
      F      C      G       Am            F
Every fear I lay at your feet, I'll sing through the night
        C         G      C
Oh God, the battle belongs to You
```

[Verse 2]
```
C                                  F
And if You are for me, who can be against me
Am                        G         F
For Jesus there's nothing impossible for You
C                                        F
When all I see are the ashes, You see the beauty
Am                                G      C
When all I see is a cross, God You see the empty tomb
```

[Chorus]

[Bridge]
```
F           C              G
Almighty fortress, You go before us
                   Am            G         F
Nothing can stand against the power of our God
F              C                G
You shine in the shadows You win every battle
                   Am            G         F
Nothing can stand against the power of our God
```

[Chorus]
```
           F       C        G          Am            F
So when I fight, I'll fight on my knees, with my hands lifted high
    C            G     Am
Oh God, the battle belongs to You
      F      C      G       Am            F
Every fear I lay at your feet, I'll sing through the night
        C         G      C
Oh God, the battle belongs to You
```

Play along!
https://www.youtube.co
m/
watch?v=l11l4K5ko7U

VL-22

The Battle Belongs

Phil Wickham

Chords Used: C(I) F(IV) G(V) Am(vi)

Verse 1

When all I see is the battle, you see my

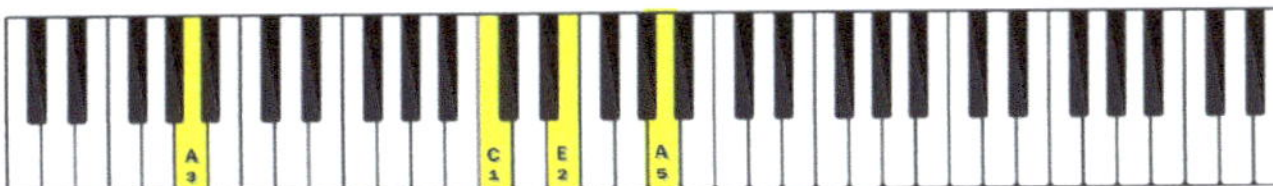

victory!

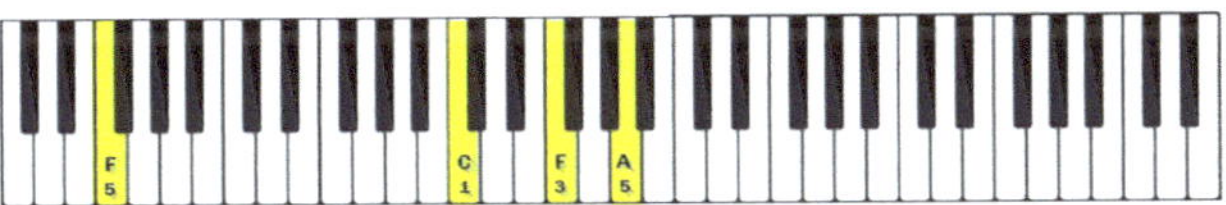

When all I see is the mountain, you see a

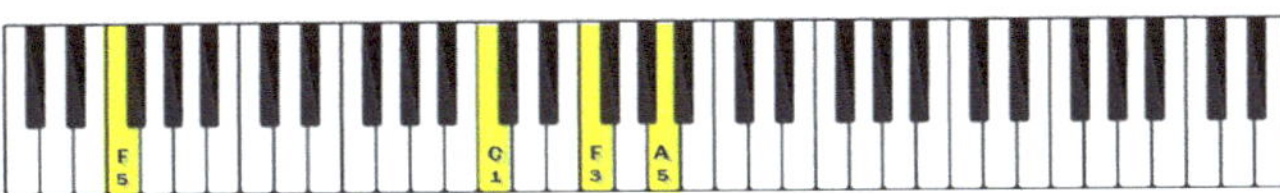

mountain

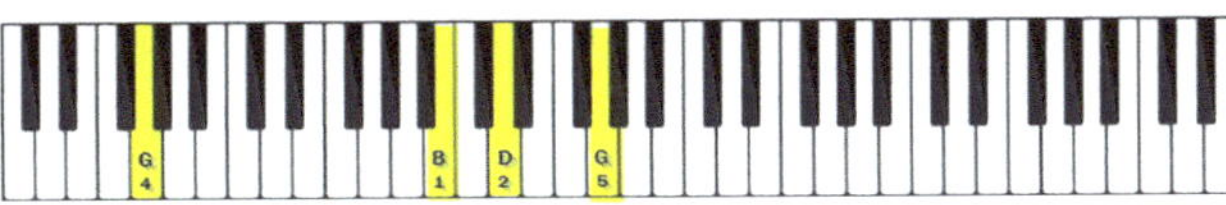

moved!

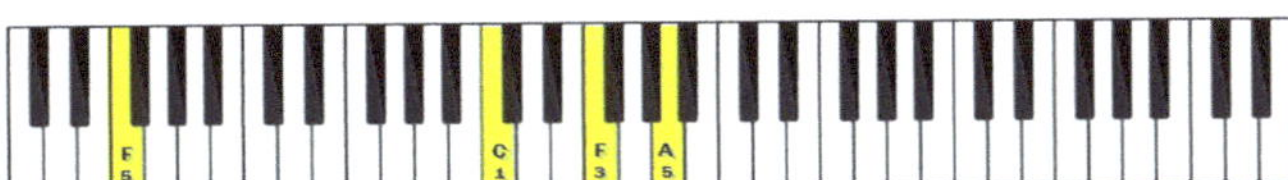

And as I walk through the shadows, your

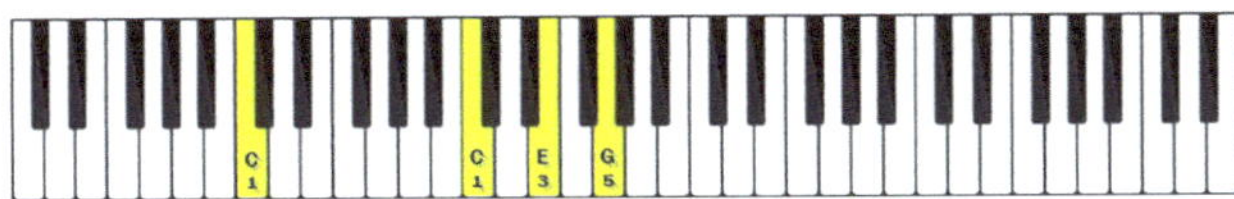

surrounds me!

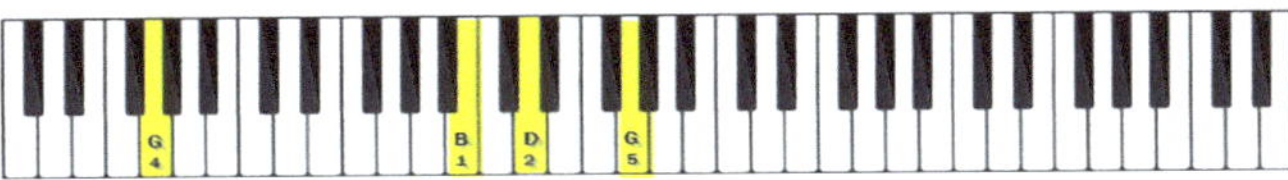

There's nothing to fear now, for I am

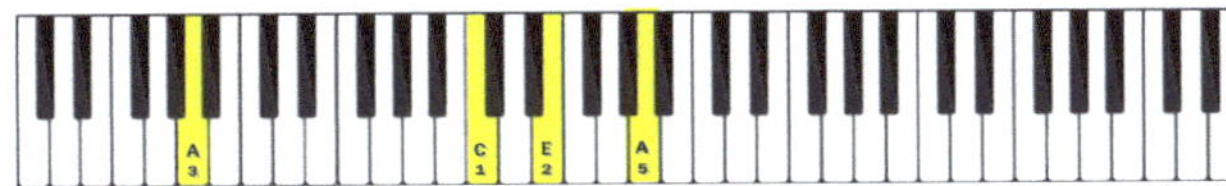

safe with

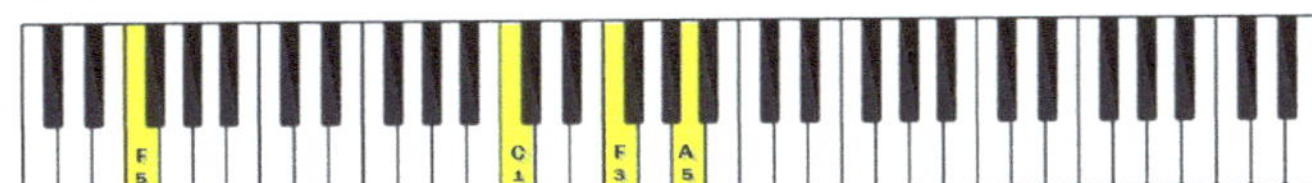

you! So when I

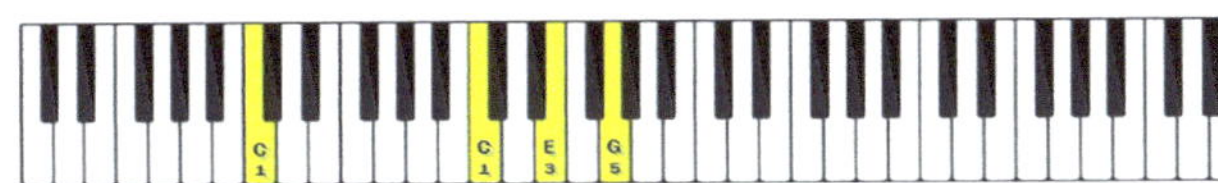

Chorus *fight, I'll*

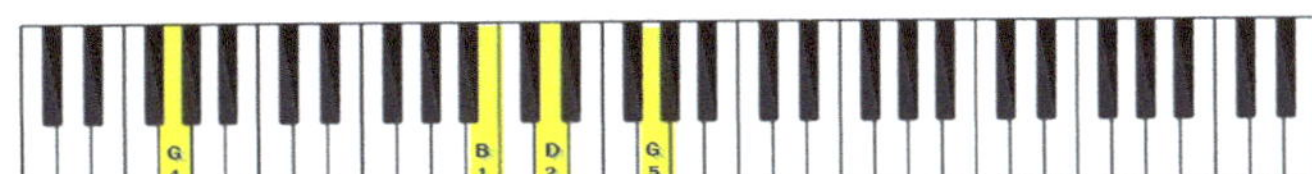

fight on my

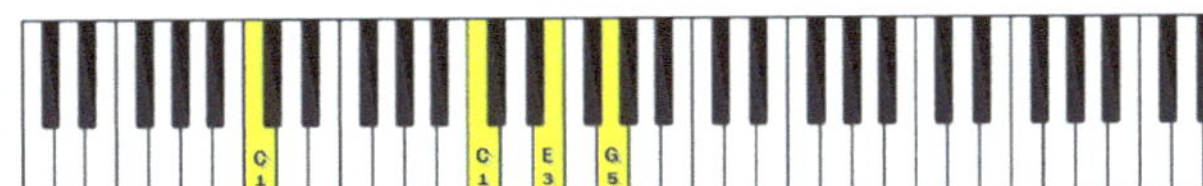

knees, with my

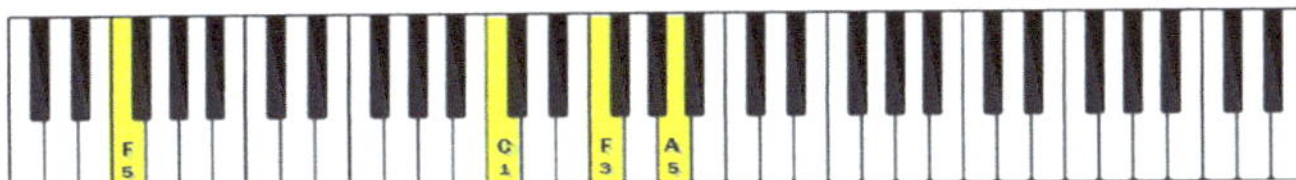

hands lifted

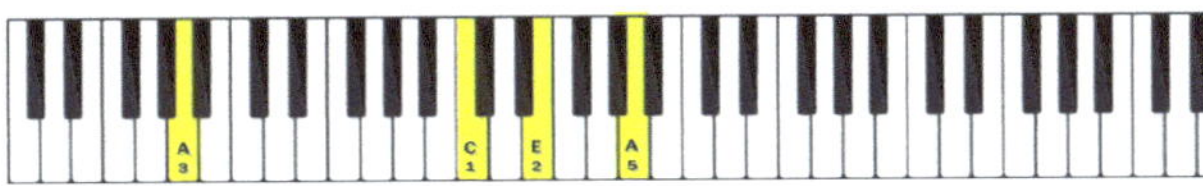

high Oh

God! The battle be-

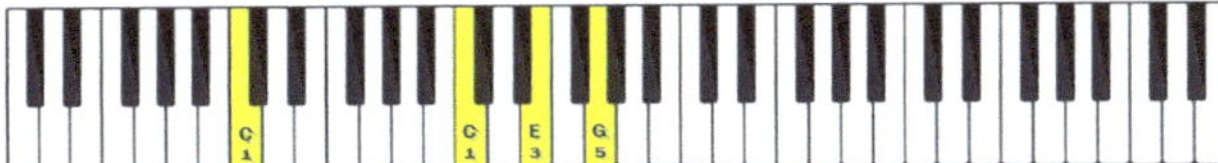

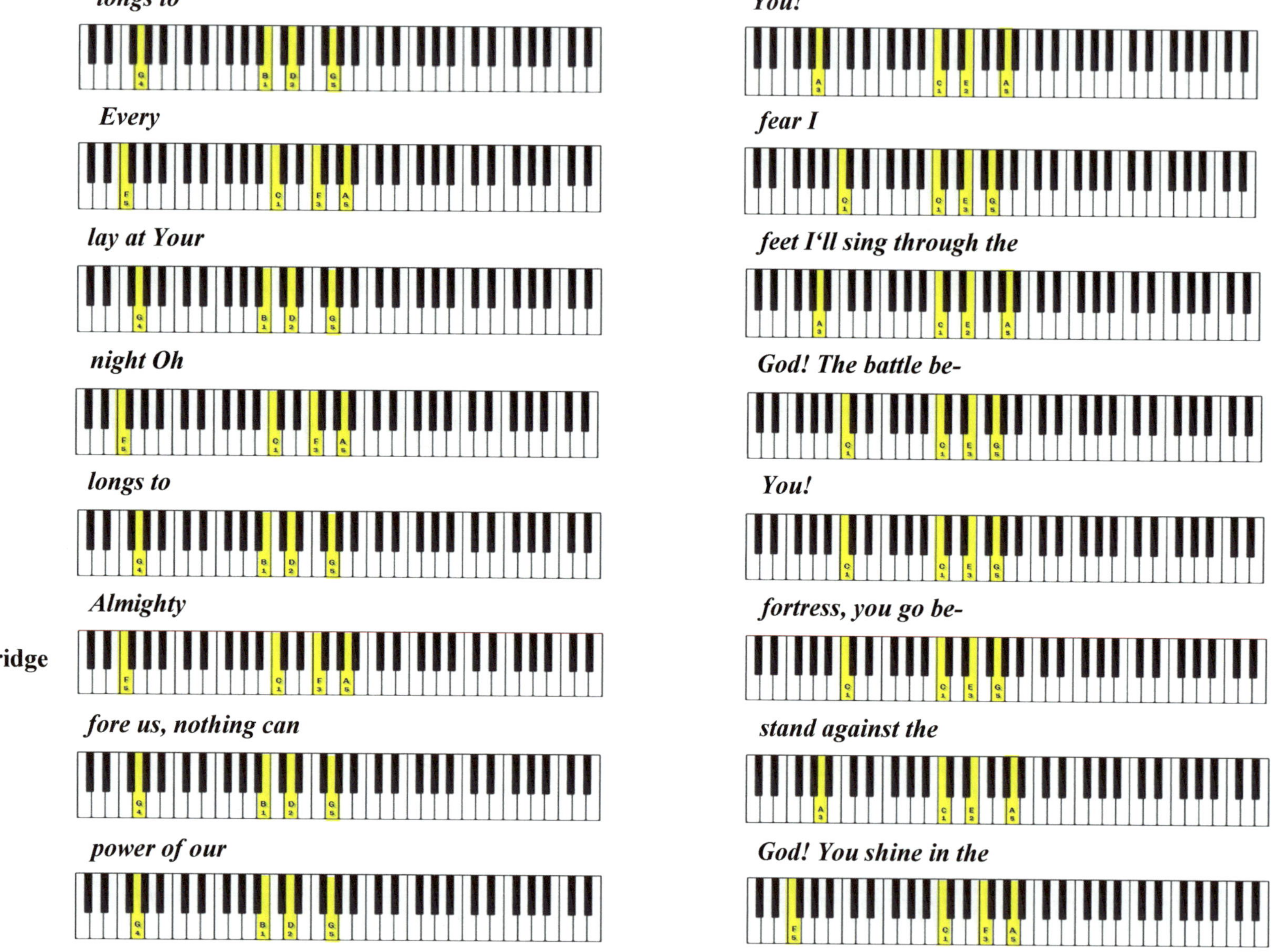

longs to
Every
lay at Your
night Oh
longs to
Almighty
Bridge
fore us, nothing can
power of our
You!
fear I
feet I'll sing through the
God! The battle be-
You!
fortress, you go be-
stand against the
God! You shine in the

shadows you win every

stand against the

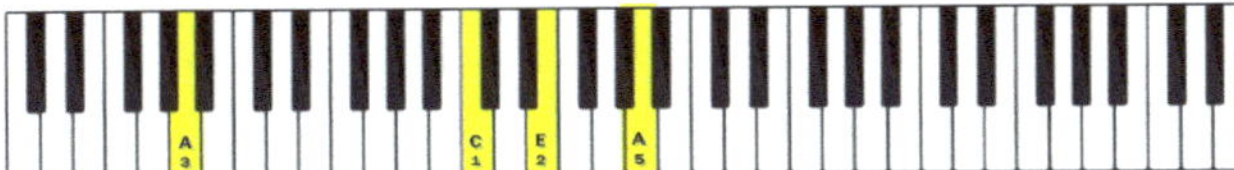

God! Almighty

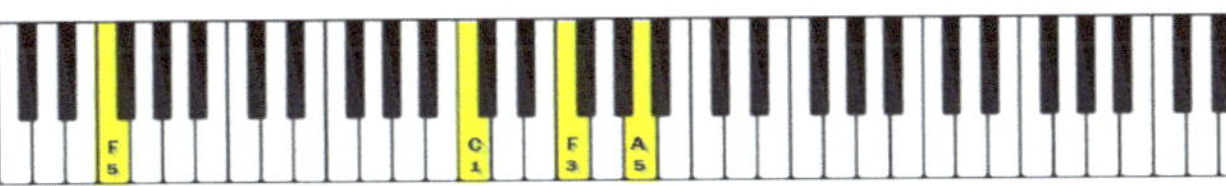

fore us, nothing can

power of our

shadows you win every

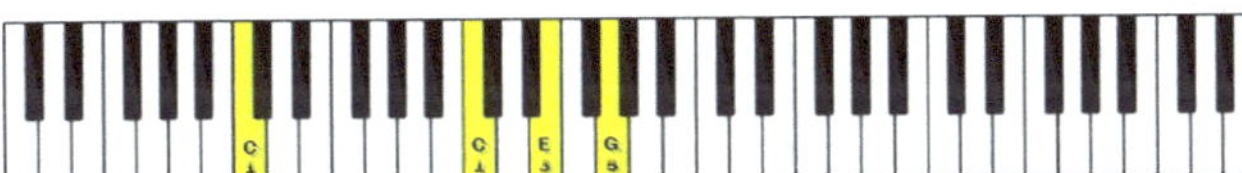

stand against the

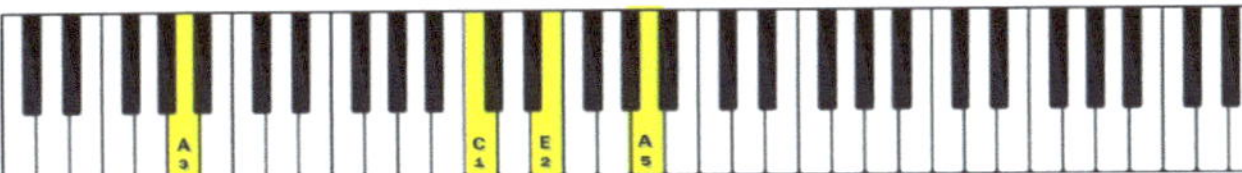

God!

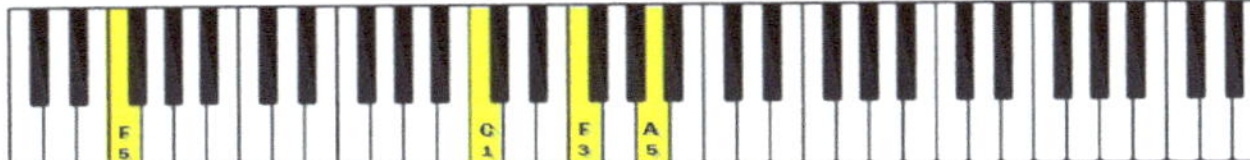

battle! Nothing can

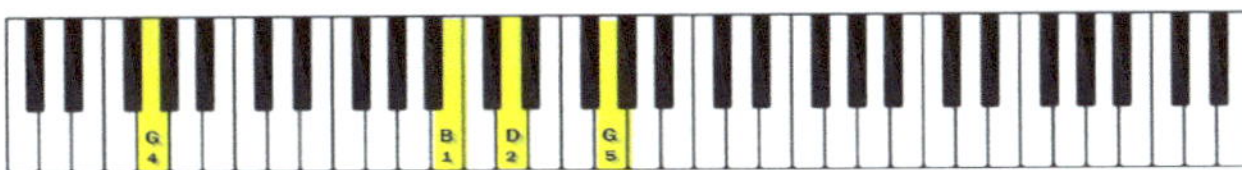

power of our

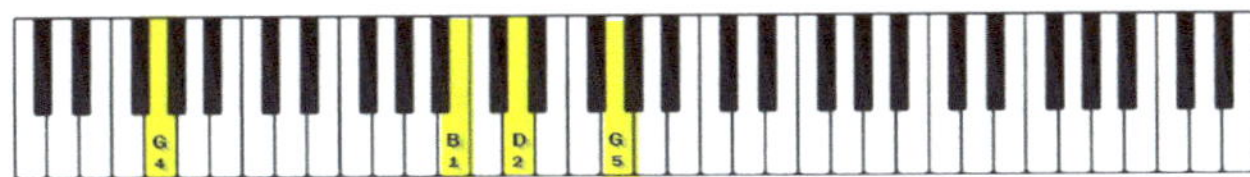

fortress, you go be-

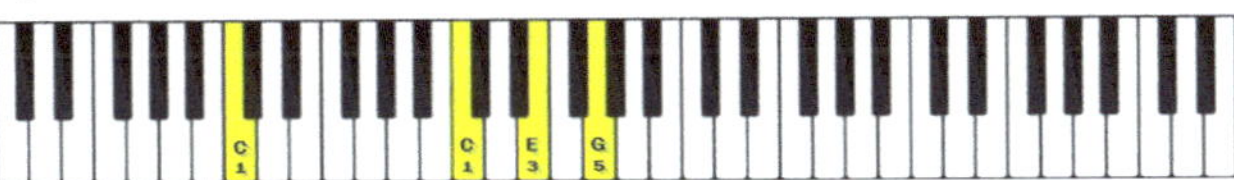

stand against the

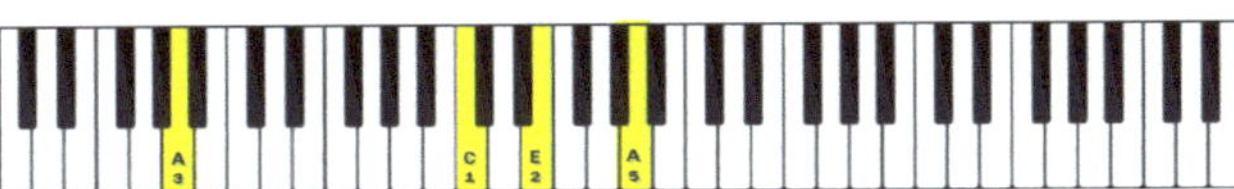

God! You shine in the

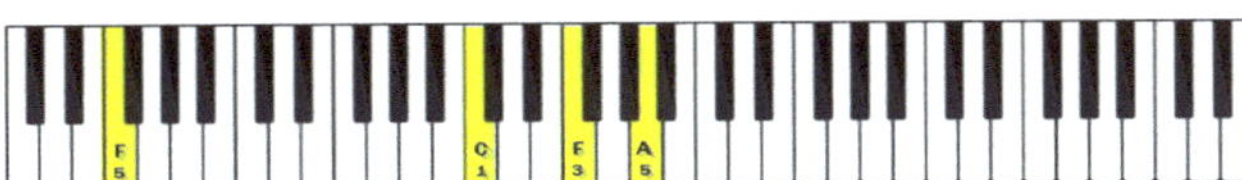

battle! Nothing can

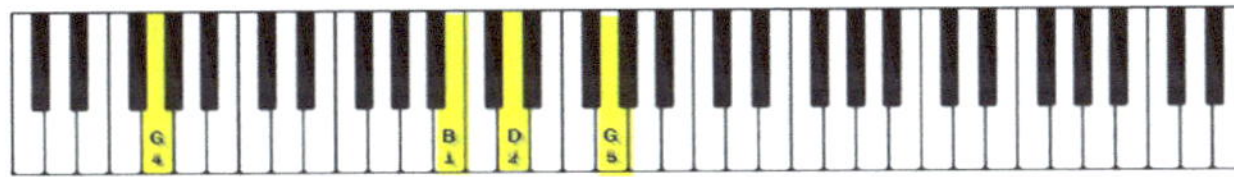

power of our

Same God

Brandon Lake

Time = 4

[Verse 1]
```
C                      F C
I'm calling on the God of Jacob
C                          F C
Whose love endures through generations
Am                              F
I know that You will keep Your covenant
C                      F C
I'm calling on the God of Moses
C                      F C
The One who opened up the ocean
Am                      F              C
I need You now to do the same thing for me
```

[Chorus]
```
C              G
O God, my God, I need You
Am         G         F
O God, my God, I need You now
      C       F    G
How I need You now
C              G
O Rock, O Rock of Ages
Am              G      F
I'm standing on Your faithfulness
C     F     G  C
On Your faithfulness
```

[Verse 2]
```
C                      F C
I'm calling on the God of Mary
```

```
C                          F C
Whose favor rests upon the lowly
Am                                  F
I know with You all things are possible
```

```
C                      F C
I'm calling on the God of David
C                          F C
Who made a shepherd boy courageous
Am
I may not face Goliath
F
but I've got my own giants
```

[Chorus 2]

[Bridge]
```
C
You heard Your children then
Am
You hear Your children now
F
You are the same God
F            G
You are the same God
C
You answered prayers back then
Am
And You will answer now
F          C
You are the same God
F            G
You are the same God
```

```
C
You were providing then
Am
You are providing now
F                    C
You are the same God
F              G
You are the same God
```

[Bridge 2]
```
C
You freed the captives then
Am
You're freeing hearts right now
F
You are the same God
F            G
You are the same God
C
You touched the lepers then
Am
I feel Your touch right now
F
You are the same God
F            G
You are the same God
```
[End]
```
C                  F    C
I'm calling on the Holy Spirit
C                            F  C  G C
Almighty river, come and fill me again
```

Same God

Brandon Lake

Verse 1

I'm calling on the God of

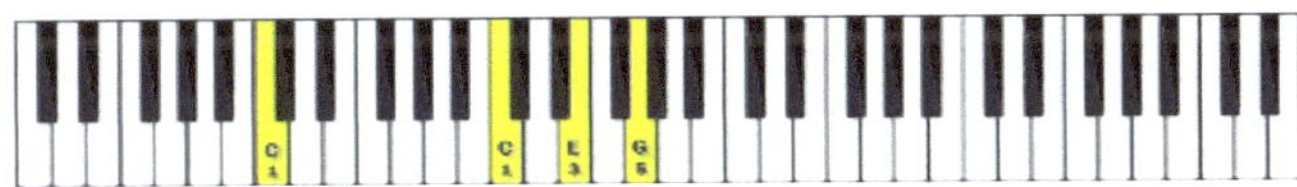

cob, whose love endures through gener-

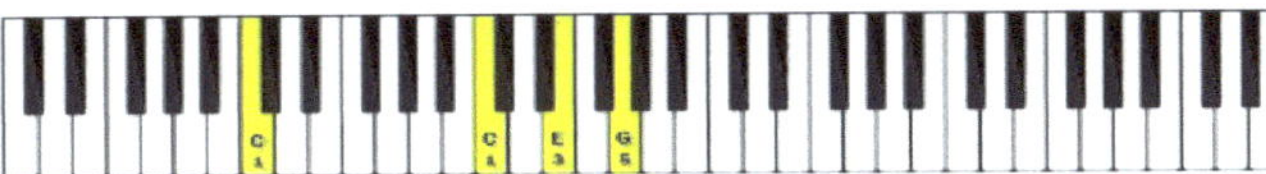

tions!

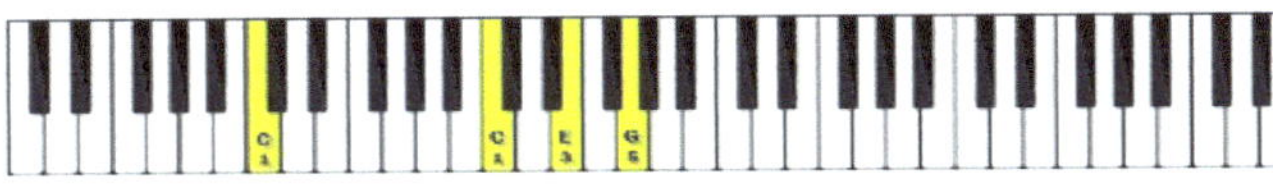

covenant

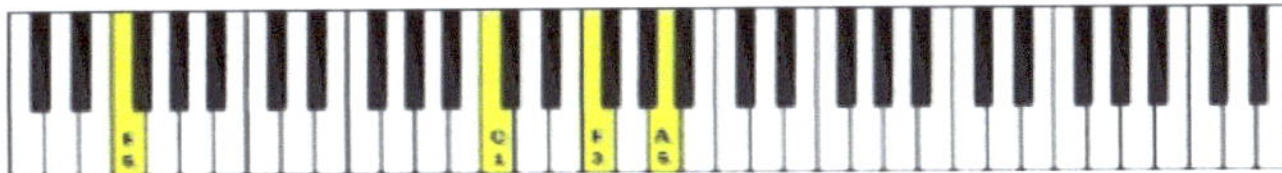

Mo-

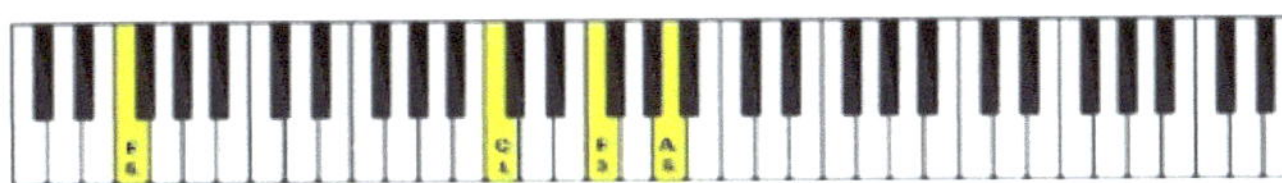

o-

I need You now to do the

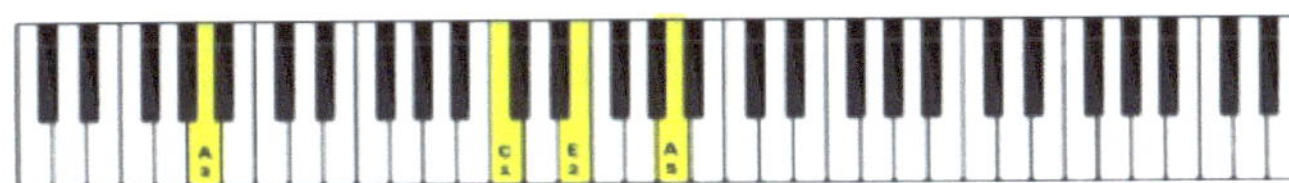

me!

Ja-

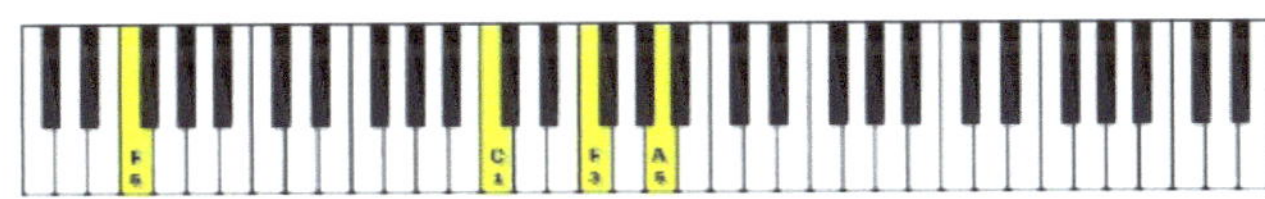

a-

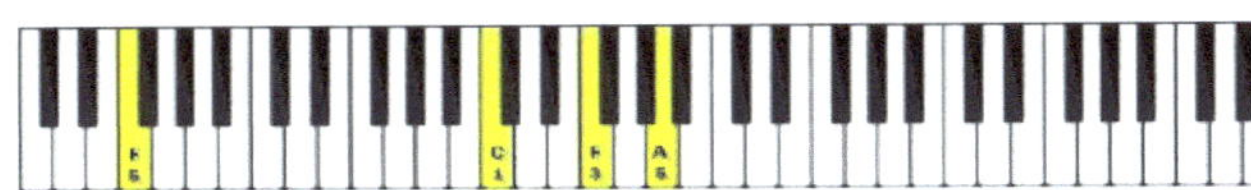

I know that You will keep Your

I'm calling on the God of

ses! The One who opened up the

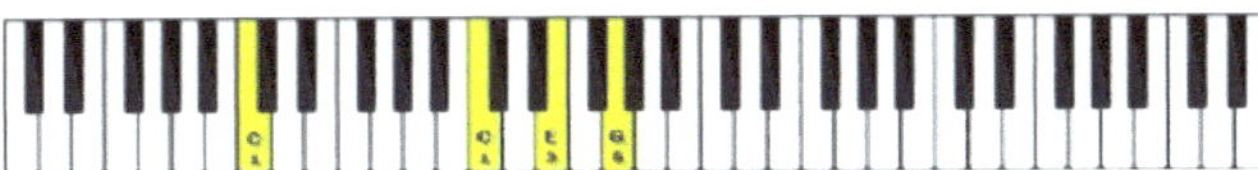

ceans!

same thing for

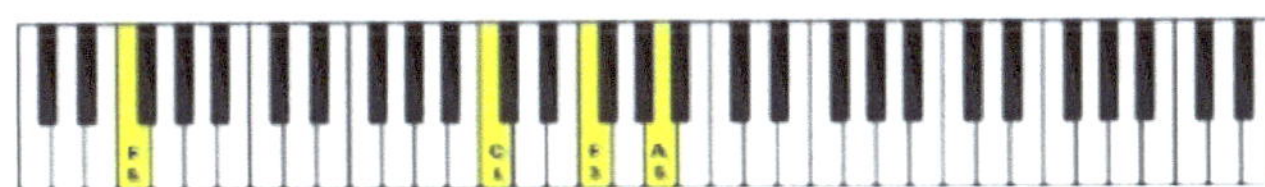

Chorus

O God, my God, I

O God, my God, I

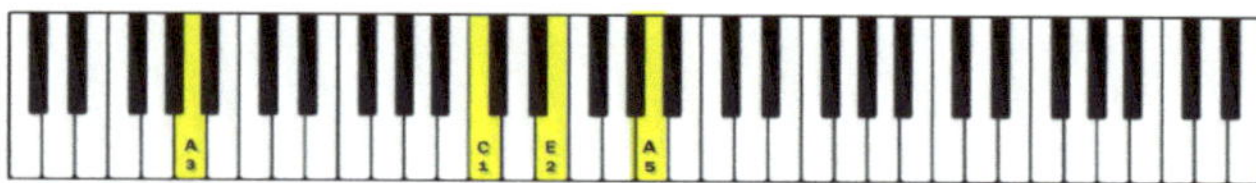

now, how I

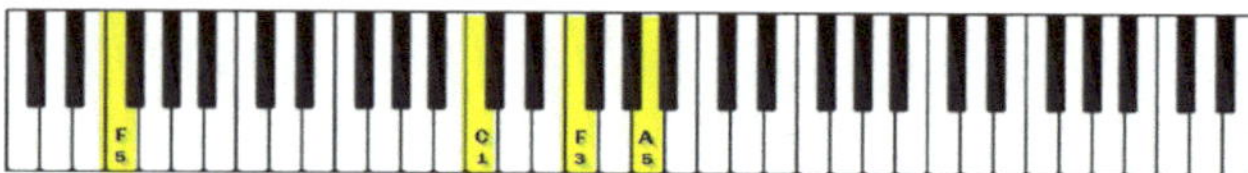

now!

O Rock, O Rock of

I'm standing on Your

ness,

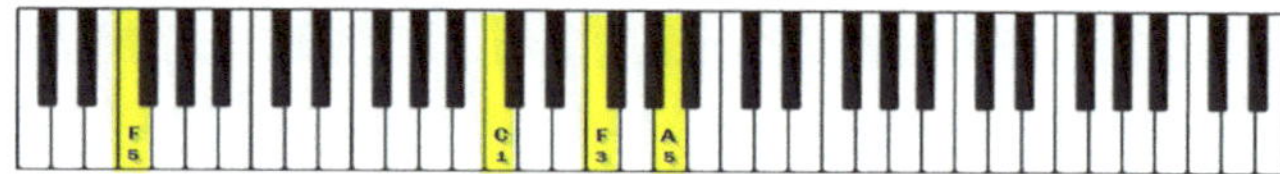

faithful-

need You

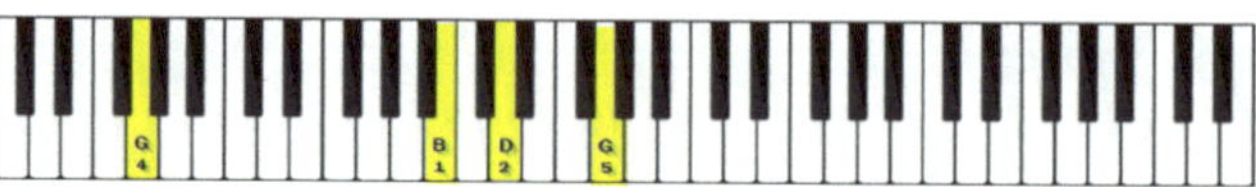

need You

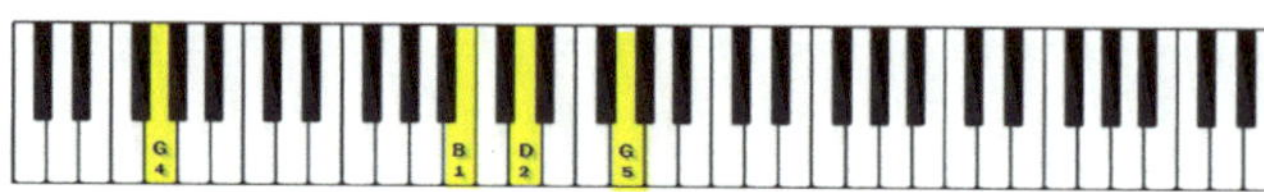

need You

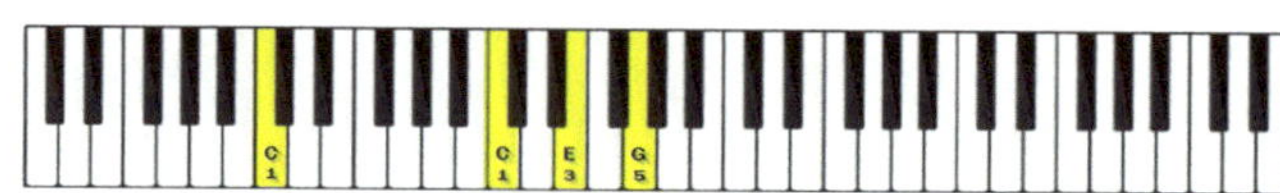

Ages

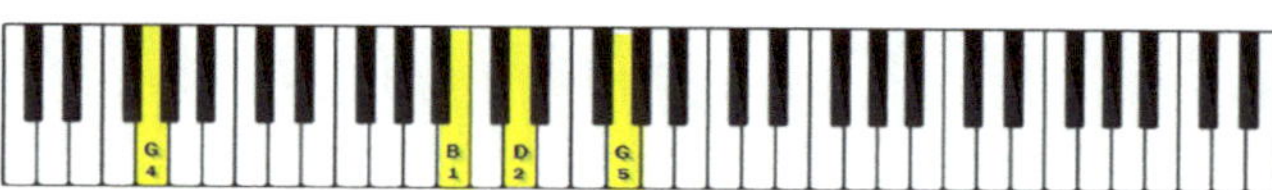

faithful-

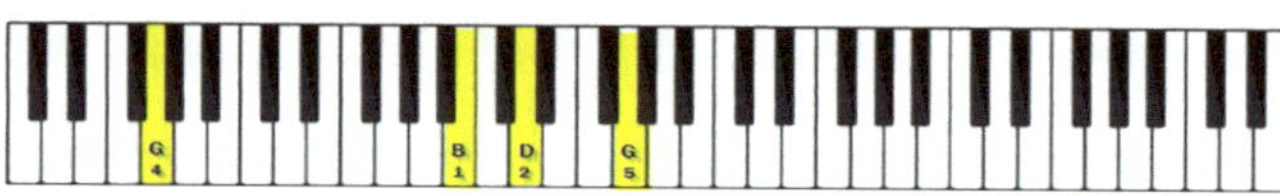

on Your

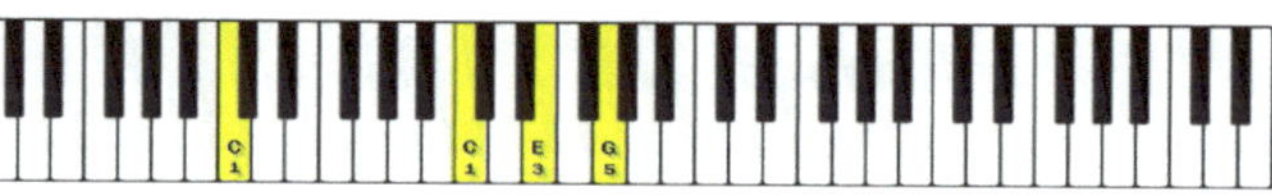

ness!

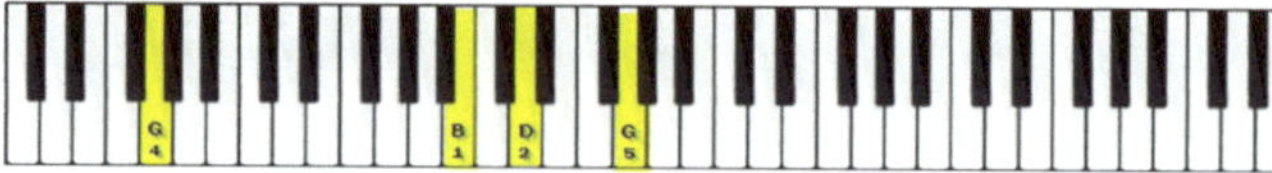

Bridge 1

You heard Your children then

You hear Your children now

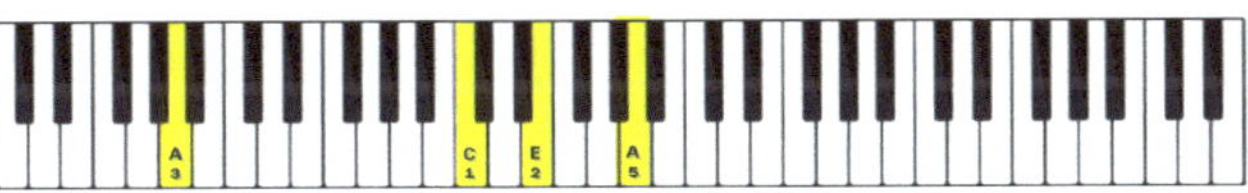

You are the same God! You are the same

God!

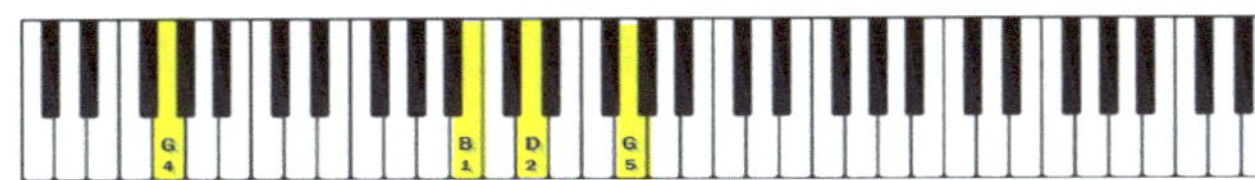

You answered prayers back then,

and You will answer now

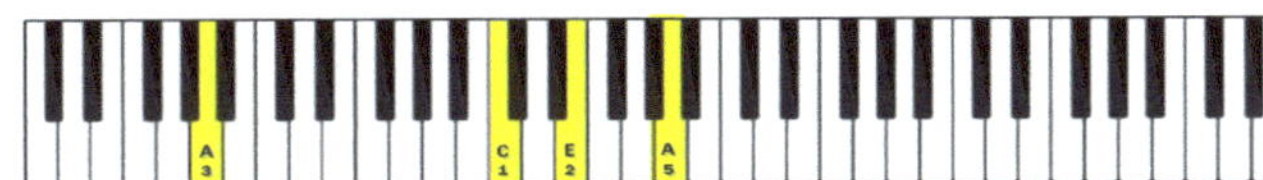

You are the same

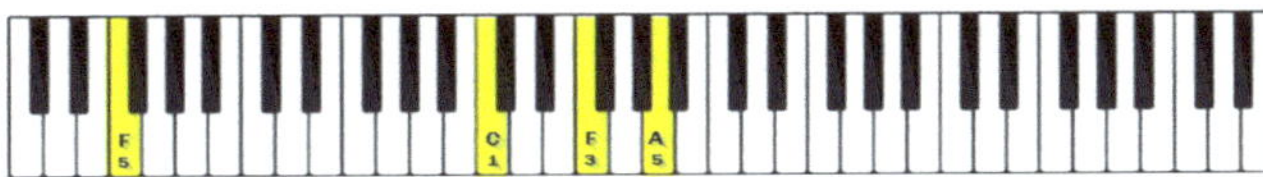

God!

You are the same

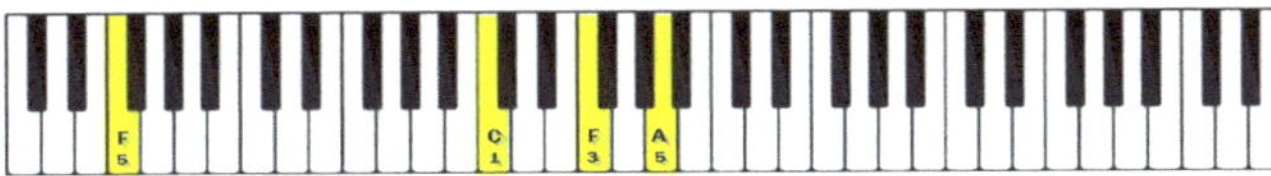

God!

You were providing then

You are providing now

You are the same

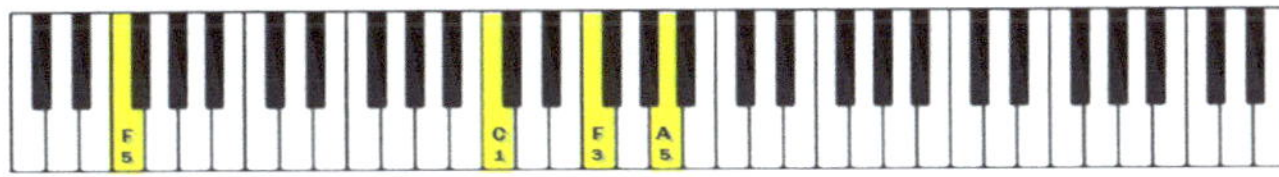

God!

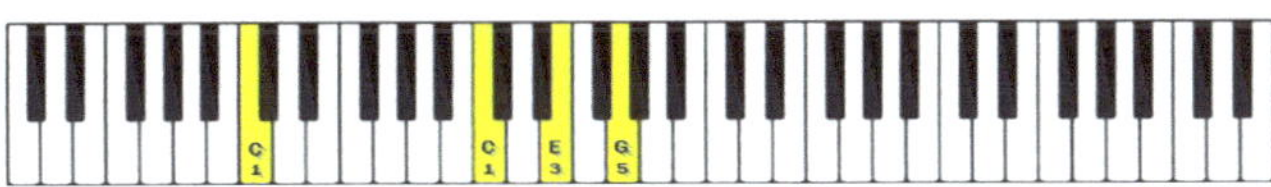

You are the same

God!

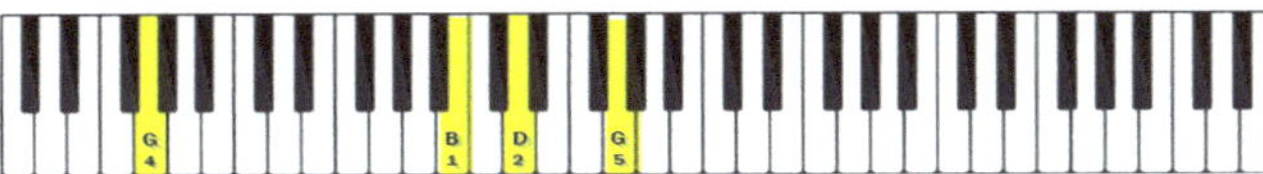

Bridge 2

You freed the captives

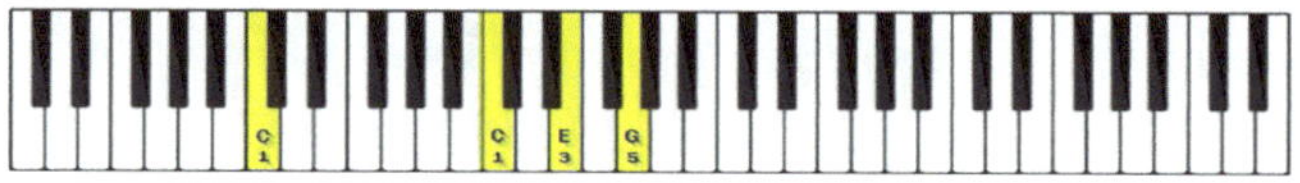

now! You are the same God! You are the same

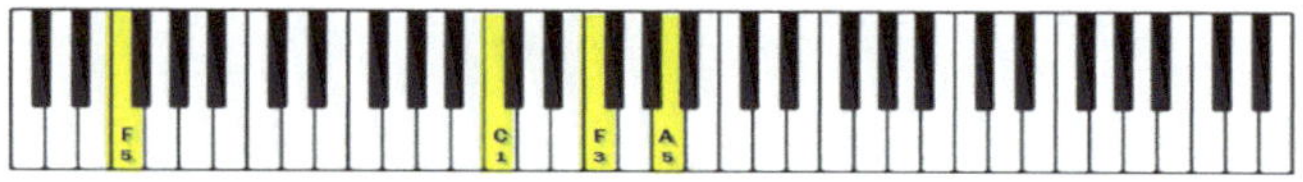

You touched the lepers then

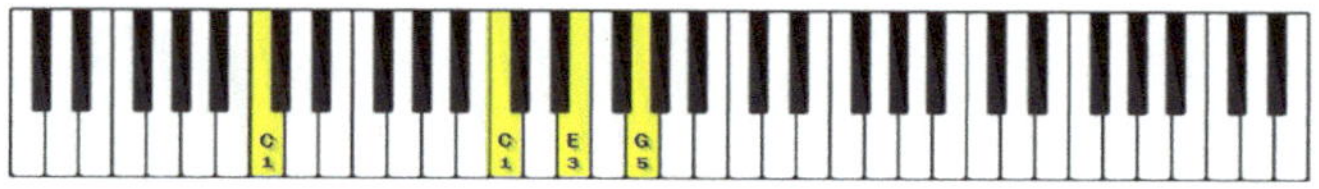

You are the same God! You are the same

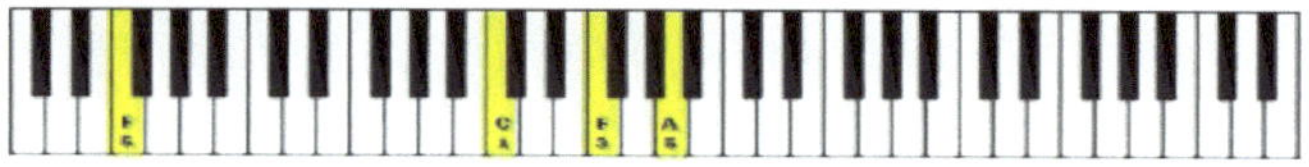

I'm calling on the Holy

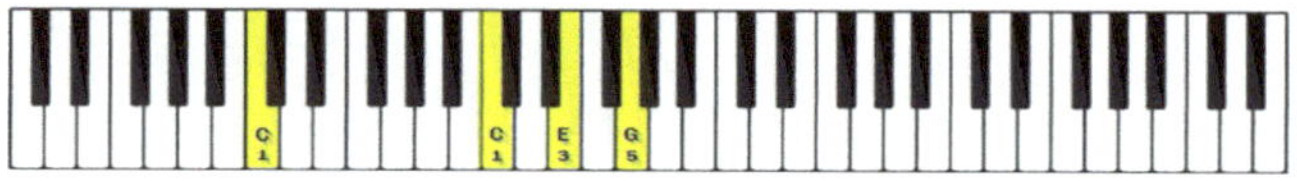

it! Almighty river, come and

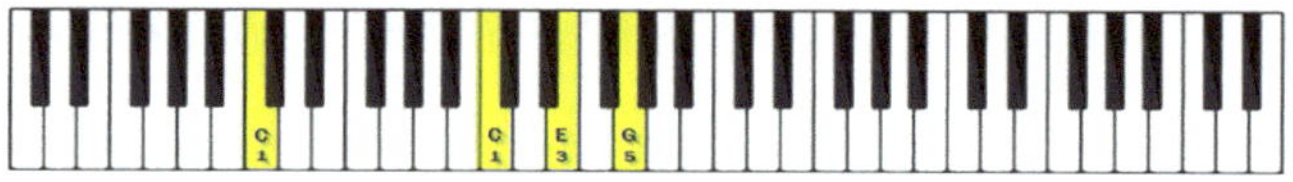

me

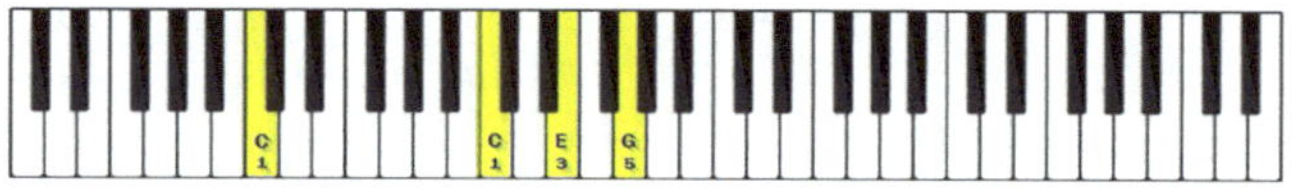

gain!

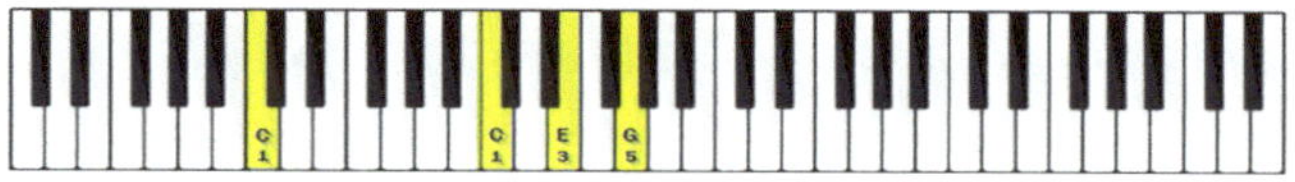

then You're freeing hearts right

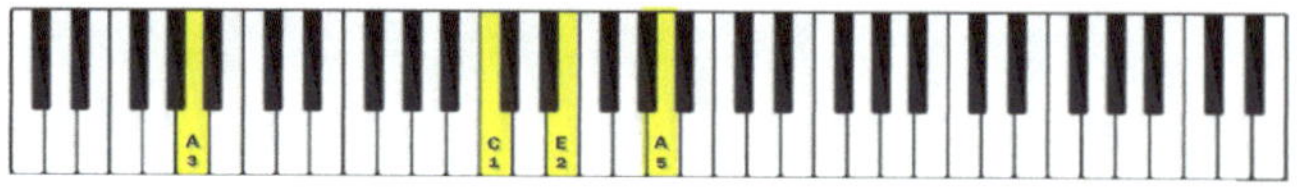

God!

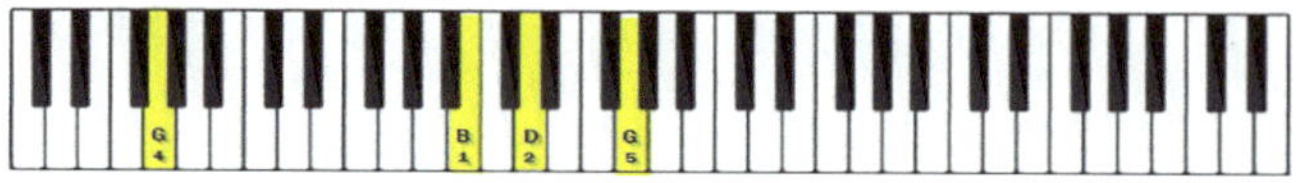

I feel Your touch right now

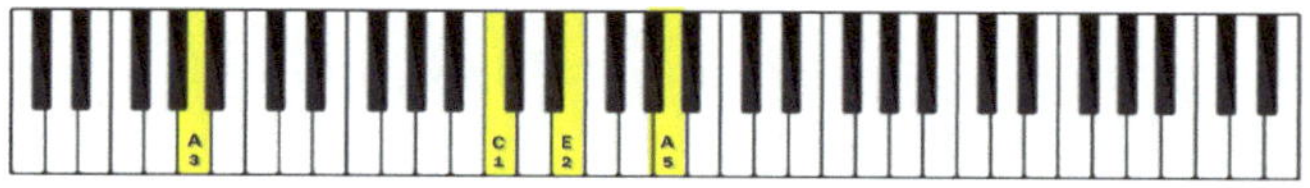

God!

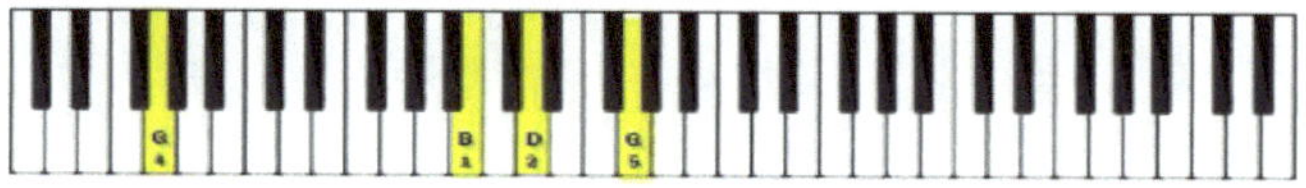

Spir-

fill

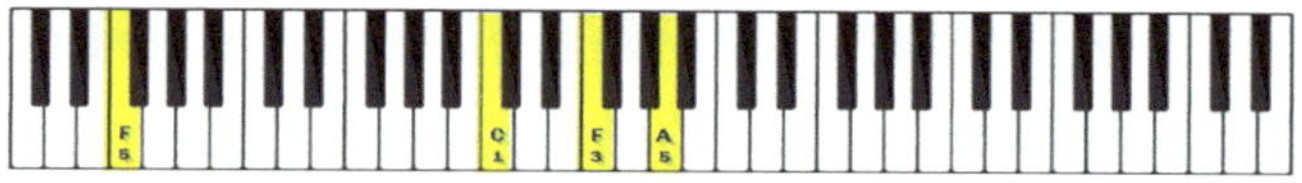

a-

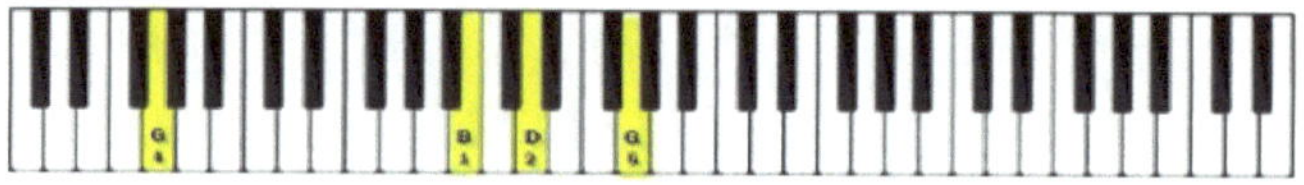

No Longer Slaves

Bethel Music

Time=4

[Verse 1]

      C
You unravel me, with a melody
      F   G   C
You surround me with a song
        C
Of deliverance, from my enemies
      F   G   C
Till all my fears are gone

[Chorus]

        F   G   C
I'm no longer a slave to fear
   Am   G   C
I am a child of God
        F   G   C
I'm no longer a slave to fear
   Am   G   C
I am a child of God

[Instrumental]
Am G C F **2X**

[Verse 2]

        C   Am
From my mother's womb, You have chosen me
F   G   C
Love has called my name
        C   Am
I've been born again, into your family
      F   G   C
Your blood flows through my veins

[Chorus] 2X

      F   G   C
I'm no longer a slave to fear
   Am   G   C
I am a child of God
        F   G   C
I'm no longer a slave to fear
   Am   G   C
I am a child of God

[Instrumental]
Am G C F **2X**

[Interlude]
Am G C F **2X**
Ohhhhh, Ohhhhh...

 [Bridge 1]
Am G   C   F
I am surrounded
Am   G   C   F
by the arms of the father
Am G   C   F
I am surrounded
Am   G   C   F
by songs of deliverance
Am   G   C   F
We've been liberated
Am   G   C F
From our bondage

Am   G   C   F
We're the sons and the daughters
Am   G   C   F
Let us sing our freedom

[Interlude]
Am G C F **2X**
Ohhhhh, Ohhhhh...

[Bridge 2]
Am   G   C   F
You split the sea so I could walk right through it
Am   G   C   F
My fears are drowned in perfect love
Am   G   C   F
You rescued me and I will stand and sing
Am   G   C
I am a child of God

Play along!

https://www.youtube.com
/watch?v=dwBC_l4ppw8
&list=RDdwBC_l4pp
w8&start_radio=1

VL-24

No Longer Slaves
Bethel Music

Chords Used: C(I) F(IV) G(V) Am(vi)

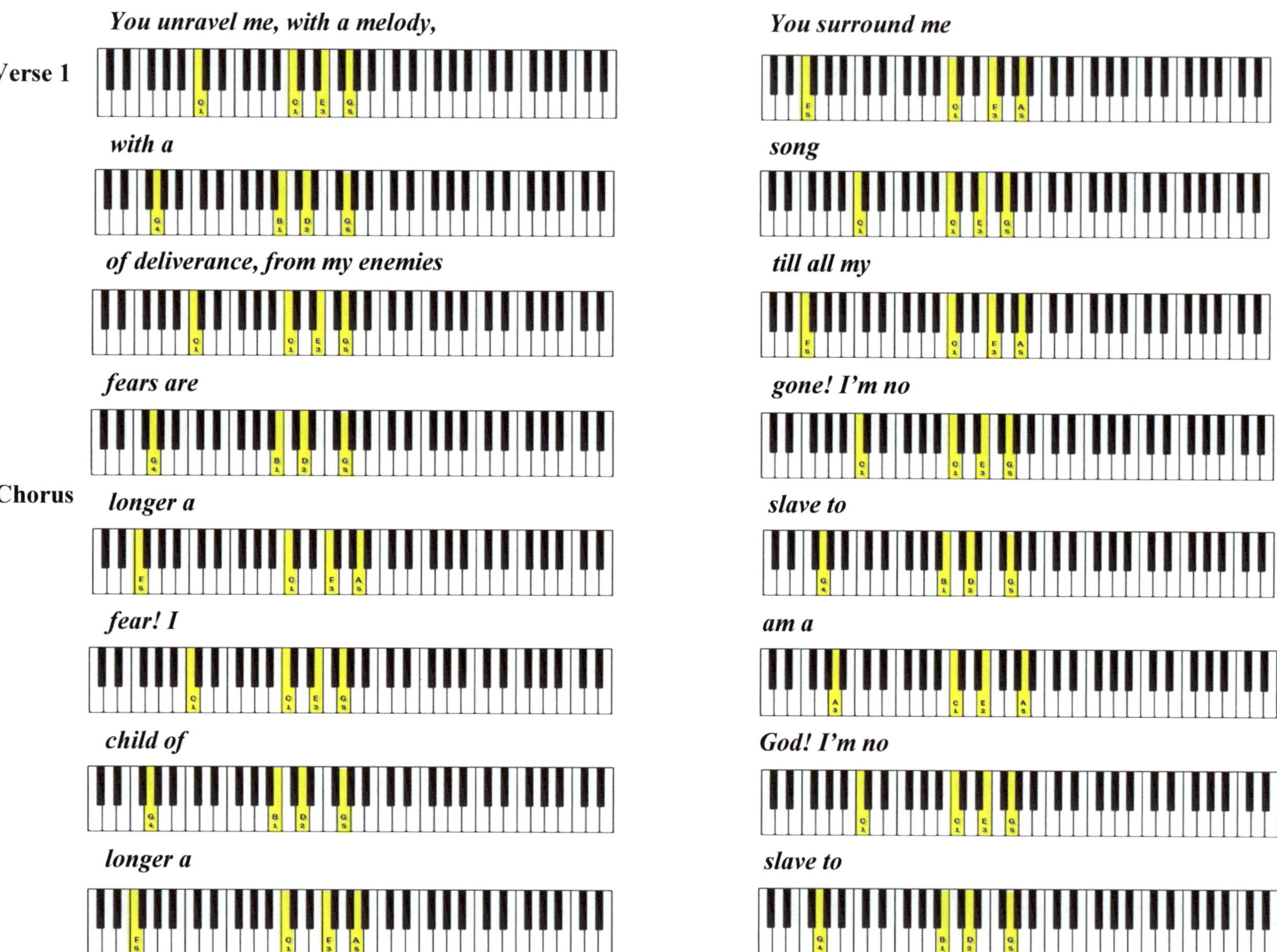

fear! I
am a
child of
God!
Bridge   I
am sur-
rounded
arms of the
by the
am sur-
Father!
I
by
rounded
de-
songs of

liver-

You split the

walk right

My fears were

perfect

You rescued

stand and

I am a

God!

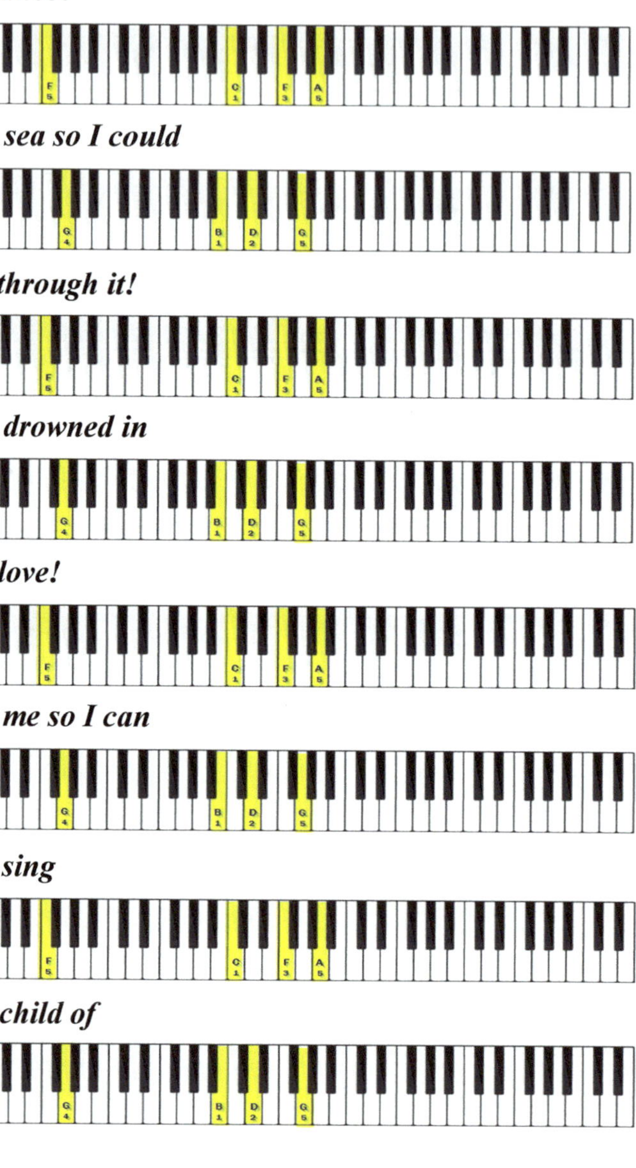

ance!

sea so I could

through it!

drowned in

love!

me so I can

sing

child of

Time=4

[Intro]
C Am F

[Verse 1]
C
I have this confidence because
Am
I've seen the faithfulness of God
               F
The still inside the storm, the promise of the shore
C
I trust the power of Your word
Am
Enough to seek Your Kingdom first
             F
Beyond the barren place, beyond the ocean waves

[Chorus 1]
C
When I walk through the waters, I won't be overcome
Am
When I go through the rivers, I will not be drowned
    F   Am   G   C
My God will make a way, so I am not afraid

[Verse 2]
C
You keep the promises You make
Am
There isn't one that is delayed
             F
So I will not lose heart, here, I will lift my arms

C
And start to sing into the night
Am
My praise will call the sun to rise
             F
Declare the battle won, declare that it is done

[Chorus 2]
C
When I walk through the waters, I won't be overcome
Am
When I go through the rivers, I will not be drowned
    F   Am   G
My God will make a way, so I am not afraid
C
When I am in the fire, I will not feel the flame
Am
I'll stand before the giant, declaring victory
    F   Am   G
My God will make a way, so I am not afraid

[Bridge]
C
Before me, behind me, always beside me
    Am
No shadow, no valley, where You won't find me
    F   G
No, I am not afraid
C
Before me, behind me, always beside me
    Am
No shadow, no valley, where You won't find me
    F   G   F   G
No, I am not afraid, I am not afraid

[Chorus]

Not Afraid

Jesus Culture

Chords Used: C(I) F(IV) G(V) Am(vi)

Verse 1

I have this confidence because

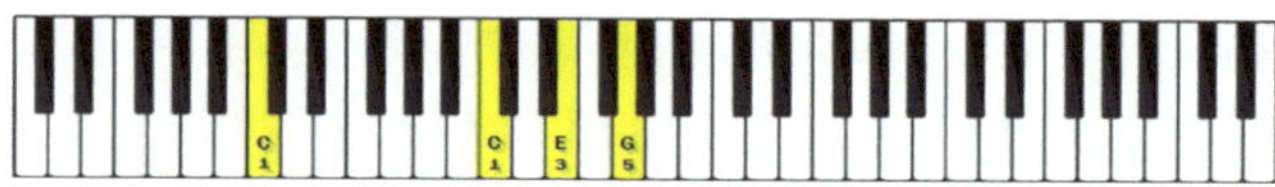

I've seen the faithfulness of God, the still inside the

storm, the promise of the shore

I trust the power of You word

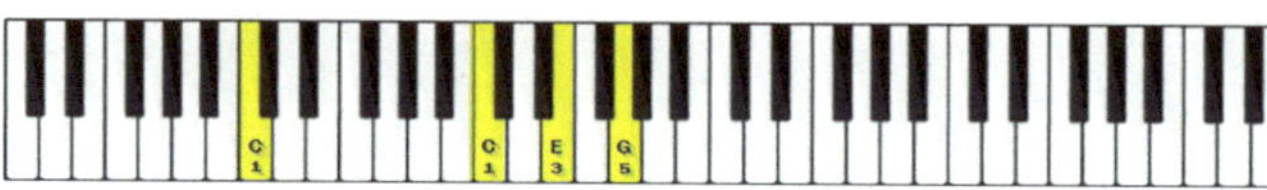

enough to seek your kingdom first, beyond the barren

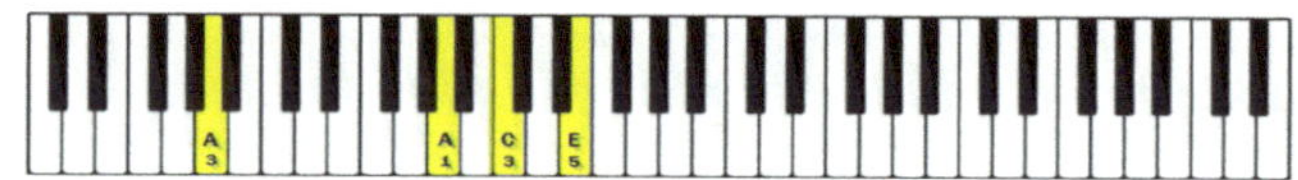

place, beyond the ocean waves!

Chorus 2

When I walk through the water, I won't be overcome!

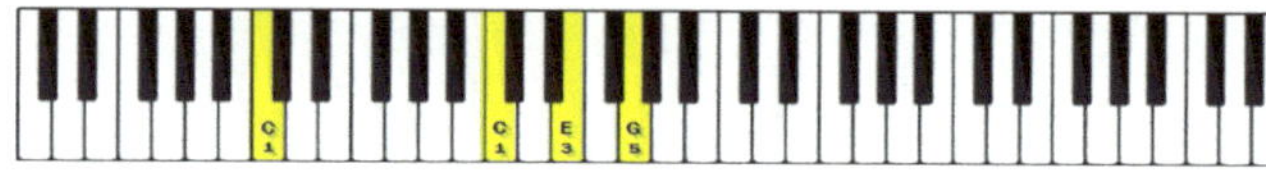

When I go through the rivers, I will not be drowned!

My God will make a way so

I am not a-

fraid! When

I am in the fire I will not feel flame, I'll

stand before the giant, declaring victory, my

God will make a way, so

I am not a-

fraid!

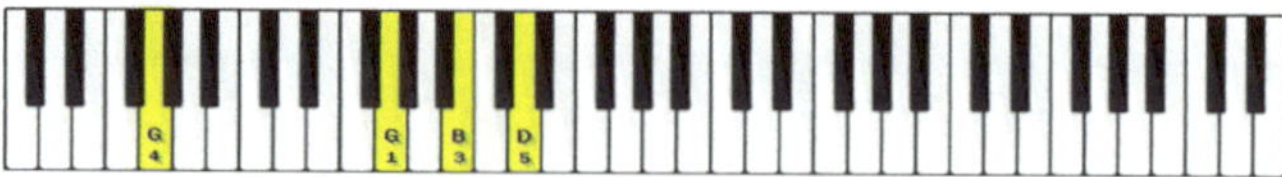

Bridge

Before me, behind me, always beside me no

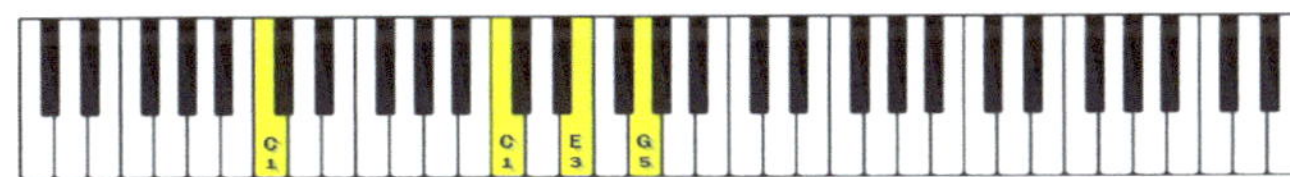

I am not a-

Before me, behind me, always beside me no

I am not a-

shadow, no valley, where You won't find me no

fraid!

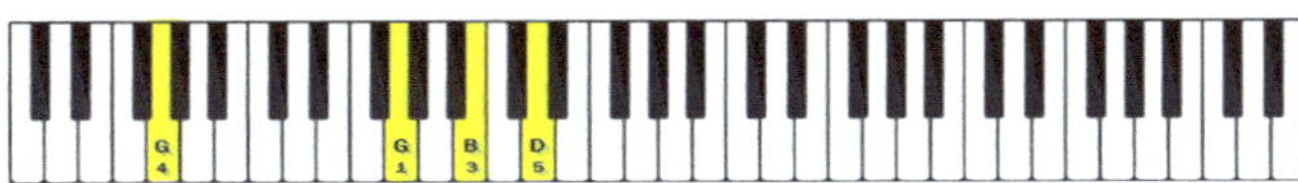

shadow, no valley, where You won't find me no

fraid!

Sometimes, especially in more traditional settings, not every verse is written with the chord symbols. The remaining verses will have just the lyrics, especially if space on the page is limited, but the chord changes will be the same.

Time=3

[Verse 1]

```
    F    C      F    G
In Christ alone, my hope is found
C    F      G        C
He is my light my strength my song
      F    C      F    G
This Cornerstone, this solid Ground
C          F     G        C
Firm through the fiercest drought and storm
      C       F      Am    G
What heights of love, what depths of peace
      C       F      Am      G
When fears are stilled when strivings cease!
    F    C    F    G
My Comforter my All in All
C       F    G    C
Here in the love of Christ I stand
```

[Verse 2]

```
    F    C      F      G
In Christ alone! - who took on flesh
C      F    G      C
Fullness of God in helpless babe!
      F    C      F      G
This Gift of love and righteousness
C          F     G      C
Scorned by the ones He came to save
C        F      Am  G
Till on that cross as Jesus died
C          F      Am G
The wrath of God was satisfied
F        C      F      G
For every sin on Him was laid:
C        F    G      C
Here in the death of Christ I live
```

[Verse 3]

There in the ground His body lay
Light of the world by darkness slain
Then bursting forth in glorious Day
Up from the grave He rose again!

And as He stands in victory
Sin's curse has lost its grip on me
For I am His and He is mine -
Bought with the precious blood of Christ

[Verse 4]

No guilt in life no fear in death
This is the power of Christ in me
From life's first cry to final breath
Jesus commands my destiny
No power of hell no scheme of man
Can ever pluck me from His hand
Till he returns or calls me home
Here in the power of Christ I'll stand!

VL-26

In Christ Alone
Traditional

Verse 1

Chords Used: C(I) F(IV) G(V) Am(vi)

love, what

peace, when

stilled when

cease,

ter, my

all,

love of

stand!

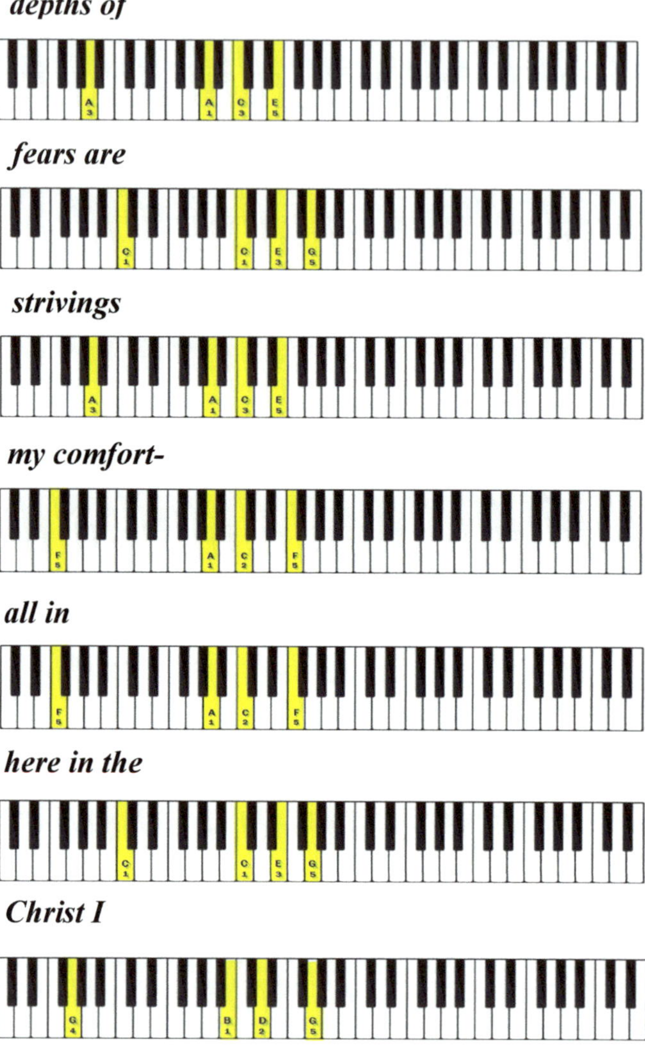

depths of

fears are

strivings

my comfort-

all in

here in the

Christ I

A chord played over a key is shown on a chord chart with 2 chords separated by a / (example: C/E). This symbol simply means that the key on the right side of the / is the lowest key played. This symbol can be synonymous with some inversions if only a triad were being played. When playing keys, this would indicate that the left hand would play the key indicated on the right side of the /.

Examples:

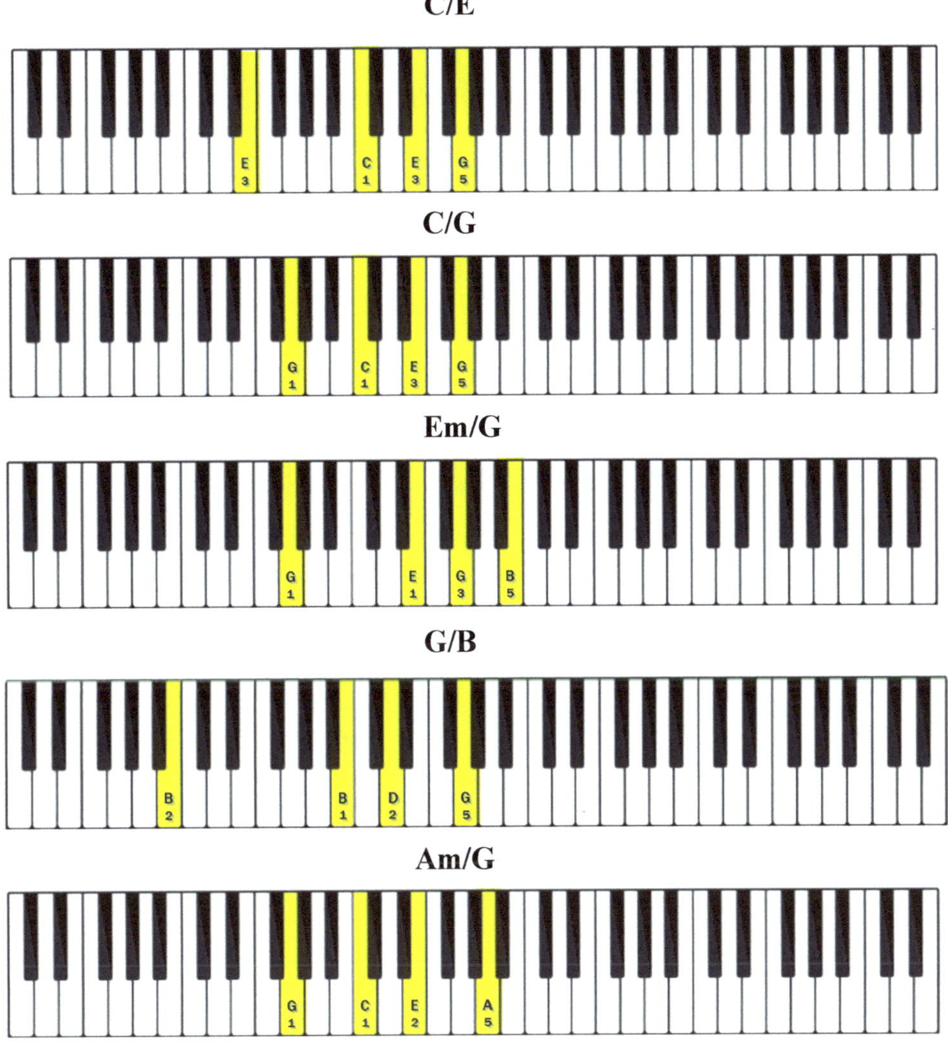

Goodness of God

Bethel Music

Time=4

[Verse]
```
          C              F           C
I love You, Lord for Your mercy never fails me
G/B      Am           F        G
All my days I've been held in Your hand
                     Am      F          C  G/B Am
From the moment that I wake up until I lay my head
           F        G          C
Oh, I will sing of the goodness of God
```

[Chorus]
```
F                              C
'Cause all my life You have been faithful
F                          C    G
And all my life You have been so so good
F                       C G/B Am
With every breath that I am able
        F       G        C
I will sing of the goodness of God
```

[Verse]
```
          C              F           C
I love Your voice, You have led me through the fire
  G/B     Am          F          G
In darkest night You are close like no other
                  Am     F              C  G/B Am
I've known You as a father, I've known You as a friend.
           F       G        C
And I have lived in the goodness of God
```

[Chorus]
```
F                              C
'Cause all my life You have been faithful
F                          C    G
And all my life You have been so, so good
F                       C G /B Am
With every breath that I am able
        F       G        C
I will sing of the goodness of God
```

[Bridge] 2X
```
C              F           G         C
Your goodness is running after, it's running after me
C              F           G         C
Your goodness is running after, it's running after me
            C          F         G       Am
With my life laid down I surrender now I give You everything
C              F           G         C
Your goodness is running after, it's running after me
```

[Chorus]
```
F                              C
'Cause all my life You have been faithful
F                          C    G
And all my life You have been so, so good
F                       C G/B Am
With every breath that I am able
        F       G       Am
I will sing of the goodness of God
        F       G       C
I will sing of the goodness of God
```

Play along!
https://
www.youtube.com/
watch?v=azXfZik1KCA

Goodness of God

Bethel Music

Chords Used: C(I) F(IV) G(V) Am(vi)

Verse 1

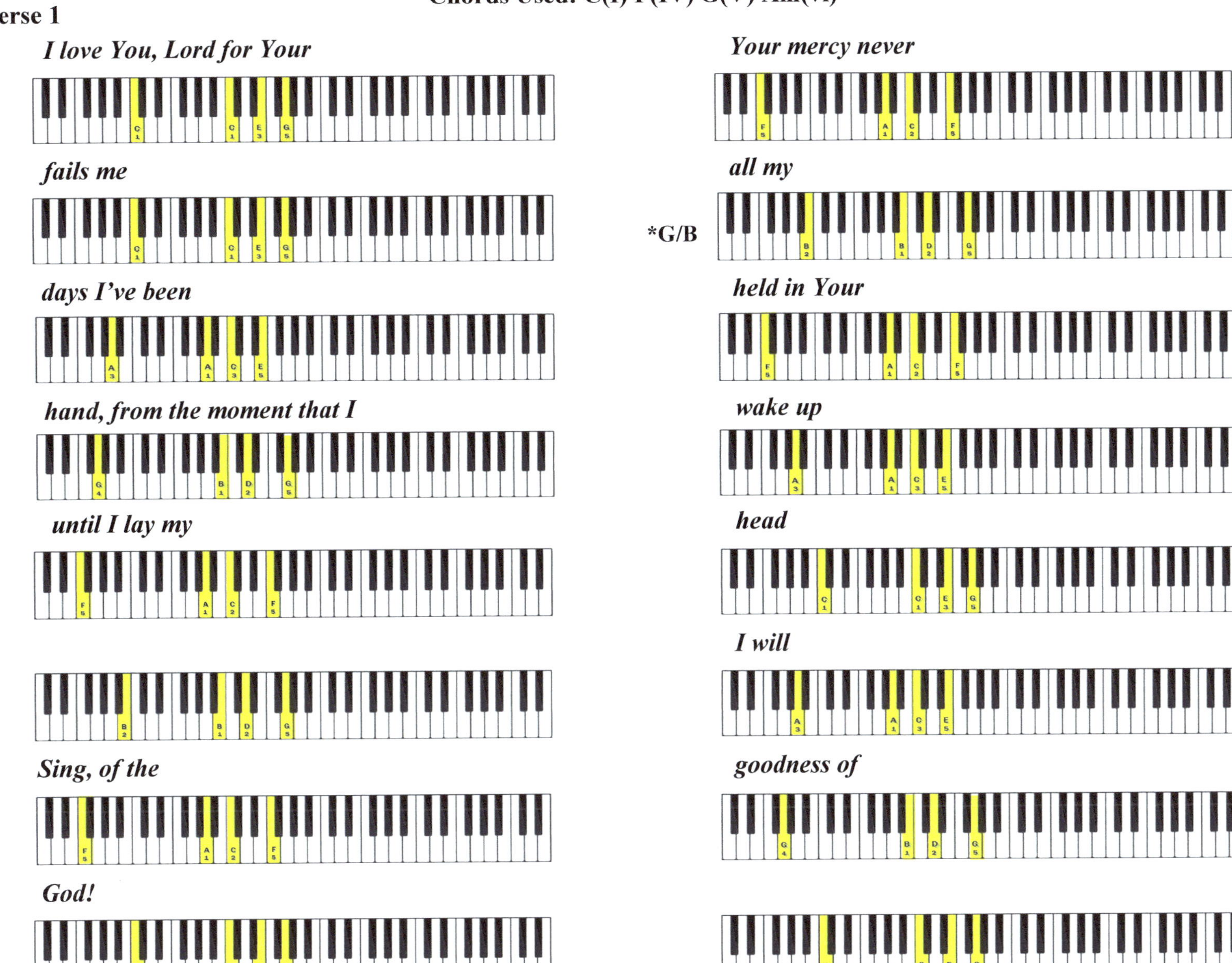

Chorus

'Cause all my life You have been
faithful
and all my life You have been
so, so
good!
With every breath that I am
able
I will
sing of the
Goodness of
God!
Your goodness is
running after, it's
running after
me!

Your goodness is

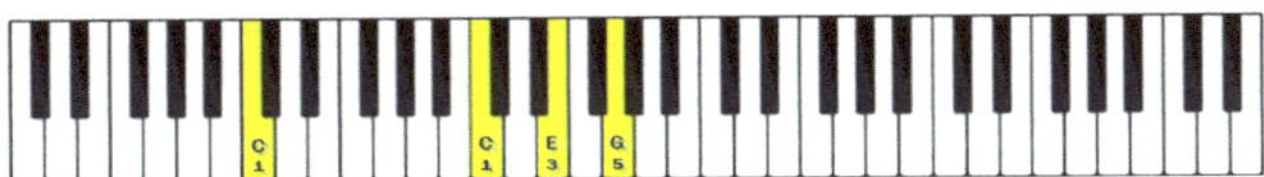

running after

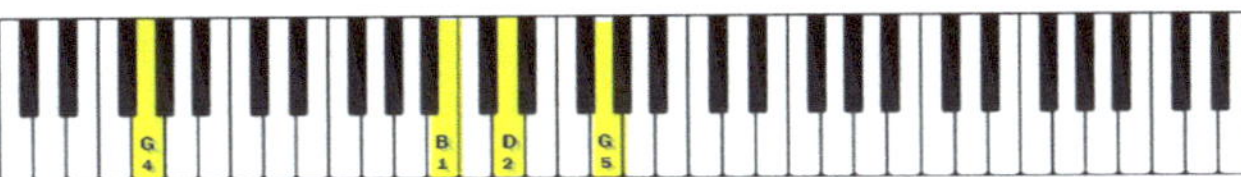

with my life laid down

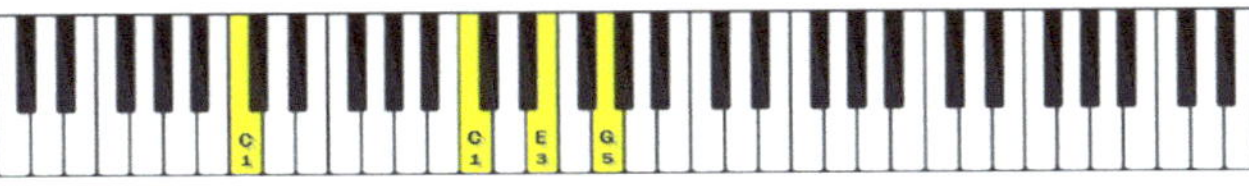

give You every-

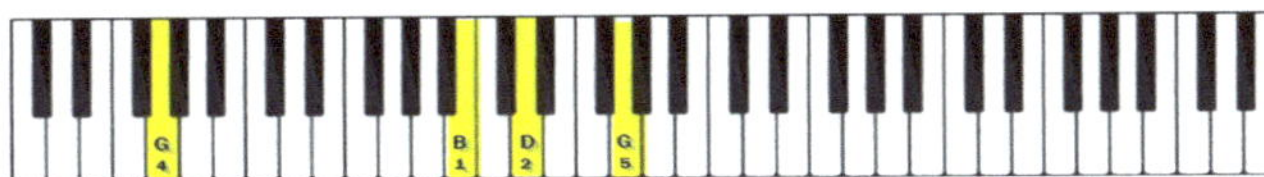

Your goodness is

running after

running after, it's

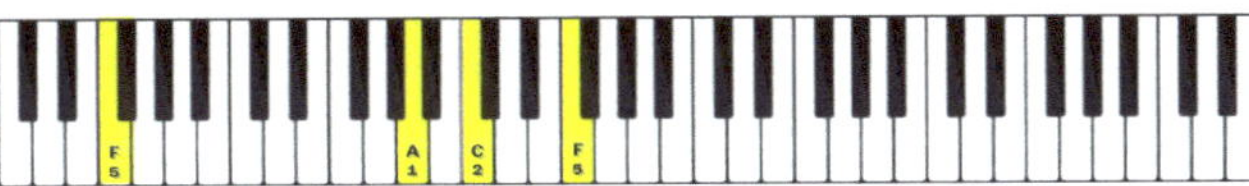

me!

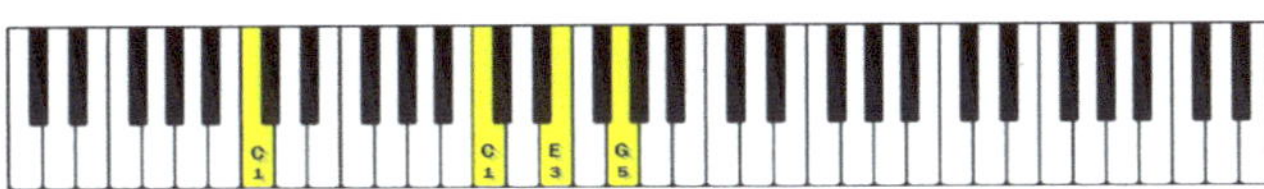

I surrender now I

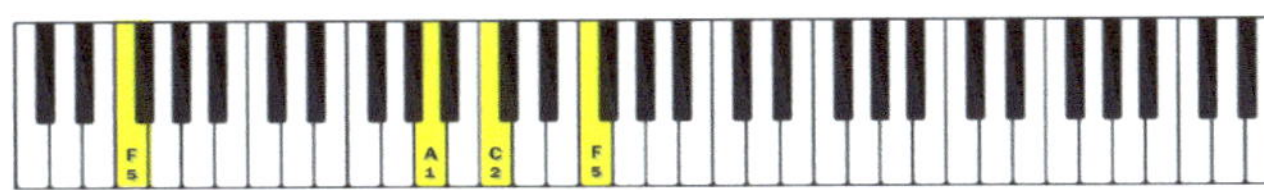

thing!

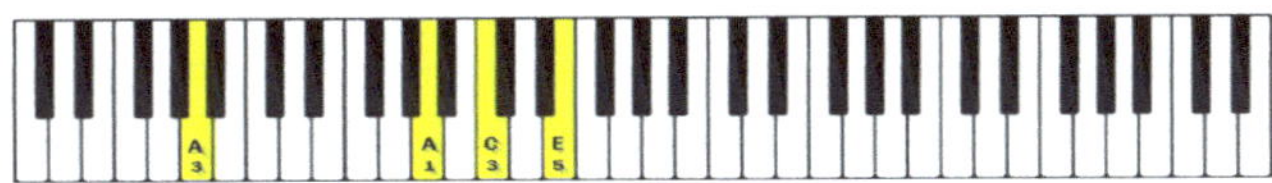

running after, it's

me!

Build My Life

Barrett, Brett Younker, Karl Martin,
Kirby Kaple, and Matt Redman

Time=4

[Intro]
|C |F | C/E | |F |
|C |F | C/E | |F |

[Verse 1]
C   F
Worthy of every song we could ever sing
C/E   F
Worthy of all the praise we could ever bring
C   F
Worthy of every breath we could ever breathe
        C/E   F
We live for You

[Verse 2]
C   F
Jesus, the name above every other name
C/E   F
Jesus, the only one who could ever save
C   F
Worthy of every breath we could ever breathe
        C/E   F
We live for You

[Chorus]
F   Dm
Holy, there is no one like You
        C/G
There is none beside You
        Am
Open up my eyes in wonder

F
Show me who You are
      Dm
And fill me with Your heart
      C/G
And lead me in Your love to
Am
those around me

[Instrumental 1]
|F | G | Am | C/E |
[Bridge]
F   G   Am
I will build my life upon Your love
        C/E
It is a firm foundation
F   G   Am
I will put my trust in You alone
        C/E
And I will not be shaken
F   G   Am
I will build my life upon Your love
        C/E
It is a firm foundation
F   G   Am
I will put my trust in You alone
        C/E
And I will not be shaken

[Chorus] 2X
F   Dm
Holy, there is no one like You
        C/G
There is none beside You
        Am
Open up my eyes in wonder
F
Show me who You are
      Dm
And fill me with Your heart
      C/G
And lead me in Your love to
Am
those around me

[Outro]
|F |G |Am |C/E |
|F |G |Am |C/E |F |

Play along!
https://www.youtube.com/
watch?v=lEuldF9RQ00

VL-29

Build My Life

Barrett, Brett Younker, Karl Martin,
Kirby Kaple, and Matt Redman

Verse 1 — Chords Used: C(I) Dm (ii) F(IV) G(V) Am (vi)

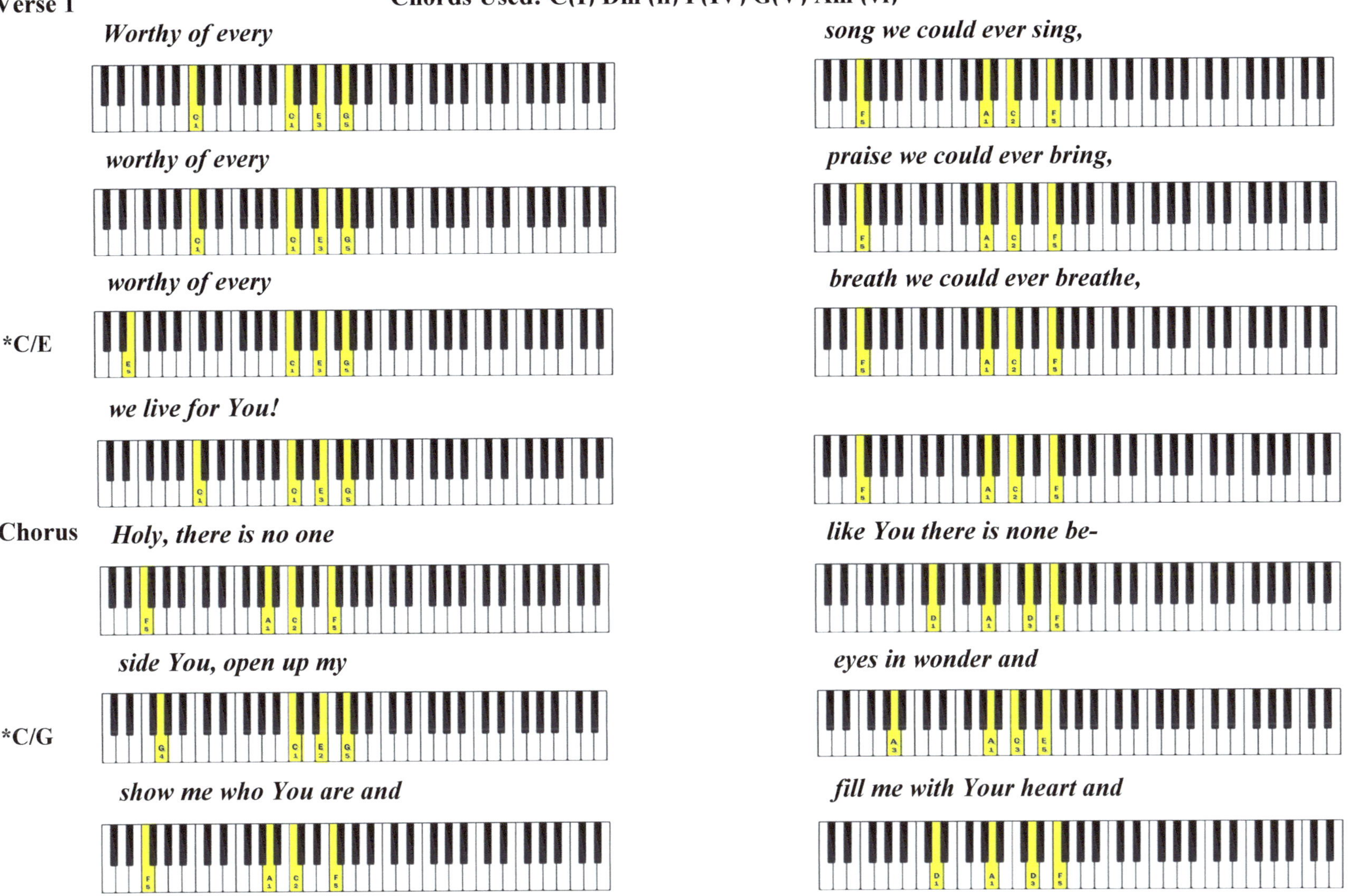

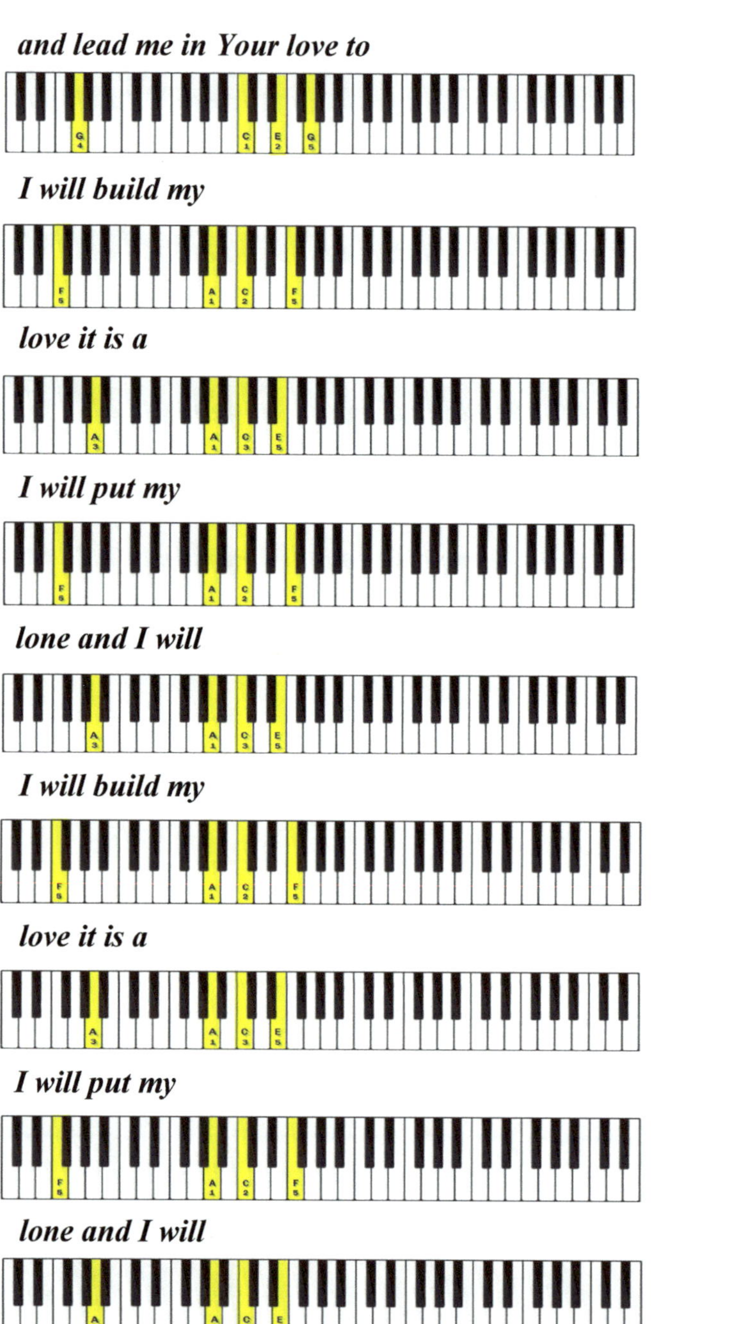

and lead me in Your love to
Bridge   I will build my
love it is a
I will put my
lone and I will
I will build my
love it is a
I will put my
lone and I will

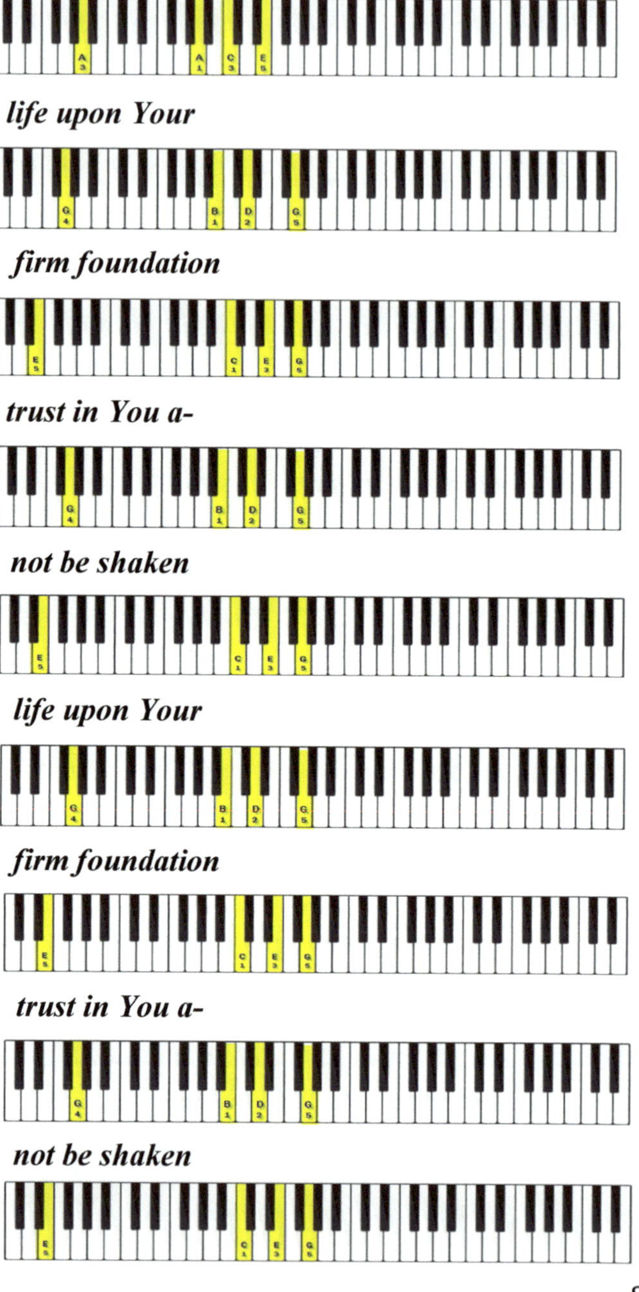

those around me
life upon Your
firm foundation
trust in You a-
not be shaken
life upon Your
firm foundation
trust in You a-
not be shaken

Cornerstone

Hillsong Worship

Time=4

[Intro]
C Am F G

[Verse 1]
C
My hope is built on nothing less
F   G
Than Jesus' blood and righteousness
Am   Em/G
I dare not trust the sweetest frame
F   G   C
But wholly trust in Jesus' name
C
My hope is built on nothing less
F   G
Than Jesus' blood and righteousness
Am   Em/G
I dare not trust the sweetest frame
F   G   C
But wholly trust in Jesus' name

[Chorus]
C/E   F   Am   G
Christ alone, Cornerstone
C/E   F   Am   G
Weak made strong in the Savior's love
C/E   F
Through the storm
Am   G   C
He is Lord, Lord of all

[Verse 2]
C
When darkness seems to hide His face
F   G
I rest on His unchanging grace
Am   Em/G
In every high and stormy gale
F   G   C
My anchor holds within the veil

[Chorus]
C/E   F   Am   G
Christ alone, Cornerstone
C/E   F   Am   G
Weak made strong in the Savior's love
C/E   F
Through the storm
Am   G   C
He is Lord, Lord of all

[Chorus]

C/E   F   Am   G
Christ alone, Cornerstone
C/E   F   Am   G
Weak made strong in the Savior's love
C/E   F
Through the storm
Am   G   C
He is Lord, Lord of all

[Verse 3]
C
When He shall come with trumpet sound
F   G
Oh may I then in Him be found
Am   Am/G
Dressed in His righteousness alone
F   G   C
Faultless, stand before the throne

[Chorus]

Play along!
https://www.youtube.
com/
watch?v=izrk-erhDdk

Chords Used: C(I) Em (iii) F(IV) G(V) Am(vi)

Verse 1

My hope is built on nothing less

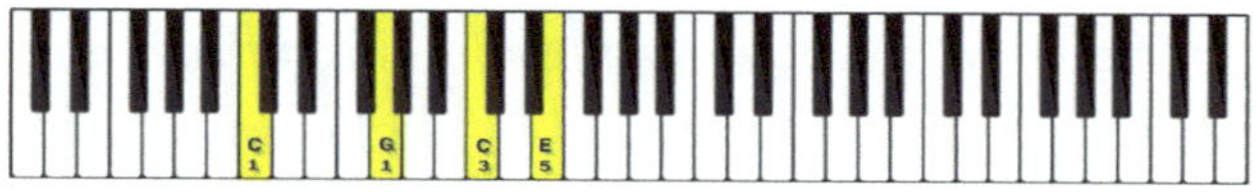

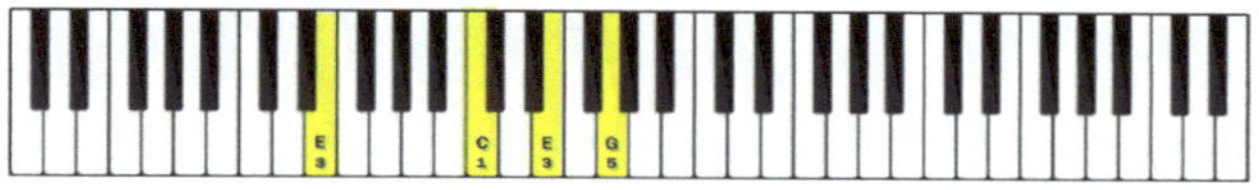

than Jesus' blood and

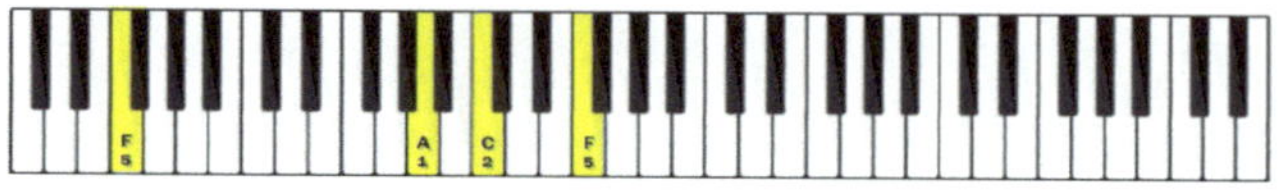

righteousness,

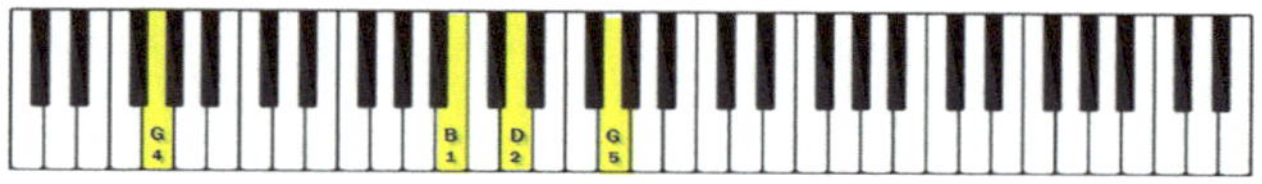

I dare not trust the

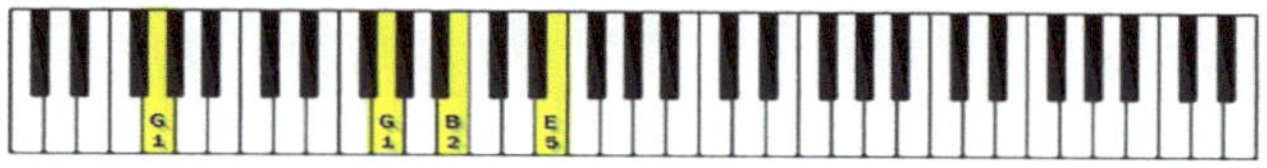

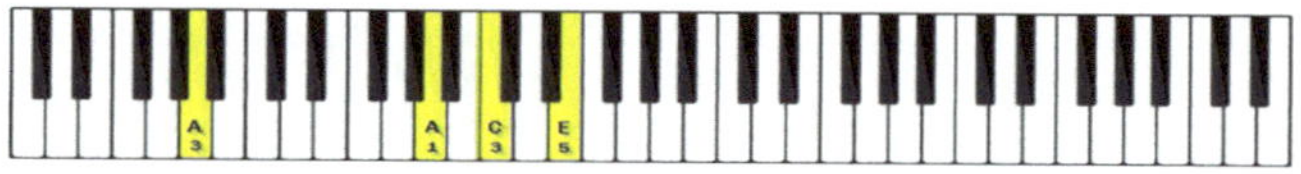

sweetest frame

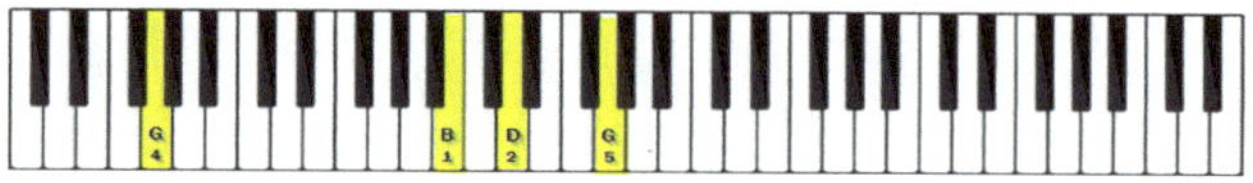

but wholly

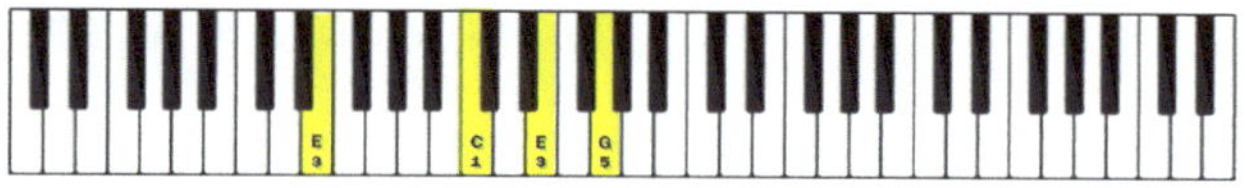

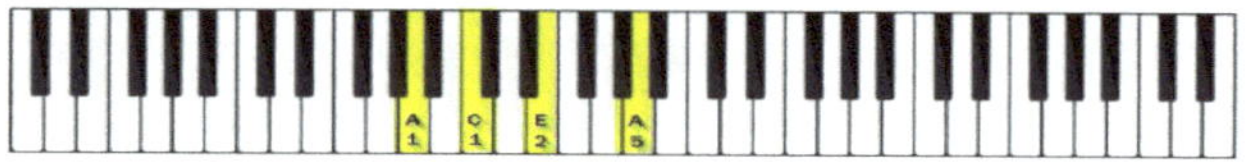

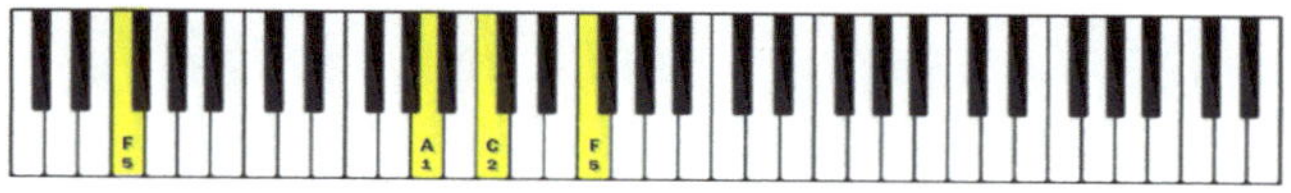

trust in Jesus'

name!

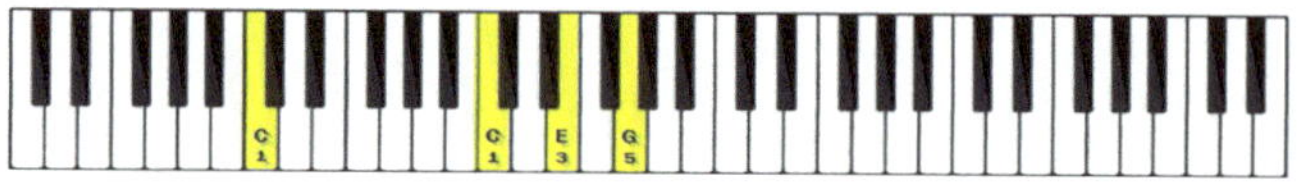

Chorus *Christ*

alone,

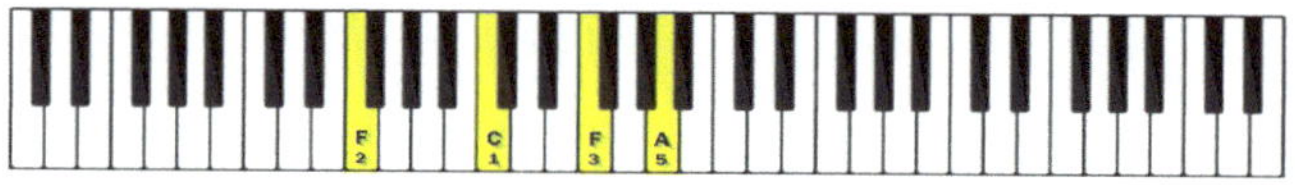

Corner-

stone

weak made

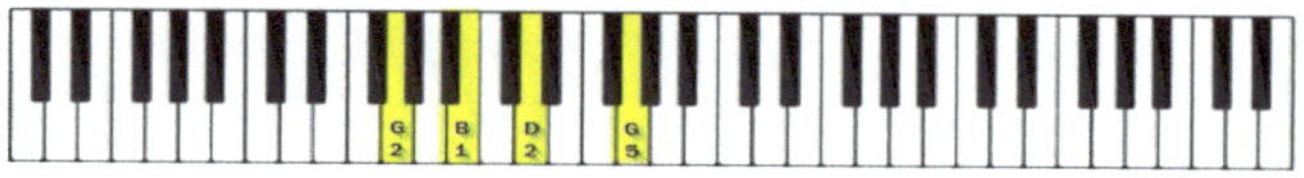

strong in the

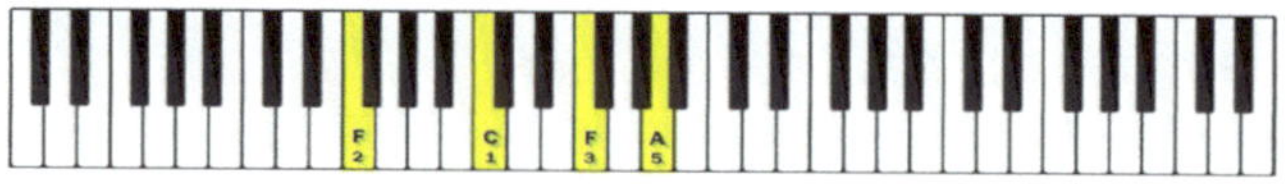

Savior's

love

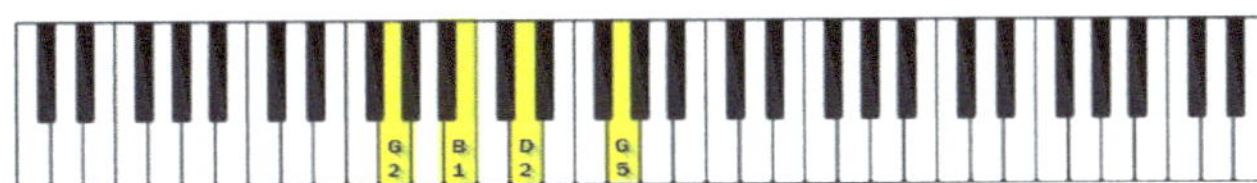

through the

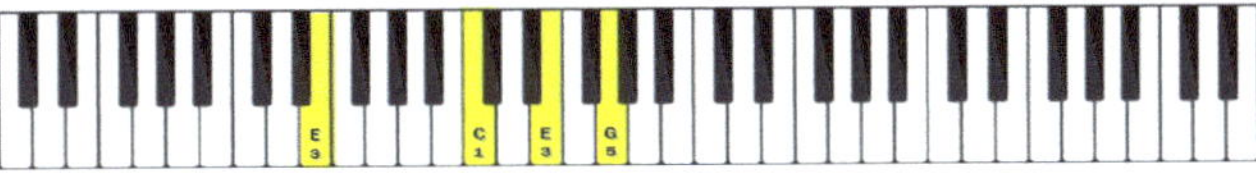

storm

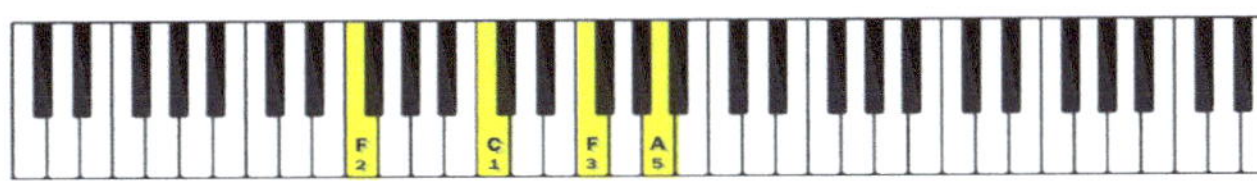

He is

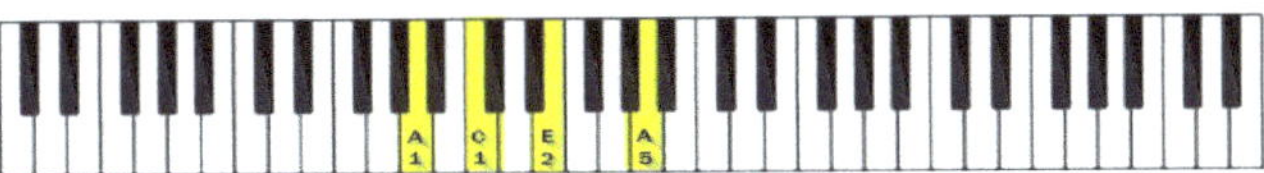

Lord, Lord of

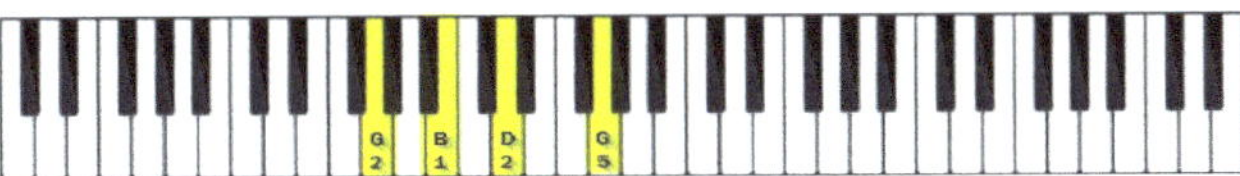

all!

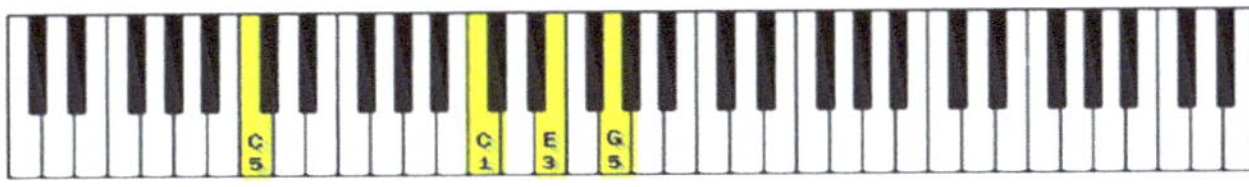

Variations to the Triad

Oftentimes a chord chart will display a variation of a triad. One way this is represented is by a number following the chord symbol. For example, C2. To explain this, let's review the concept of how a triad is built.

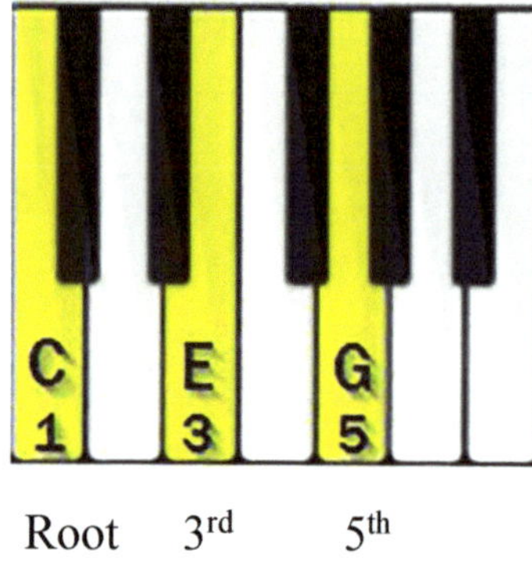

Root   3rd   5th

The major triad is built by playing the root, 3rd and 5th. In a C triad, the D would be the "2nd" and the F would be the "4th". To play a **C2,** the D (2nd) would be played. Sometimes the chord chart will indicate (no3). If this notation is not there, the player can play both the 3rd and the 2nd if desired, but the 2nd must be played. If this notation is there, then the player would only play the 2nd.

C2

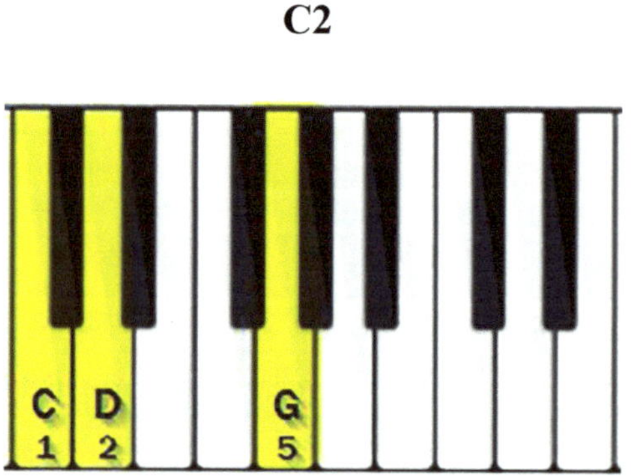

G2

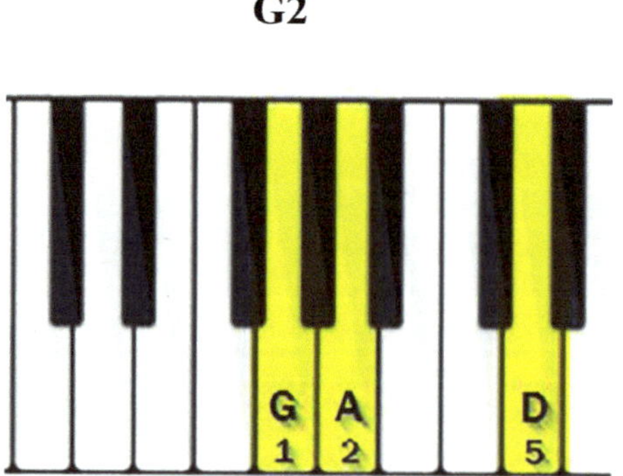

Another common variation is a triad which adds the 6th (example, C6). Just as we added the 2nd to the previous example, the 6th of a C major triad is A. When a 6 is shown on a chord symbol, the 5th and 6th should be played.

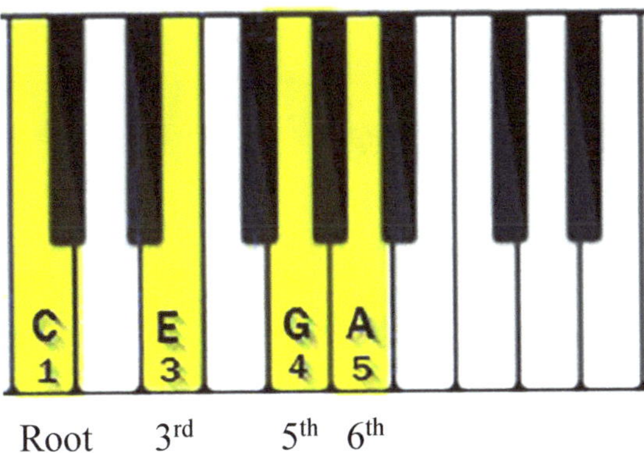

Sus (Suspended) Chords

The sus chord is very common in worship music. This symbol stands for "suspended" and it refers to playing the 4th of the triad is place of the 3rd. Frequently, especially in more traditional music, this sound will resolve to the 3rd of the major triad. Sus chords can also be written as a chord with a 4 instead of the sus indicating that the fourth key is to be played.

Examples

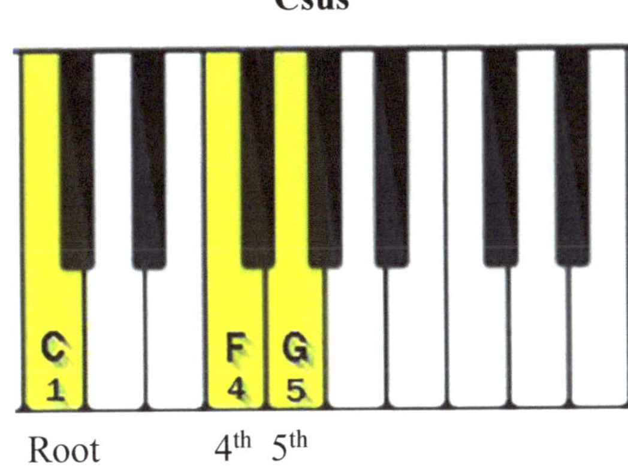

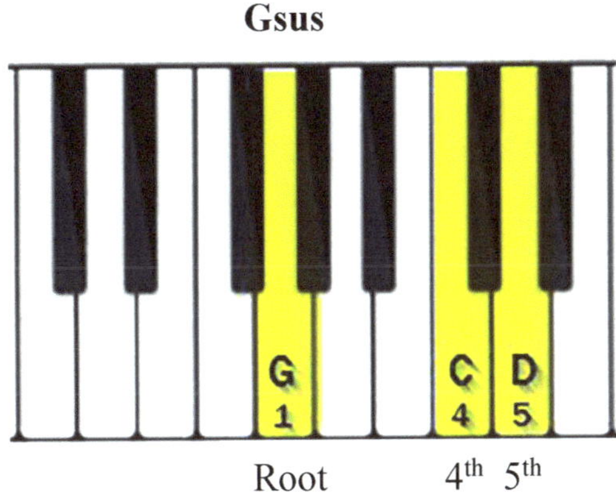

VL-31

House of the Lord

Phil Wickham

Time=4

[Intro]
C C2 C Gsus F2 Gsus F2 **2X**

[Verse 1]
C
We worship the God who was,
C
we worship the God who is
C   Am   Gsus   F2
We worship the God who evermore will be
C
He opened the prison doors,
C
He parted the raging sea my God,
    Am   Gsus F2
He holds the victory, yeah

[Chorus]
C
 There's joy in the house of the Lord
                             G   F2
There's joy in the house of the Lord today
                                    F/G   C
And we won't be quiet, we shout out Your praise!
C
There's joy in the house of the Lord
               G F2
our God is surely in this place
              F/G   C
and we won't be quiet,we shout out Your praise!

[Interlude]
C   C2 | C   Gsus | F2   Gsus | F2   Gsus
|**[Verse 2]**

C
We sing to the God who heals,
C
we sing to the God who saves
C   Am   Gsus   F2
we sing to the God who always makes a way
        C
'cause He hung up on that cross,
        Dm
then He rose up from that grave
                        Am   Gsus F2
my God's still rolling stones away!

[Chorus]

[Bridge] 2X
                              C
('Cause) We were the beggars,
       G/C C
now we're royalty
            C
we were the prisoners,
        G/C   C
now we're running free
(G/B) Am
we are forgiven,
        F   C
accepted, redeemed by His grace
       G   F   C
let the house of the Lord sing praise!

[Chorus]2X

[Ending]
C   C2   C   Gsus
  we shout out Your praise!
F
There is joy in this house
                                    C C2
there is joy in this house today!
C   Gsus   F2
  We shout out Your praise!
                          Gsus
  We shout out Your praise!
C   Dm   Am   G F   C

Play along!
https://www.youtu
be.com/
watch?v=jVZGwP

VL-32

House of the Lord

Phil Wickham

Chords Used: C(I) Dm (ii) F(IV) G(V) Am(vi)

Intro 2X

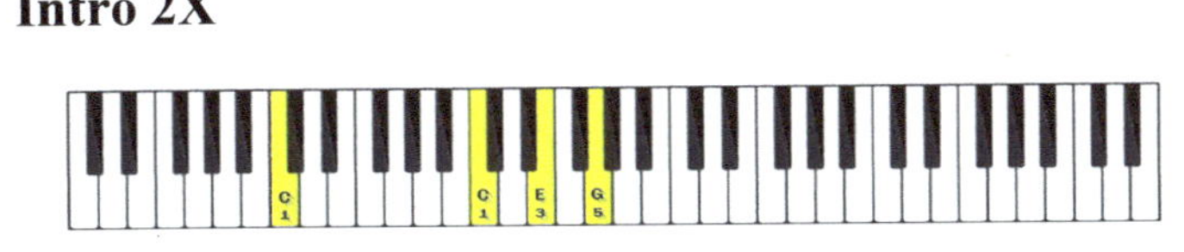

*C2

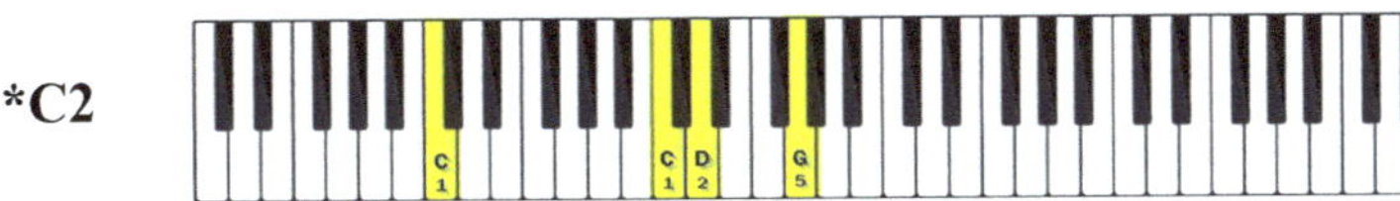

*Gsus

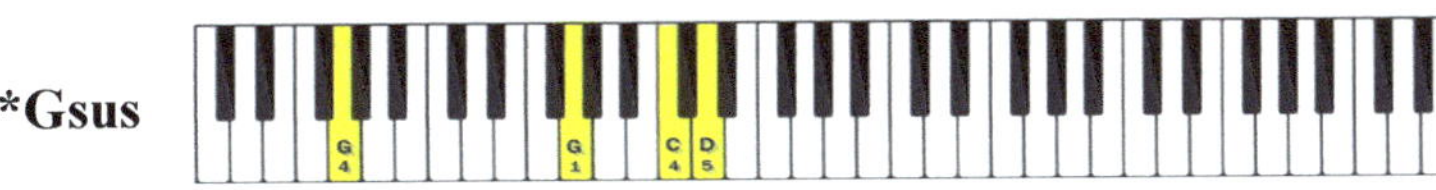

*F2

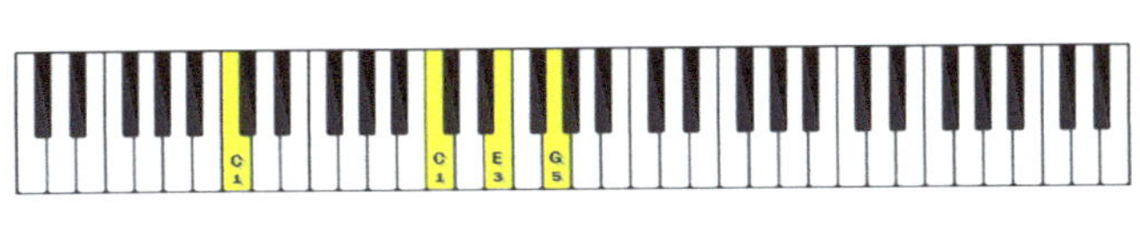

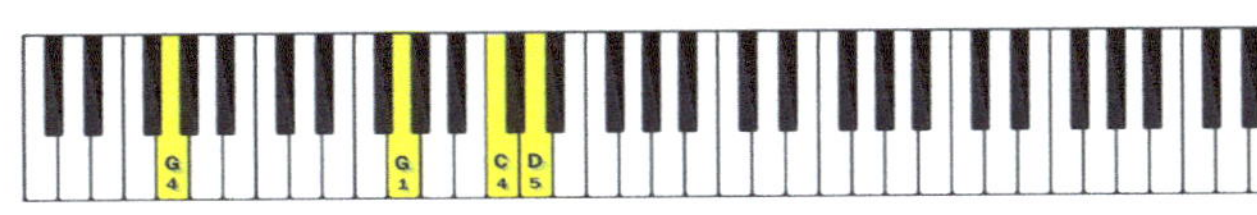

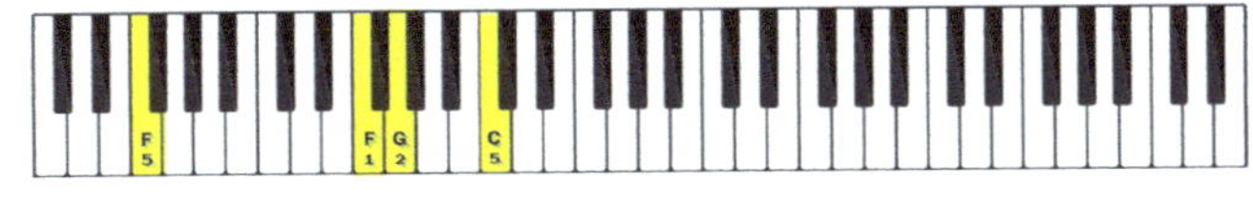

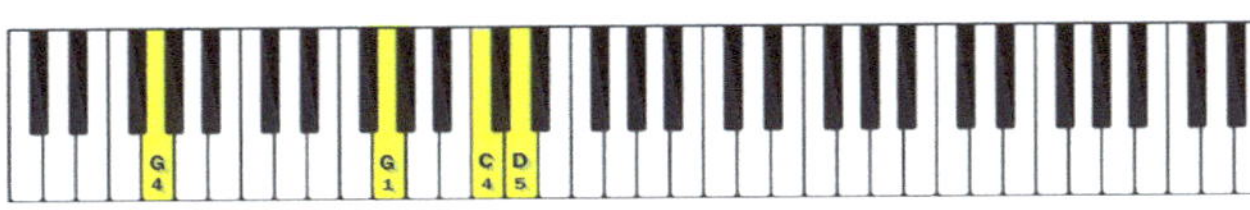

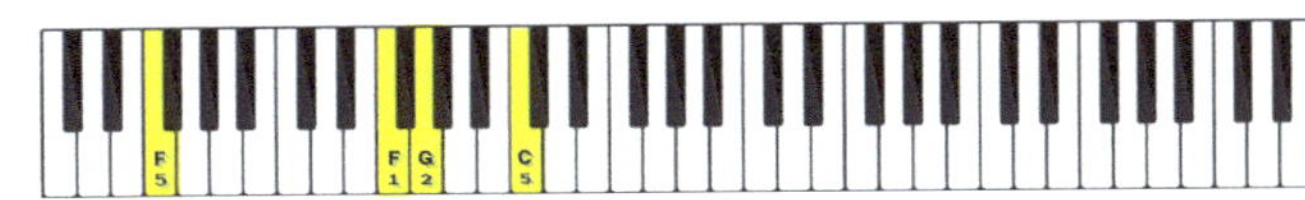

Verse 1

We worship the God who was, we worship the God who is, we worship the God who ever-

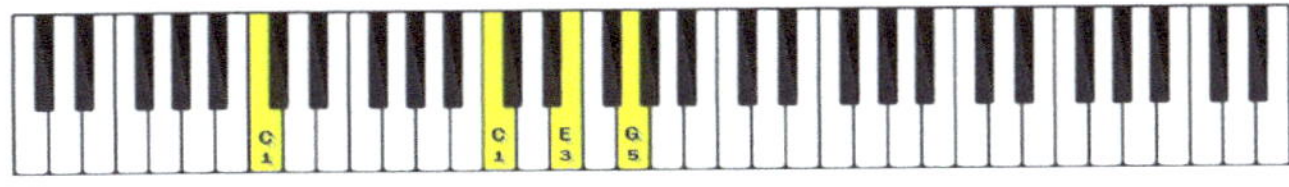

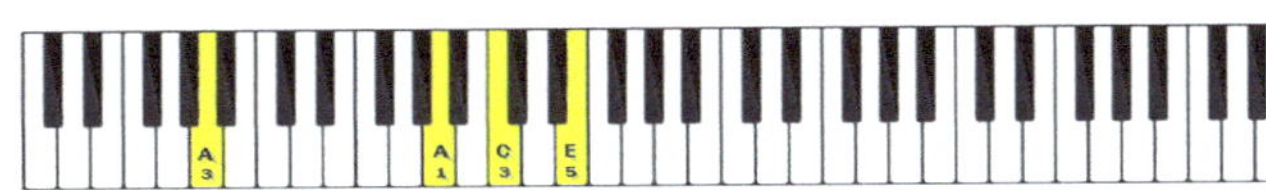

more will

be!

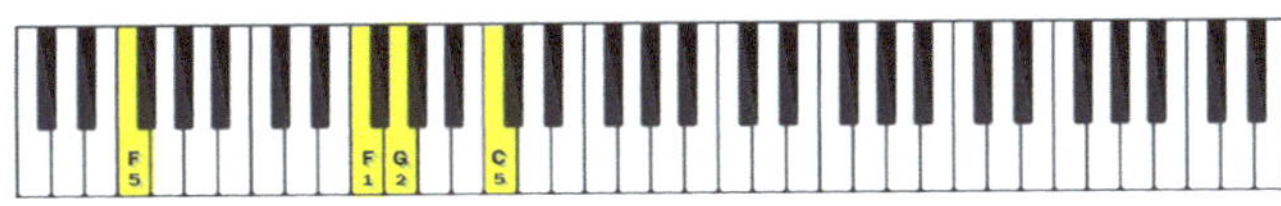

He opened the prison doors, He parted the raging sea, my God He holds the

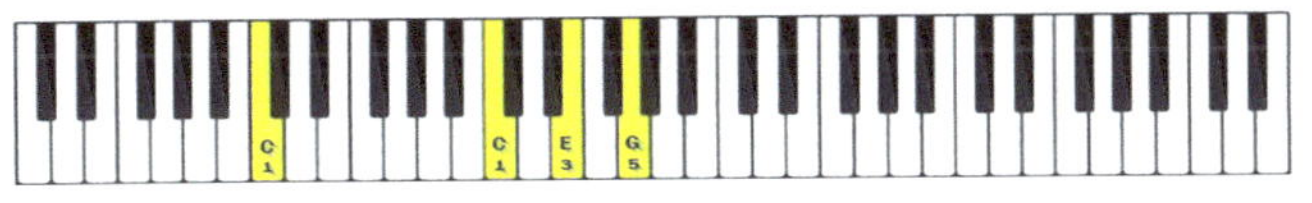

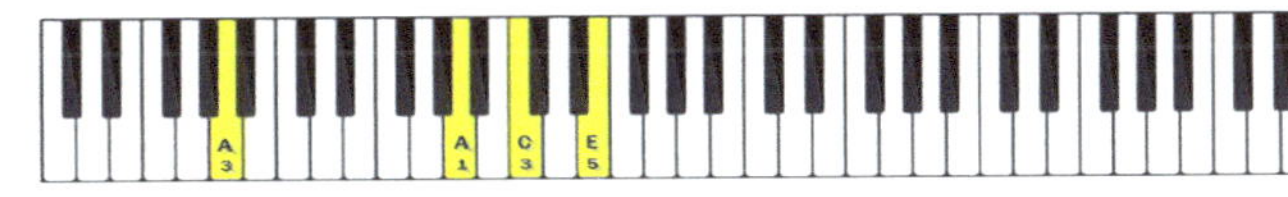

victor-

y!

Chorus
There's joy in the House of the Lord! There's joy in the house of the Lord today and we won't be quiet, we
shout out Your
*F/G
praise! There's joy in the House of the Lord! Our God is surely
in this
Place and we won't be quiet, we
should out your
Praise!
Interlude

Bridge

'Cause) We were the beggars, now we're

ty! We were the prisoners, now we're

free!

forgiven, accepted

Grace let the

Lord sing

royal-   **G/C*

running

We are

redeemed by His

house of the

praise!

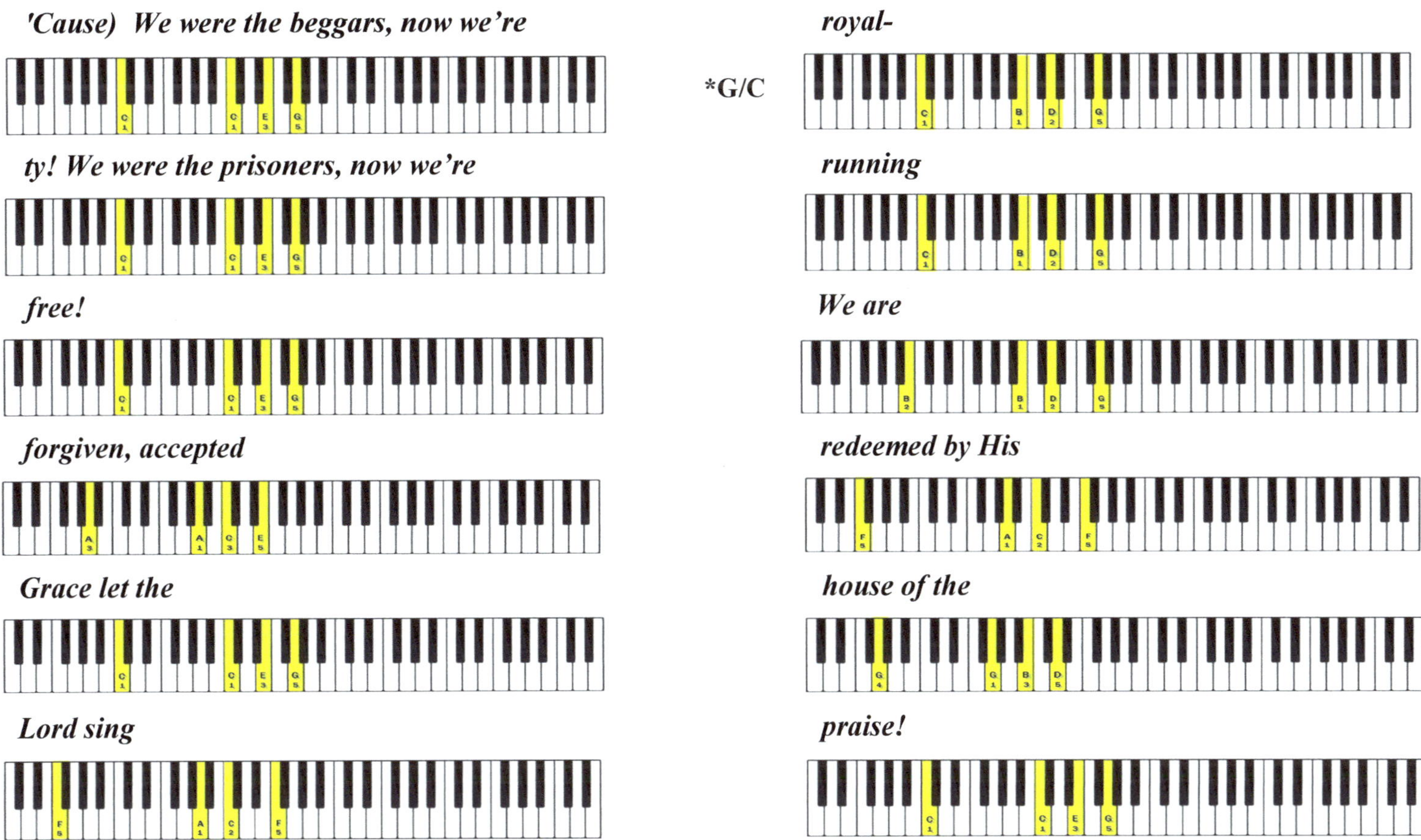

O Praise The Name

Hillsong Worship

Time=4

[Intro]
C C/E F
C C/E F

[Verse 1]
      C
I cast my mind to Calvary
           G   Am
Where Jesus bled and died for me
        F   C/E
I see His wounds, His hands, His feet
        G   C   C/E F
My Savior on that cursed tree

[Verse 2]
      C
His body bound and drenched in tears
          G   Am
They laid Him down in Joseph's tomb
          F   C/E
The entrance sealed by heavy stone
        G   C   C/E F
Messiah still and all alone

[Chorus]
  C   F   C
O praise the Name of the Lord our God
  Am   Gsus   G
O praise His Name forever - more
   C/E   F   Am
For endless days, we will sing Your praise
   F   Gsus G C   C/E F
Oh Lord, oh Lord our God

[Verse 3]
        C
Then on the third, at break of dawn
        G   Am
The Son of heaven rose again
            F   C/E
O trampled death, where is your sting
        G   C
The angels roar for Christ the King

[Chorus]

  C   F   C
O praise the Name of the Lord our God
  Am   Gsus   G
O praise His Name forever - more
   C/E   F   Am
For endless days, we will sing Your praise
   F   Gsus G C   C/E F
Oh Lord, oh Lord our God

[Verse 4]
        C
He shall return in robes of white
        G   Am
The blazing sun shall pierce the night
          F   C/E
And I will rise among the saints
        G   C
My gaze transfixed on Jesus' face

[Chorus]

VL-33

O Praise The Name

Hillsong Worship

Verse 1

Chords Used: C(I) F(IV) G(V) Am(vi)

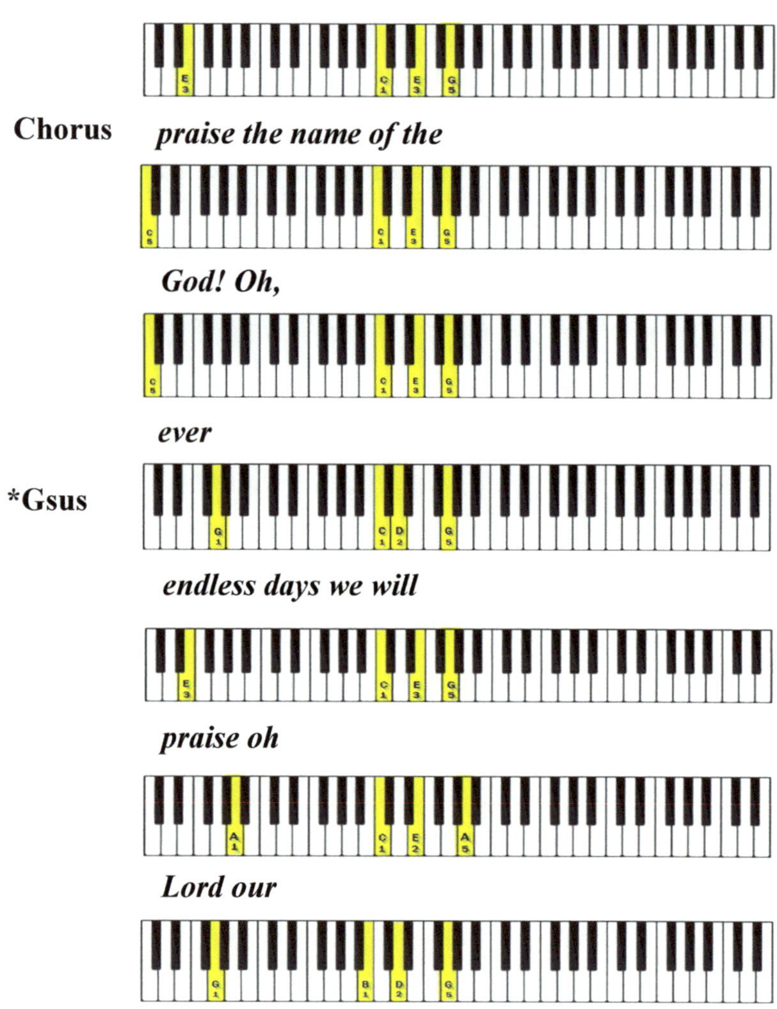

Chorus
praise the name of the
God! Oh,
*Gsus
ever
endless days we will
praise oh
Lord our

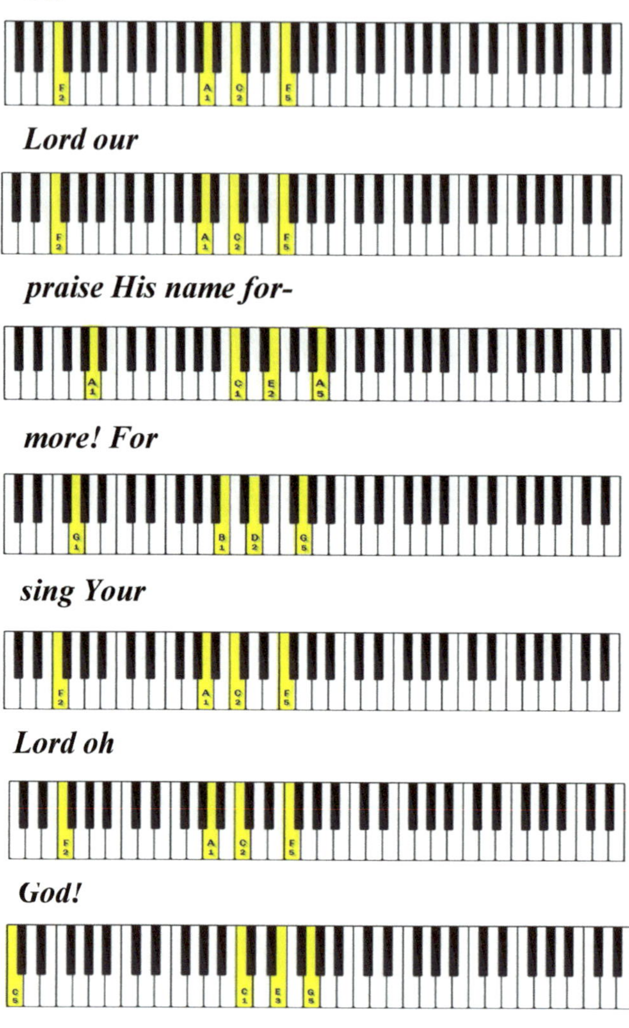

Oh
Lord our
praise His name for-
more! For
sing Your
Lord oh
God!

Yet Not I But Through Christ In Me

City Alight

Time=4

Intro:
C F6/A C/G F6/A

Verse 1

```
              C                    F
What gift of grace is Jesus my redeemer
              C          Am          G
There is no more for heaven now to give
              C                       F
He is my joy my righteousness and freedom
              C        Gsus    G      Csus   C
My steadfast love my deep and boundless peace
              F              C
To this I hold my hope is only Jesus
C/E     F       C           Gsus G
For my life is wholly bound to His
              C        Dm        C/E       F
Oh how strange and divine I can sing all is mine
        C/G           Gsus G    C
Yet not I but through Christ in me
```

Verse 2

The night is dark but I am not forsaken
for by my side, the Savior He will stay
I labor on in weakness and rejoicing
For in my need, His power is displayed
To this I hold my Shepherd will defend me
through the deepest valley He will lead
Oh the night has been won an I shall overcome
Yet not I but through Christ in me

[Turn]
C F6/A C/G F6/A

Verse 3

No fate I dread, I know I am forgiven
the future sure the price it has been paid
for Jesus bled He suffered for my pardon
And He was raised to overthrow the grave
To this I hold my sin has been defeated
Jesus now and ever is my plea
oh the chains are released I can see I am free
Yet not I but through Christ in me

[Turn]
C F6/A C/G F6/A

Verse 4

With every breath I long to follow Jesus
for He has said that he will bring me home
and day by day I know He will renew me
Until I stand with joy before the throne
To this I hold my hope is only Jesus
All the glory evermore to Him
When the race is complete still my lips shall repeat
Yet not I but through Christ in me

Play along!
https://www.yo
utube.com/
Pwatch?v=hwc
2d1Xt8gM

VL-34

Yet Not I But Through Christ In Me

City Alight

Intro

Chords Used: C(I) Dm (ii) F(IV) G(V) Am(vi)

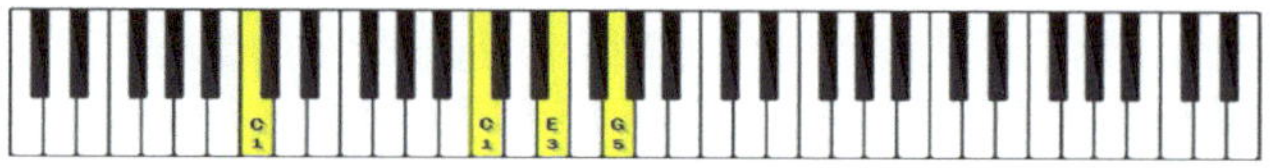

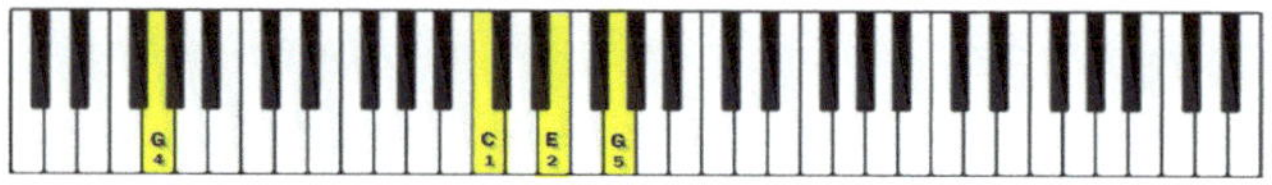

*F6/A

What gift of

Verse 1

grace is Jesus my re-

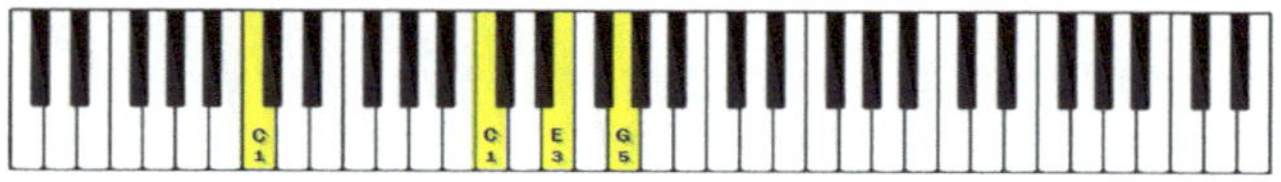

more for Heaven

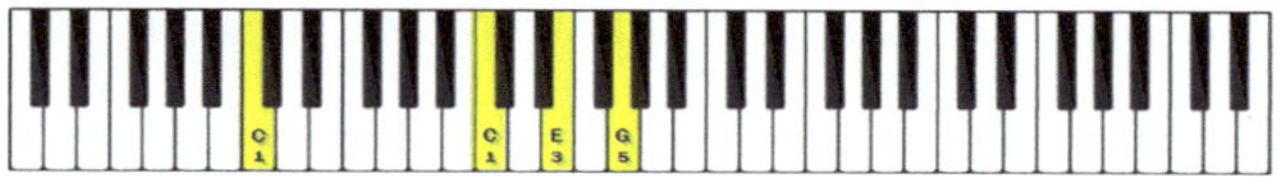

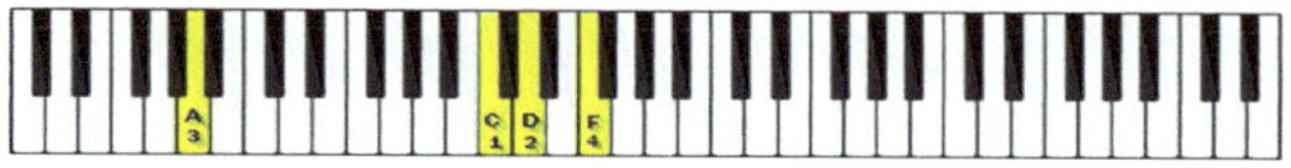

deemer, there is no

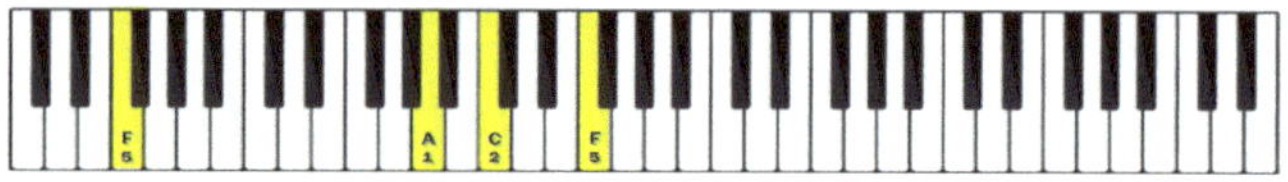

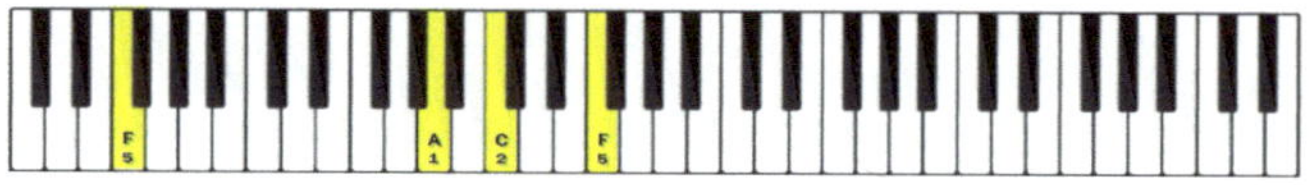

give! He is my

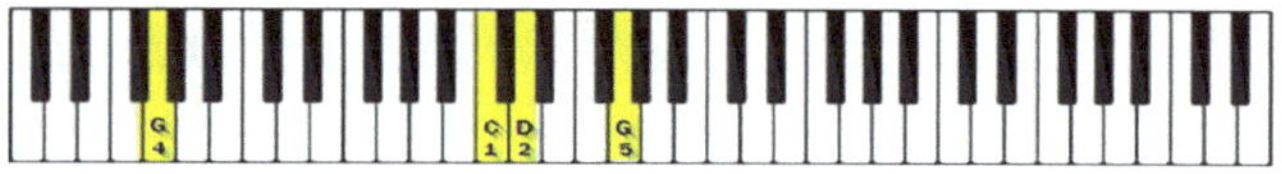

now to

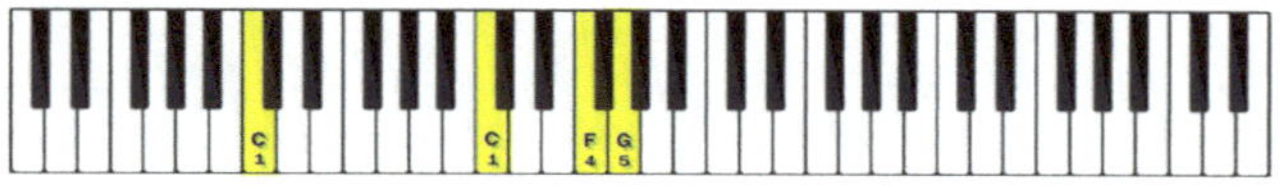

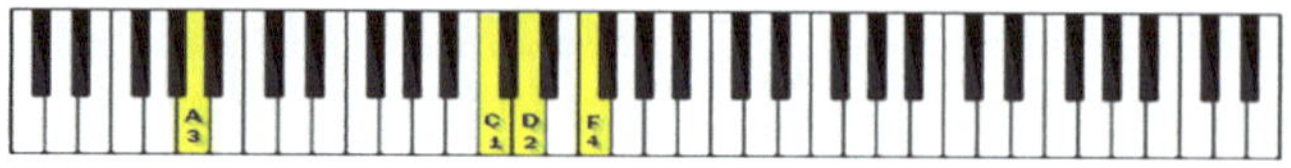

freedom, my steadfast

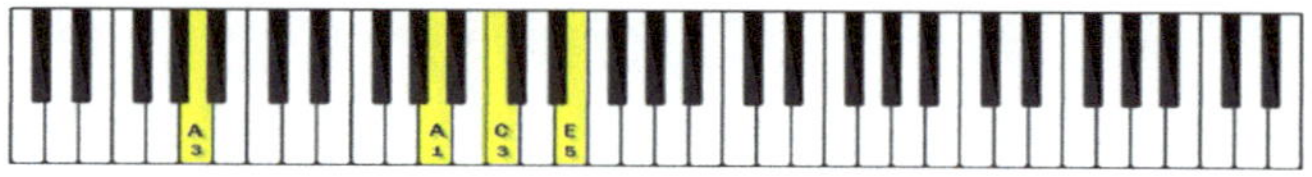

joy, my righteousness and

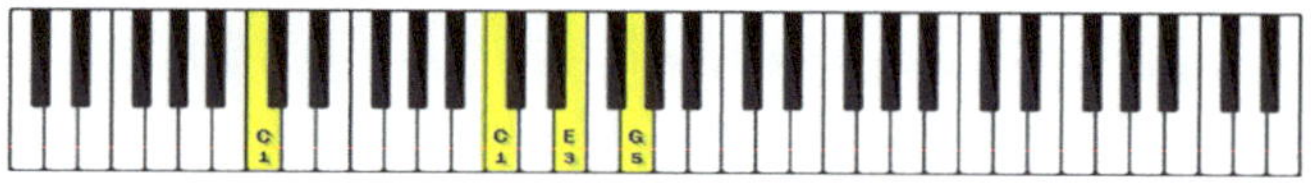

deep and

love, my

peace!

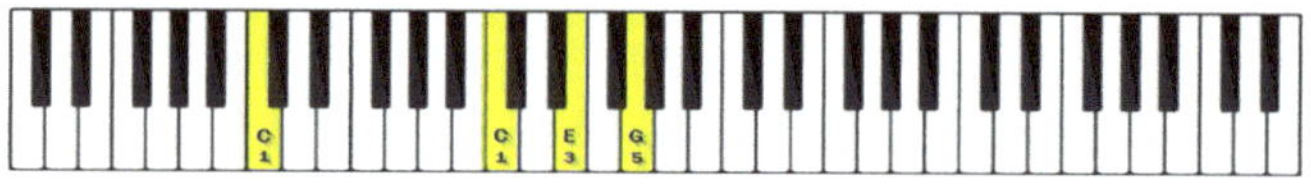

boundless

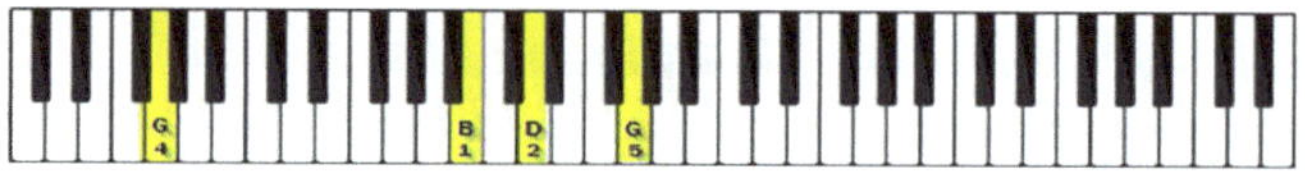

To this I

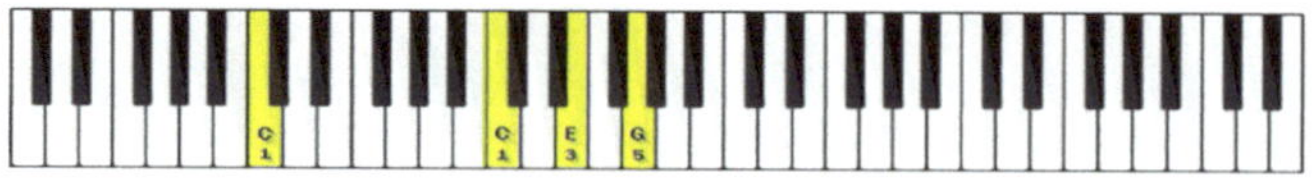

hold my hope is only
for my
wholly bound to
Oh how
divine, I can
mine yet not
Christ
me!
End
Jesus
life is
His
strange and
sing all is
I but through
in

Time=6

So far, the time (how the steady beat is grouped) of the songs presented in this method have been in 3 and 4. Another common time used in worship music is 6. Music is mathematical in nature. This can be seen and heard when we speak of the time of a song. When a song is in 6, it can be heard as a rapid 3. The beats count to 6, with an emphasis on beat 1 and beat 4. Some of the most beautiful worship songs are written with the time in 6.

How He Loves

John Mark McMillan

Time=6

[Verse 1]
C
He is jealous for me
Am
Loves like a hurricane I am a tree
G   F
Bending beneath the weight of His wind and mercy
                   C
When all of a sudden, I am unaware of these
Am
afflictions eclipsed by Glory
            G
And I realize just how beautiful You are and how
 F
great Your affections are for me

[Chorus 1]
C   Am
Oh how He loves us, so
                   G   F
Oh How He loves us, how He loves us so

[Verse 2]
C
He is jealous for me
Am
Loves like a hurricane I am a tree
G   F
Bending beneath the weight of His wind and mercy
                   C
When all of a sudden, I am unaware of these
Am
afflictions eclipsed by Glory

            G
And I realize just how beautiful You are and how
 F
great Your affections are for me

[Chorus 1]

[Instrumental]
C Am G F

[Chorus 2]
                   C
Yeah, He loves us
                   Am
Oh how He loves us
                   G
Yeah, He loves us
                   F
Oh how He loves

[Verse 3]
C
We are His portion and He is our prize
Am
Drawn to redemption by the grace in His eyes
            G   F
If His grace is an ocean we're all sinking
                   C
And, Heaven meets earth like an unforeseen kiss
                   Am
And my heart turns violently inside of my chest
      G
I don't have time to maintain these regrets when I
F
think about the way that He,

[Chorus 2]
C
He loves us
                   Am
Oh how He loves us
                   G
Oh how He loves us
                   F
Oh how He loves
                   C
Yeah He loves us
                   Am
Oh how He loves us
                   G
Oh how He loves us
                   F
Oh how He loves

**Play along!
https://
www.youtube.com/
watch?v=SUKJEhk
k2G8**

VL-35

105

Chords Used: C(I) F(IV) G(V) Am(vi)

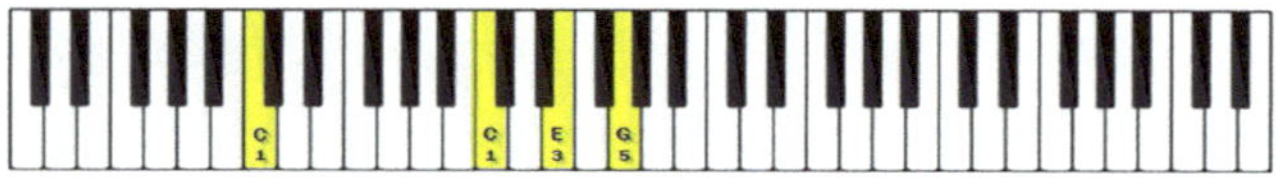

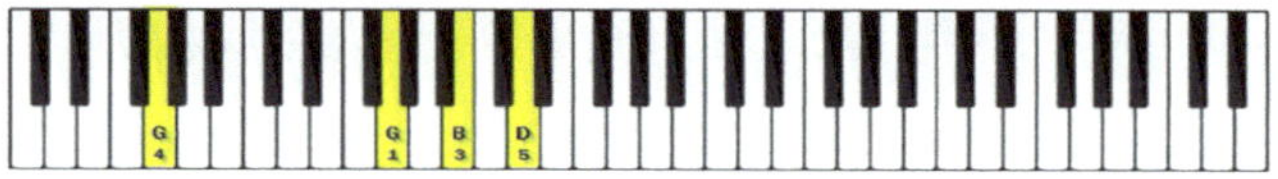

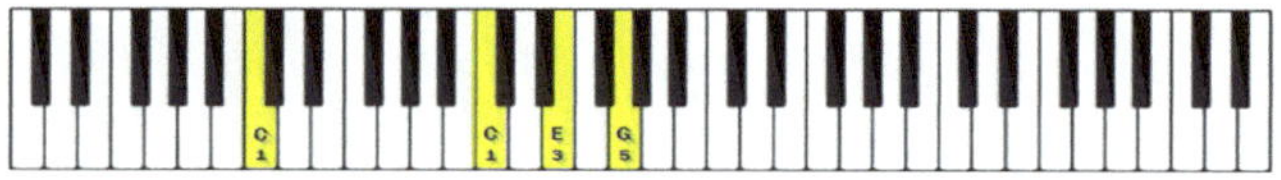

Intro

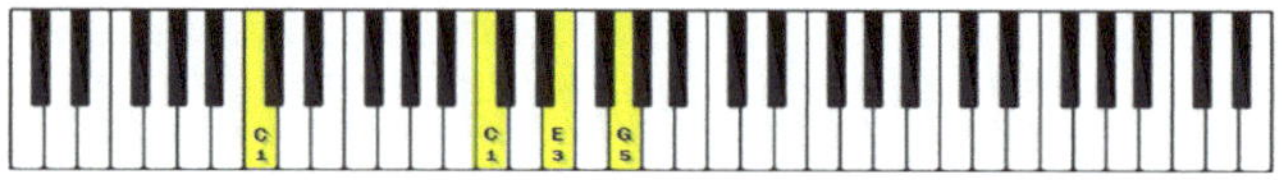

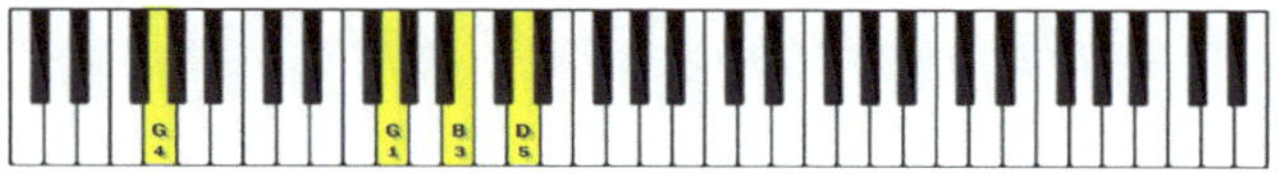

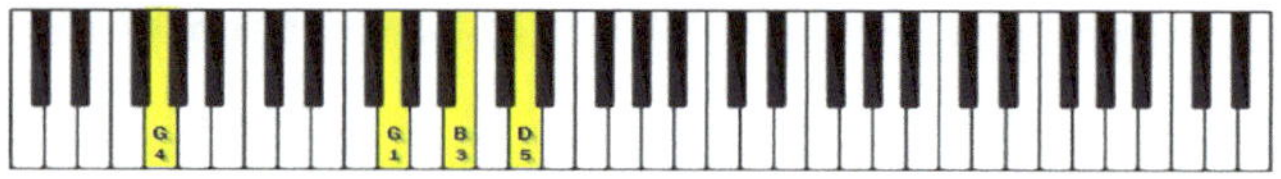

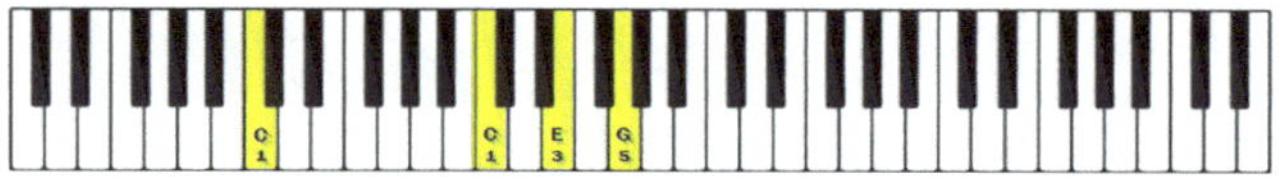

Verse 1

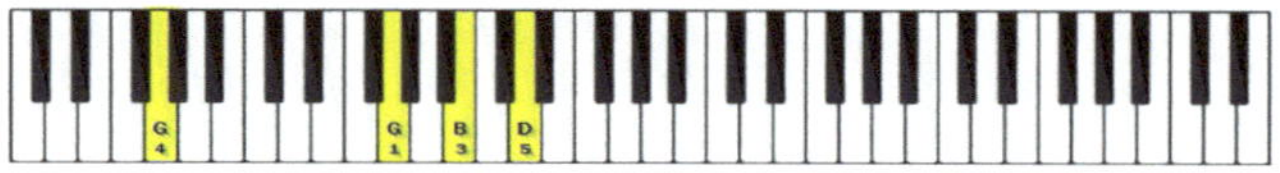

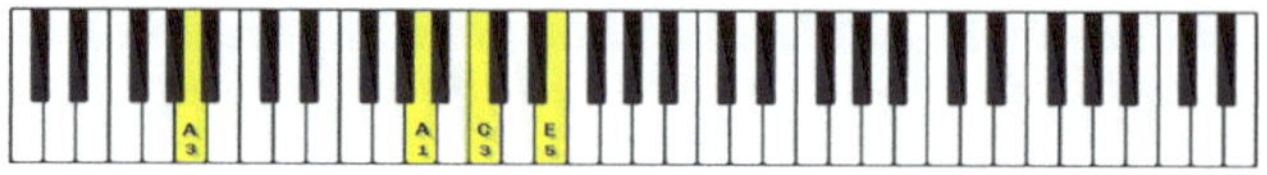

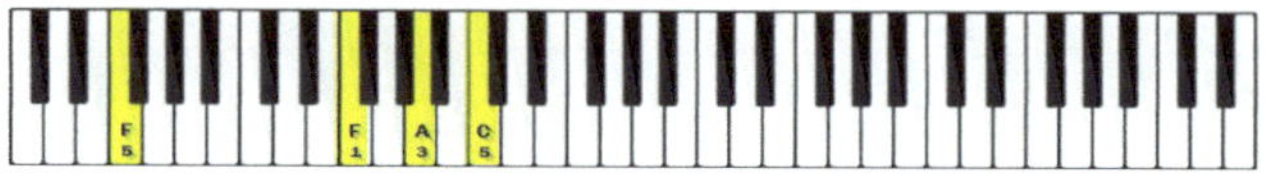

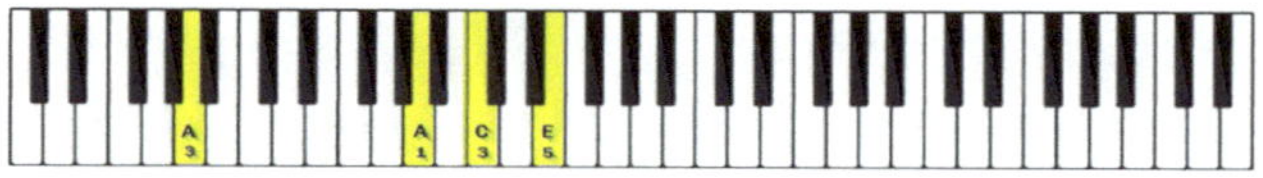

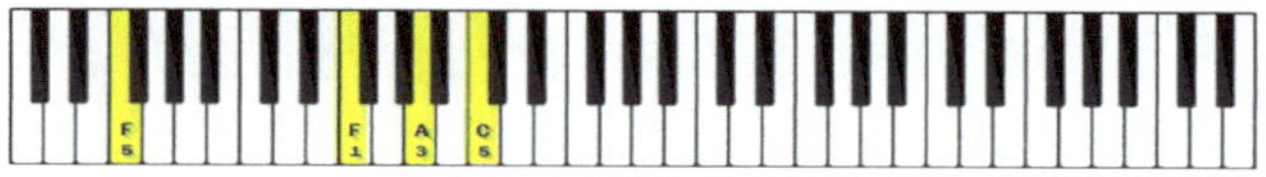

Chorus 1

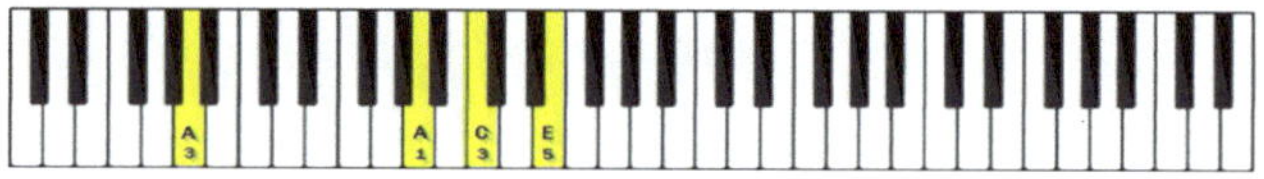

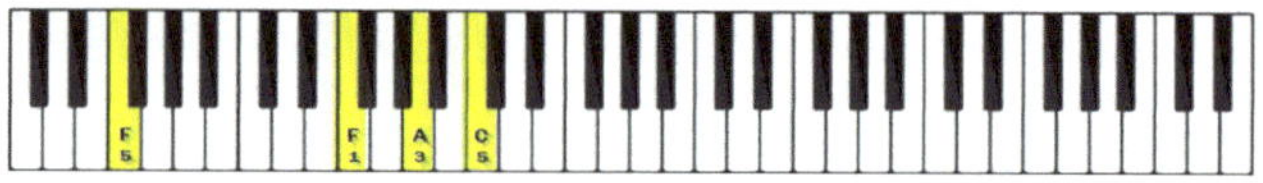

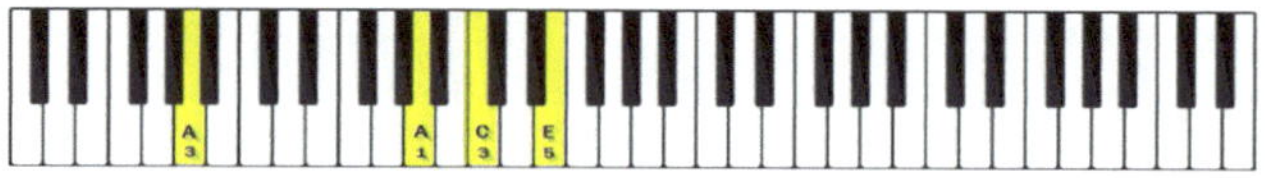

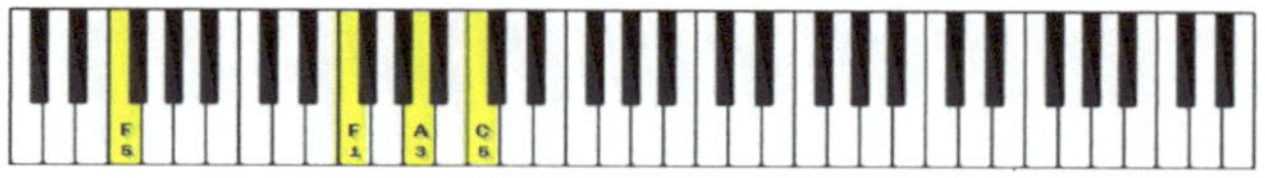

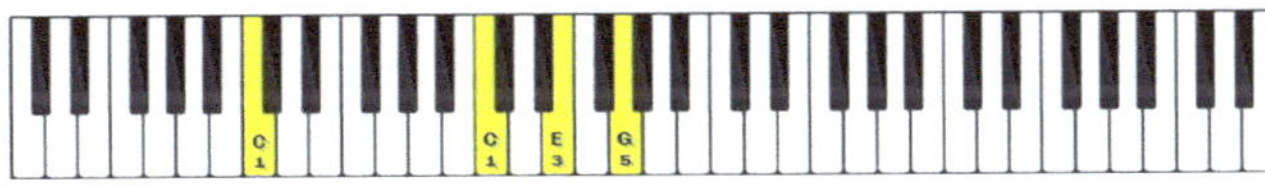

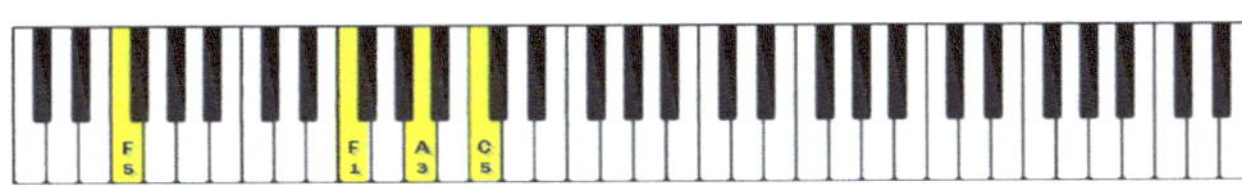

Chorus 2 *loves us, oh how*

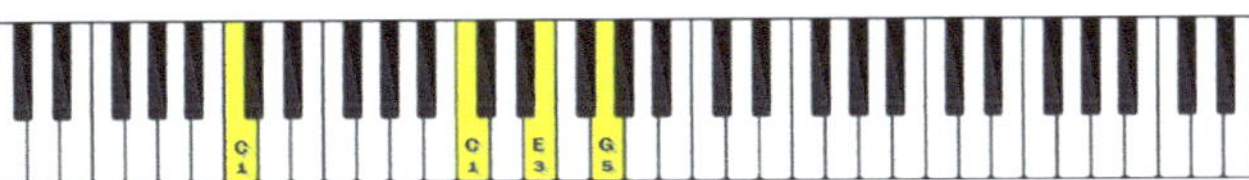

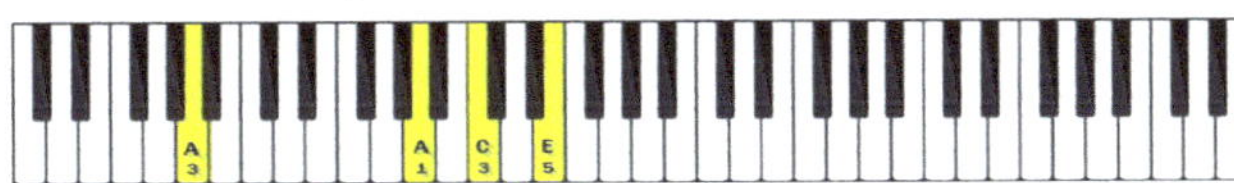

loves us, oh how

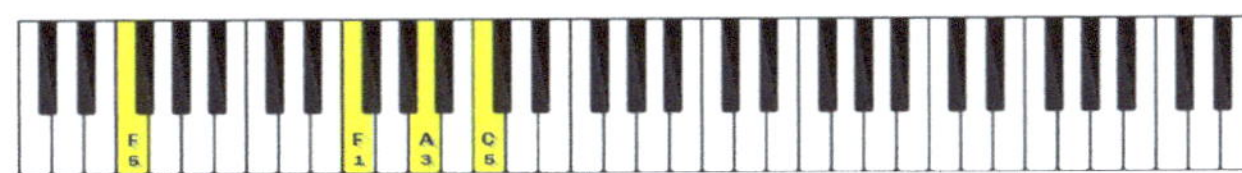

loves us, oh how

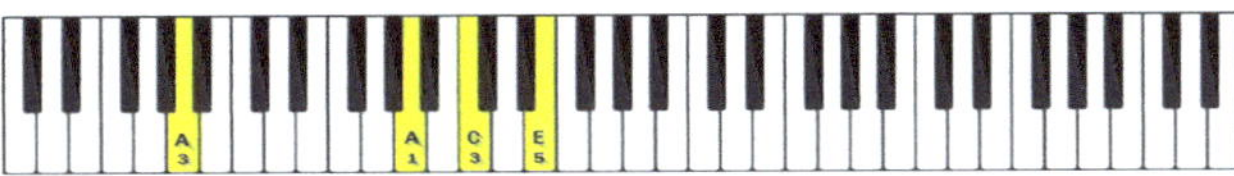

loves us, oh how

Reckless Love

Cory Asbury

Time=6

[Verse]
```
Am              G
Before I spoke a word
                      F
You were singing over me
Am          G
You have been so, so
      F
good to me
Am          G
Before I took a breath You
          F
breathed Your life into me
Am          G
You have been so, so
      F
kind to me
```

[Chorus]
```
        Am
Oh, the overwhelming
G           F           C
never-ending, reckless love of God
        Am
Oh it chases me down
G           F           C
Fights till I'm found leaves the ninety-
nine
```

```
Am              G
Oh I couldn't earn it, I don't deserve it
        F           C
Still You give yourself away
Am
Oh, the overwhelming
G           F           C
never-ending, reckless love of God
```

[Verse]
```
Am              G
When I was your foe, still
          F
Your love fought for me
Am          G
You have been so so
      F
Good to me
Am          G
When I felt no worth
          F
You paid it all for me
Am          G
You have been so so
      F
Kind to me
```

[Chorus]

[Bridge] 4X (1st time N.C.)
```
Am                      G
There's no shadow You won't light up
                  F                   C
Mountain you won't climb up coming after me
Am                  G
There's no wall You won't kick down
              F                   C
Lie You won't tear down coming after me
```

[Chorus]
```
        Am          G
Oh, the overwhelming, never-ending,
F           C
reckless love of God
        Am          G
Oh it chases me down fights till I'm found
F       C
leaves the ninety-nine
            Am          G
Oh I couldn't earn it, I don't deserve it
        F           C
Still You give yourself away
        Am          G
Oh, the overwhelming never-ending,
F           C
reckless love of God
```

Reckless Love

Cory Asbury

Chords Used: C(I) F(IV) G(V) Am(vi)

Left hand octaves optional

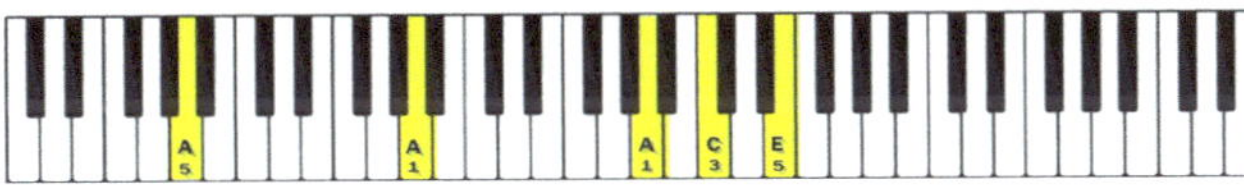

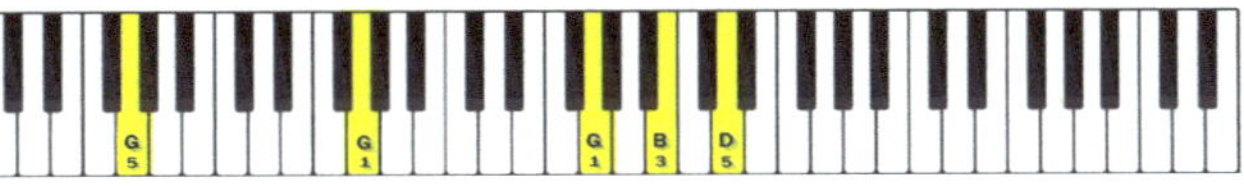

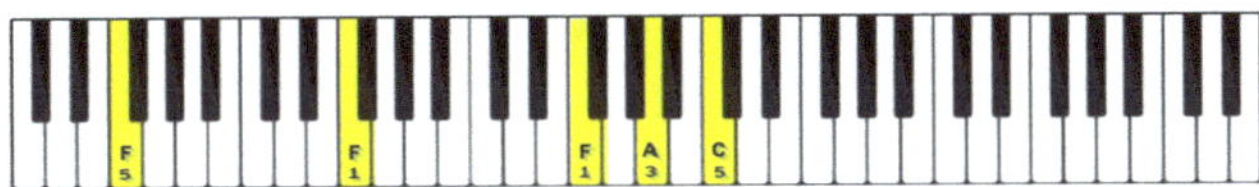

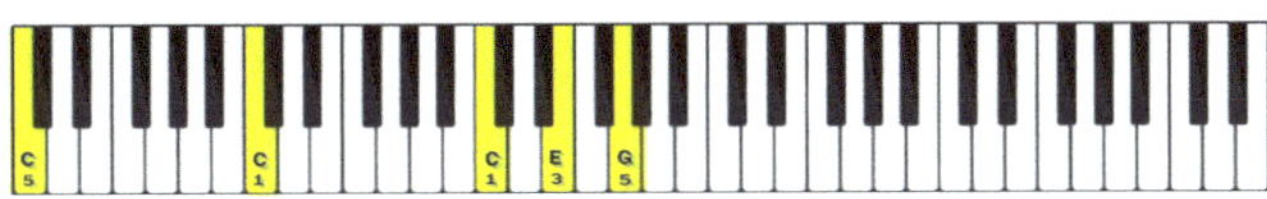

Verse 1

Before I spoke a

word You were singing

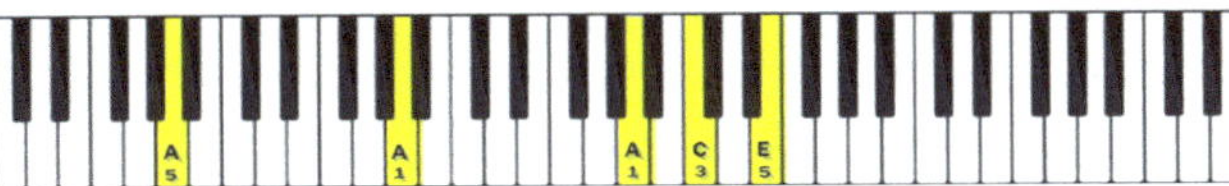

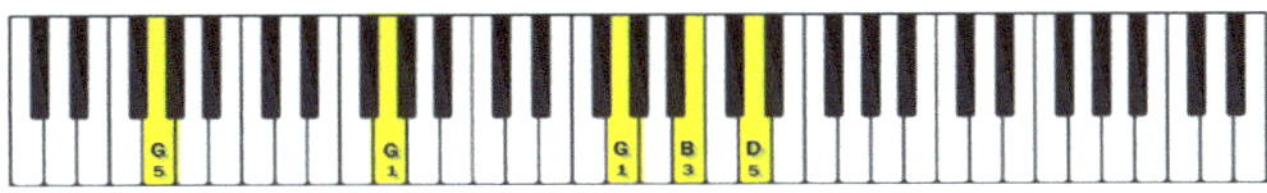

Over me!

You have been

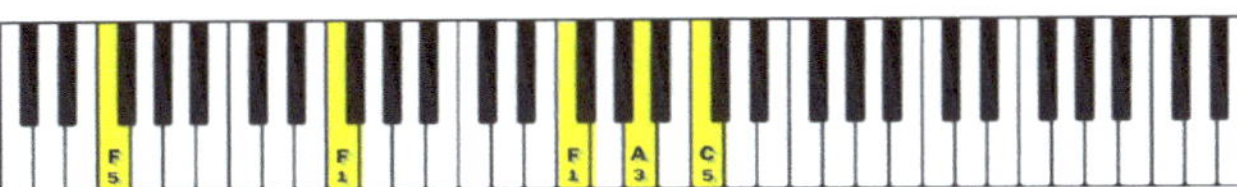

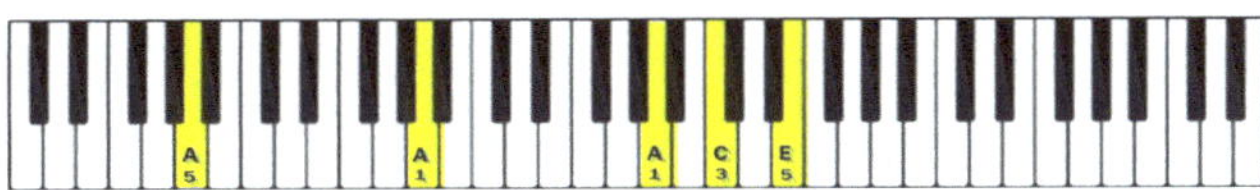

so, so good to

me!

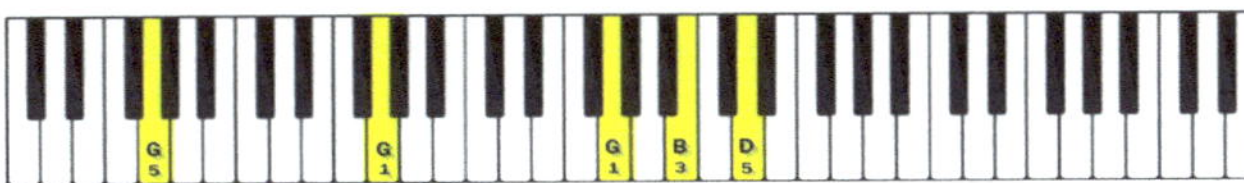

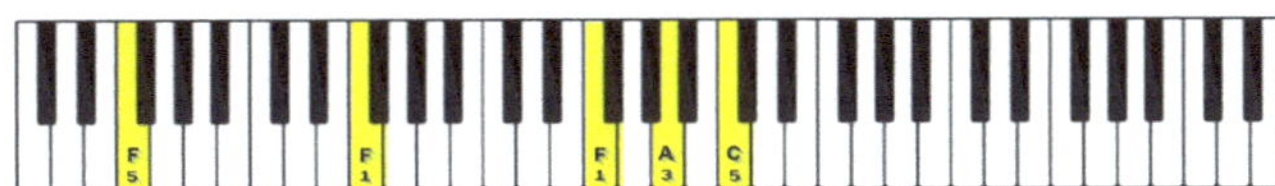

Before I took a

breath You breathed Your

life into me!

You have been

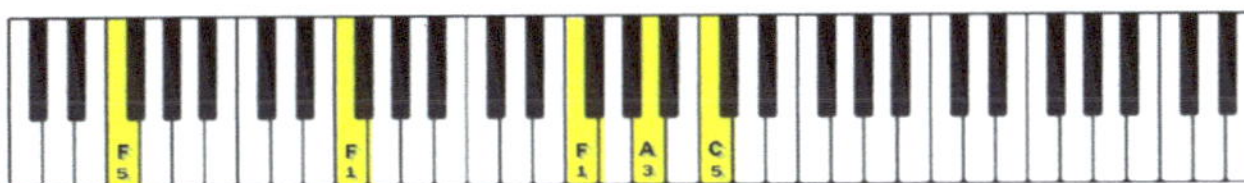

so, so good to

me! Oh the

Chorus *overwhelming,*

reckless love of

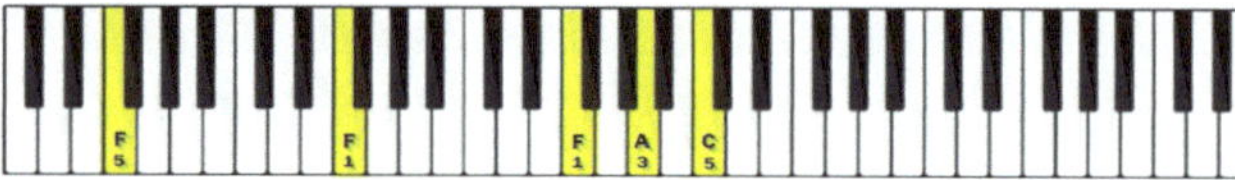

chases me down

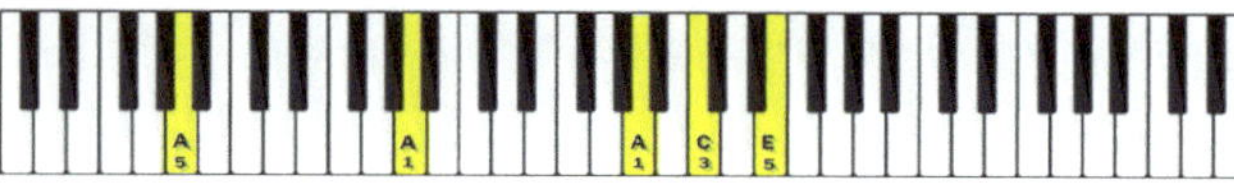

leaves the ninety-

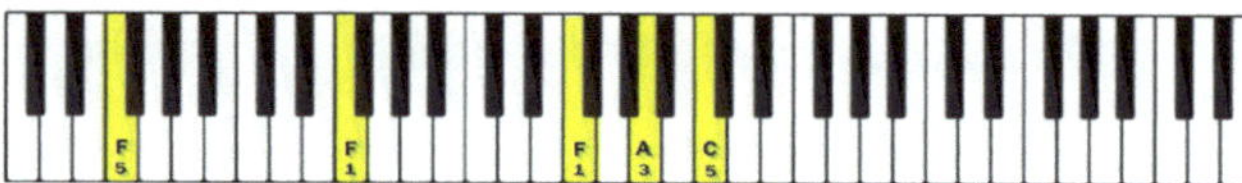

earn it, I don't

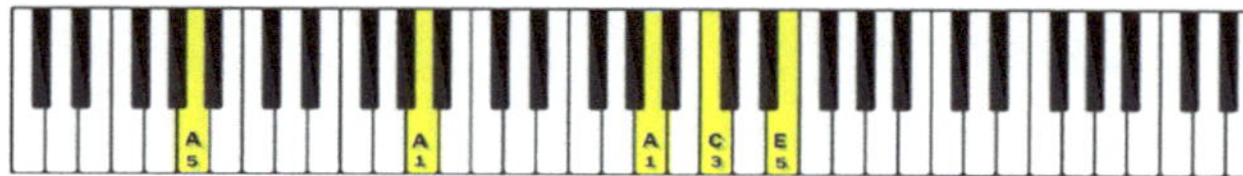

give Yourself a-

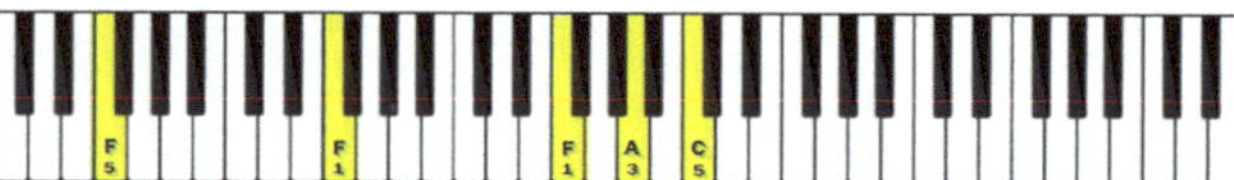

overwhelming,

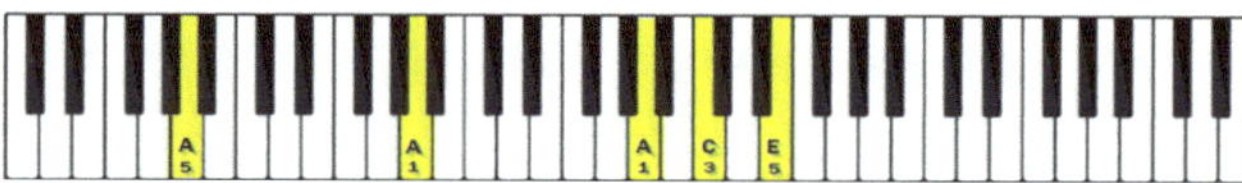

reckless love of

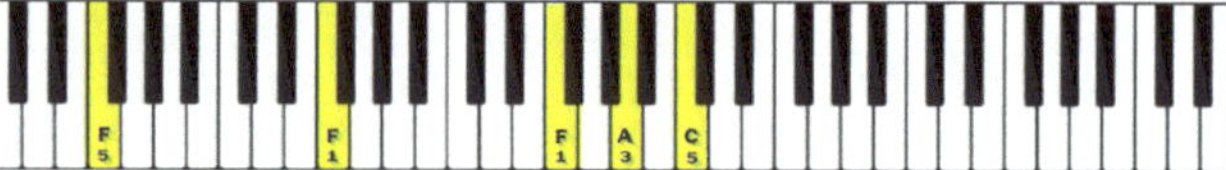

never-ending

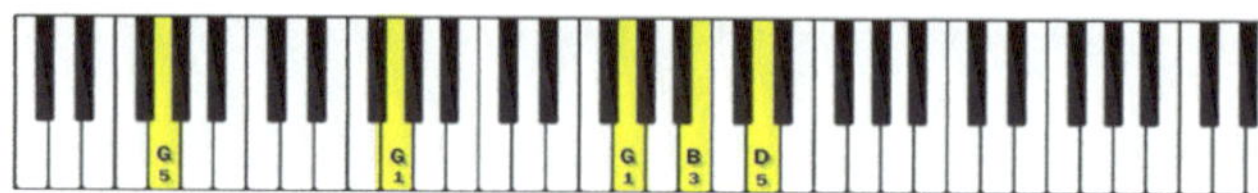

God! Oh it

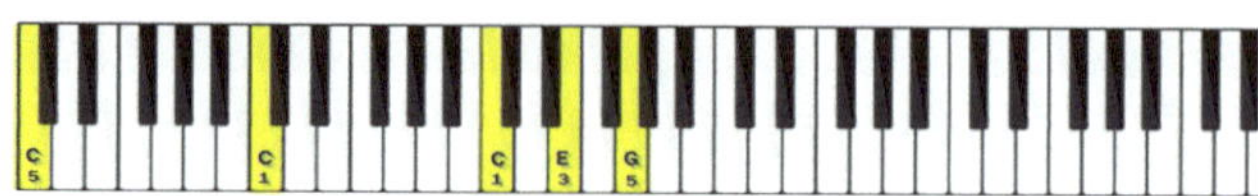

fights till I'm found

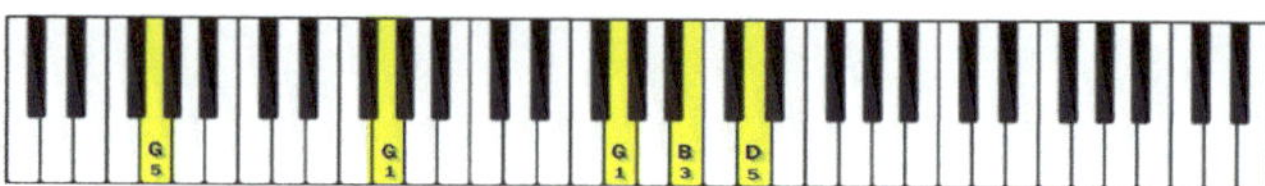

nine! Oh I couldn't

deserve it still You

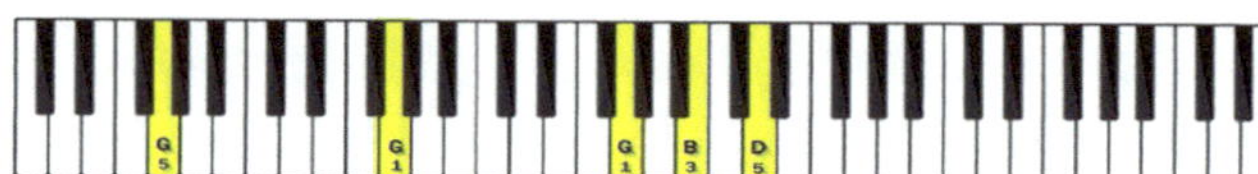

way, Oh the

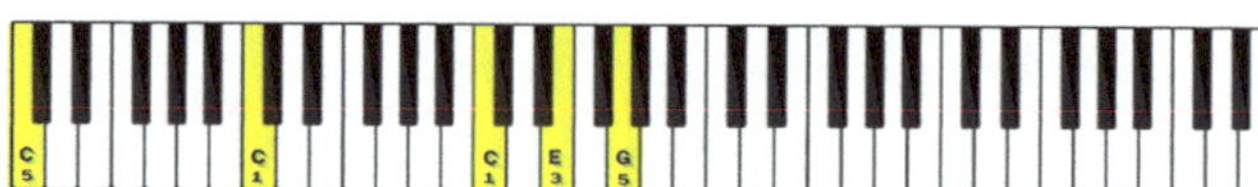

never-ending

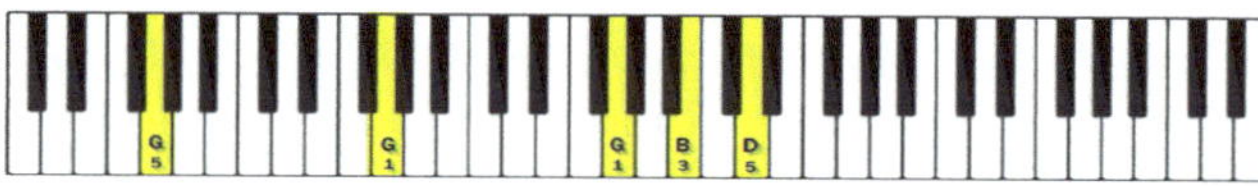

God!

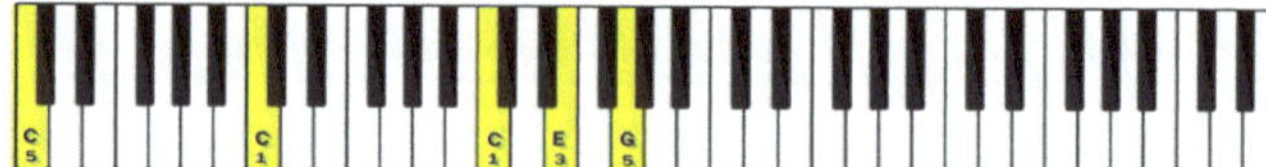

Bridge 2X

There's no shadow You won't

climb up coming after

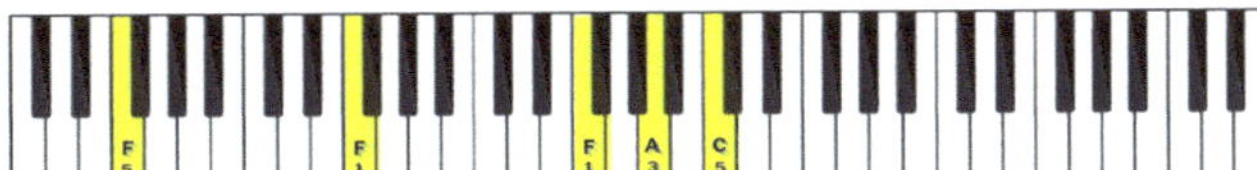

There's no wall You

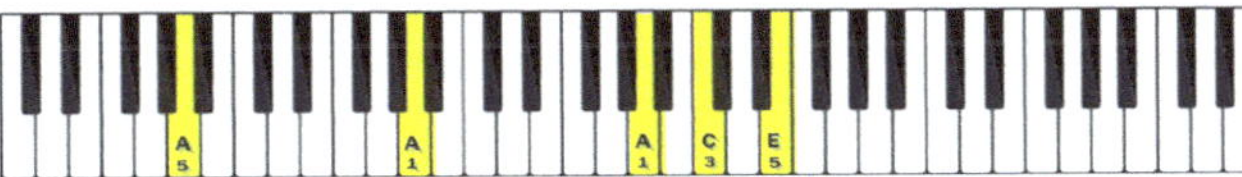

tear down coming after

There's no shadow You won't

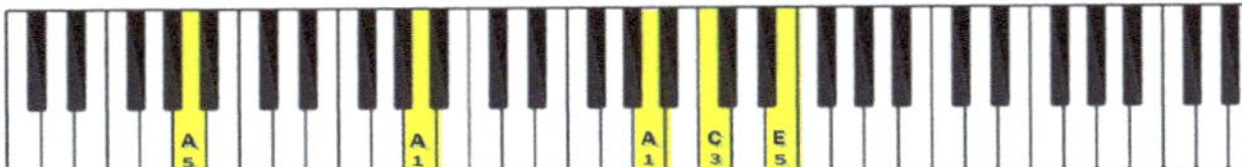

climb up coming after

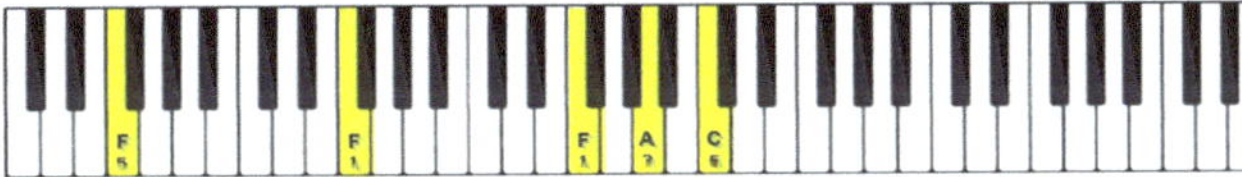

There's no wall You

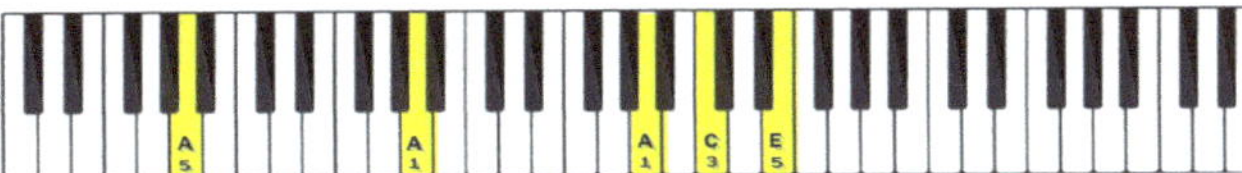

tear down coming after

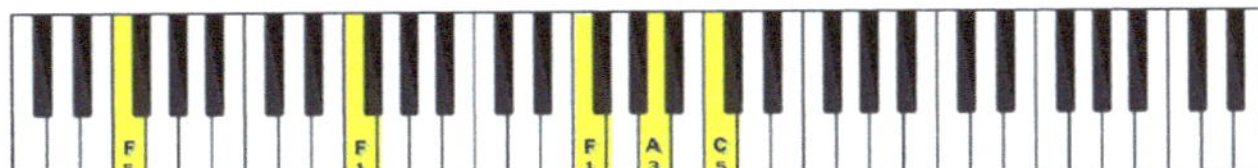

light up, mountain you won't

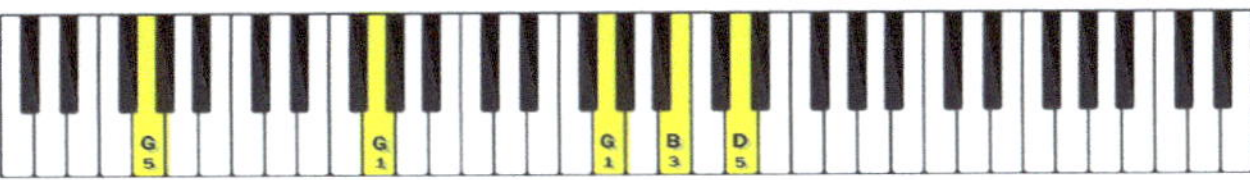

me!

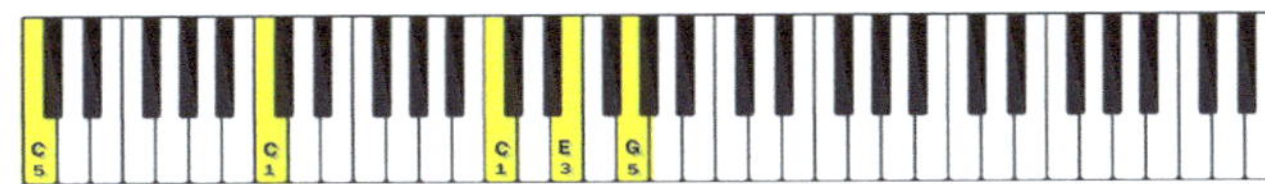

won't kick down, lie you won't

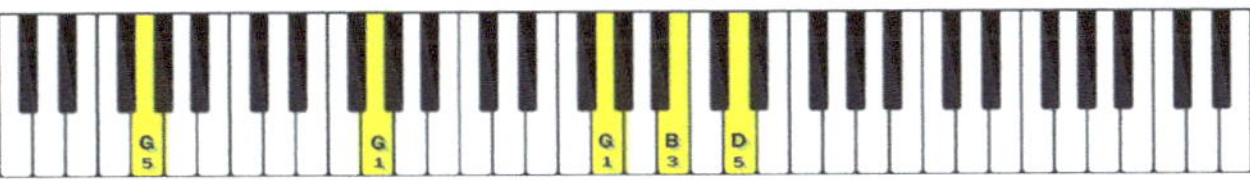

me!

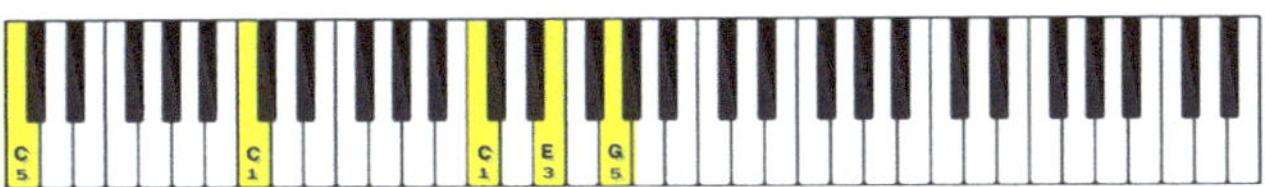

light up, mountain you won't

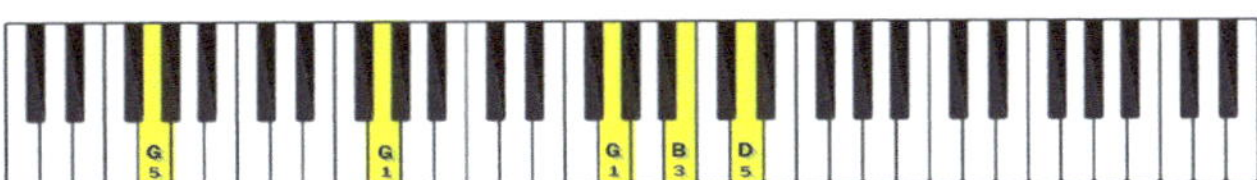

me!

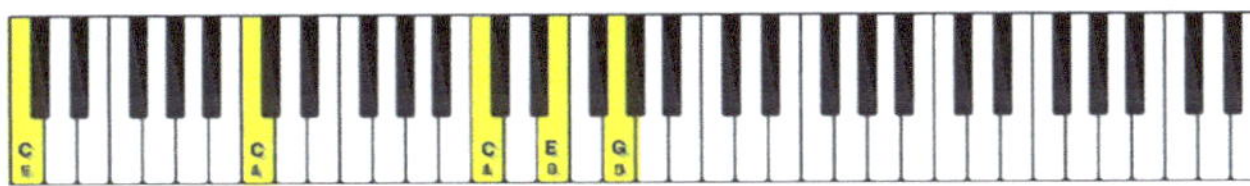

won't kick down, lie you won't

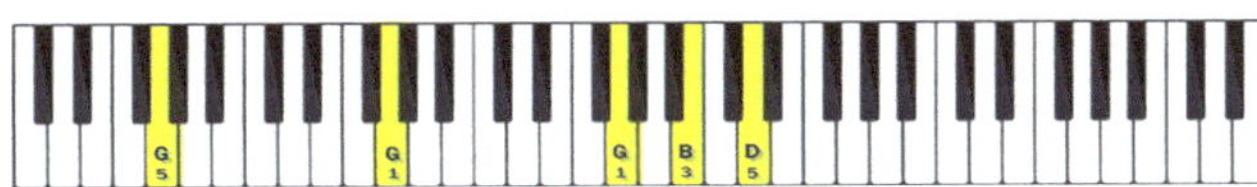

me!

Seth Condrey

Time=6

[Verse 1]

```
C                    F         C
Alone in my sorrow and dead in my sin
F                      G       Am
Lost without hope and no place to begin
      C                    F         C
Your love made a way to let mercy come in
      Am                 G  C
When death was arrested and my life began
```

[Verse 2]
```
C                    F    C
Ash was redeemed, only beauty remains
      F                 G     Am
(and) My orphan heart was given a name
      C                   F         C
My mourning grew quiet, my feet rose to dance
      Am                 G  C
When death was arrested and my life began
```

[Chorus 1]
```
        F      C        Am G
Oh Your grace so free washes over me
        F              Am            G
You have made me new, now life begins with You
```

[Verse 3]
```
  C                      F        C
Released from my chain, I'm a prisoner no more
      F             G       Am
My shame was a ransom He faithfully bore
      C                 F         C
He canceled my debt and He called me His friend
```

```
Am                      G  C
When death was arrested and my life began
```

[Chorus 2]
```
        F      C        Am G
Oh Your grace so free washes over me
        F              Am            G
You have made me new, now life begins with You
        F    C        Am       G
It's Your endless love pouring down on us
        F              Am           G
You have made us new now life begins with You
```

[Verse 4]
```
   C                      F         C
Our Savior displayed on a criminal's cross
      F                 G          Am
(and) Darkness rejoiced as though Heaven had lost
      C                  F        C
But then Jesus arose with our freedom in hand
           Am                 G      C
That's when death was arrested and my life began
           Am                 G      C
That's when death was arrested and my life began
```
[Chorus 2]
[Bridge] 2X
```
          C       F           C
Oh we're free, free, forever we're free
Am               G       C
Come join the song of all the redeemed
           C         F     C
Yes we're free, free, forever amen
           Am            G      C
//When death was arrested and my life began//
```

Death Was Arrested

Seth Condrey

Chords Used: C(I) F(IV) G(V) Am(vi)

Verse 1

Alone in my sorrow and

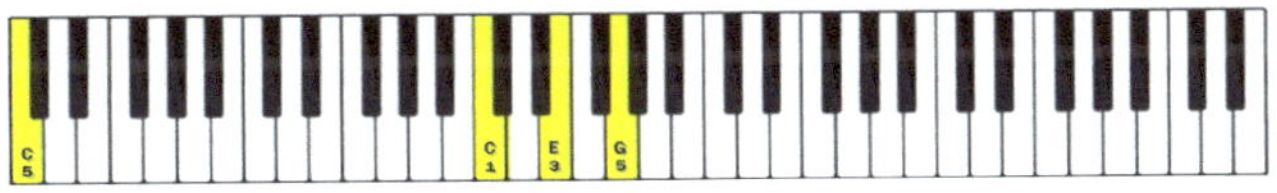

dead in my

sin!

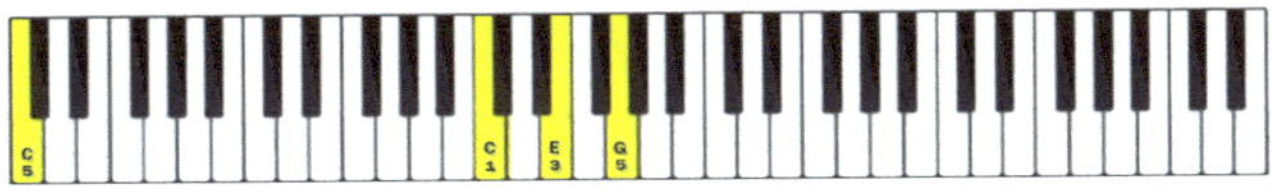

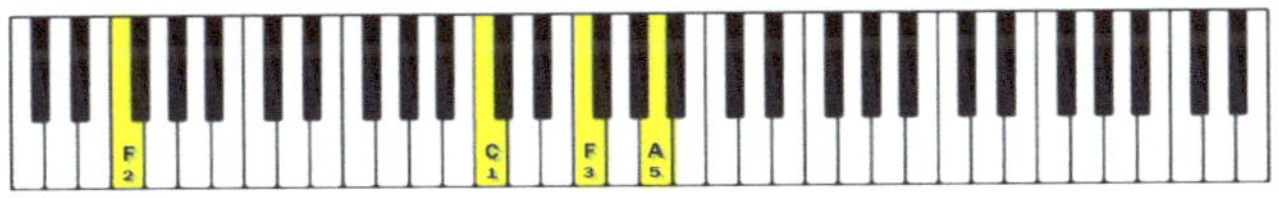

Lost without hope and no-

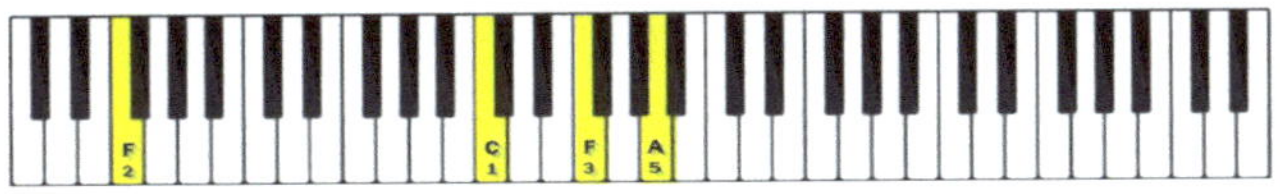

place to be-

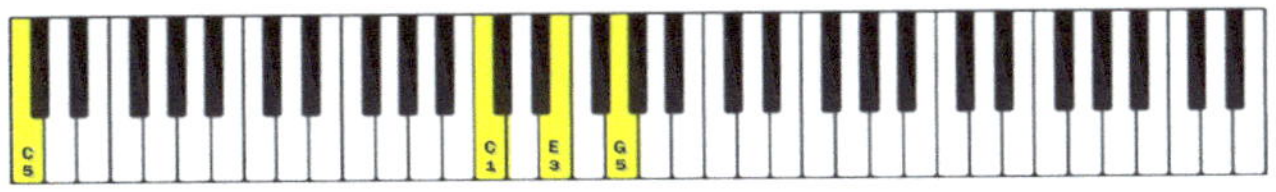

gin, Your

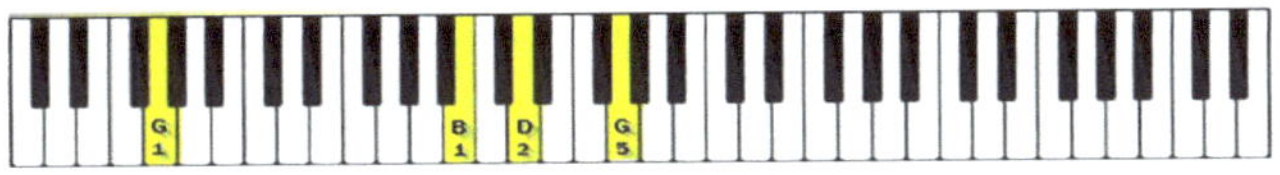

love made a way to let

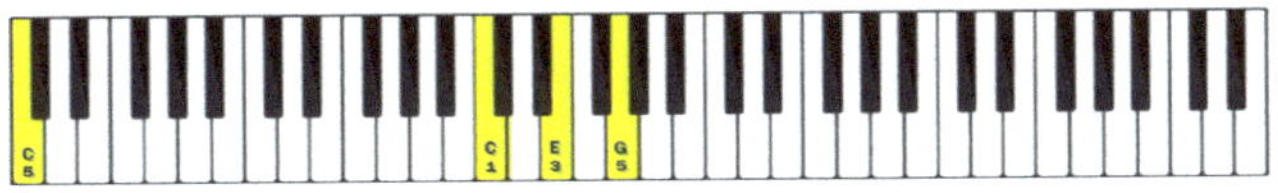

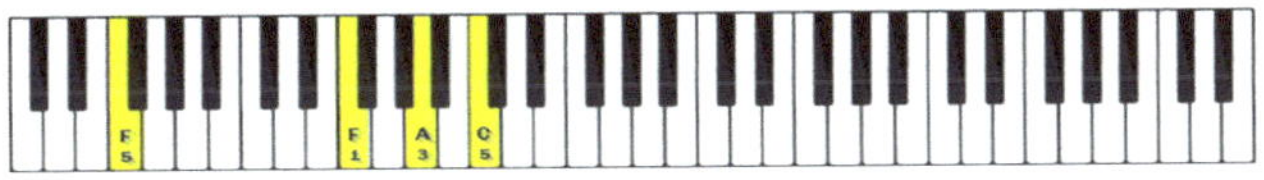

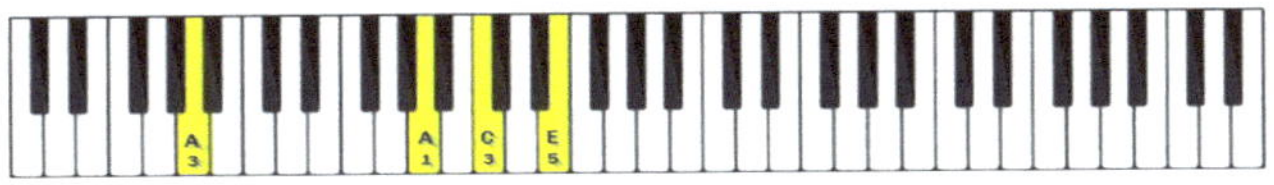

mercy come

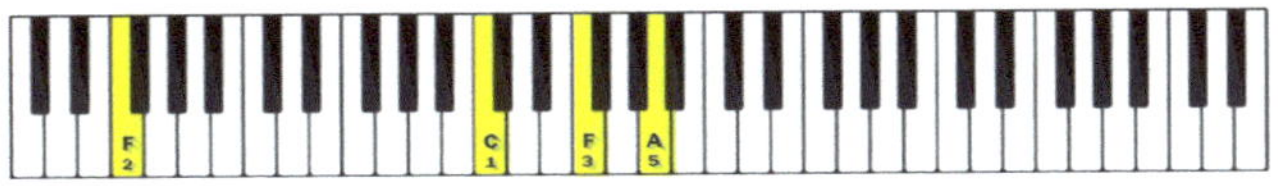

in! When

death was arrested and

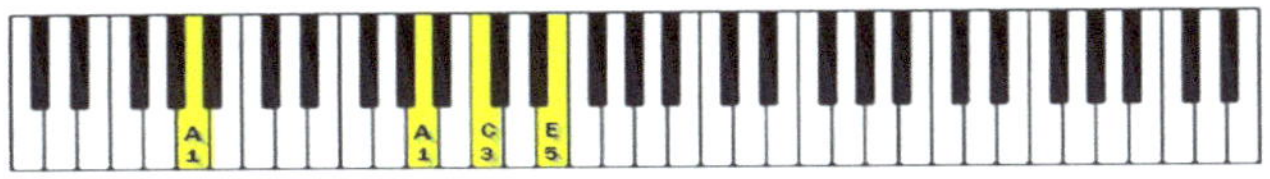

my life be-

gan! Oh Your

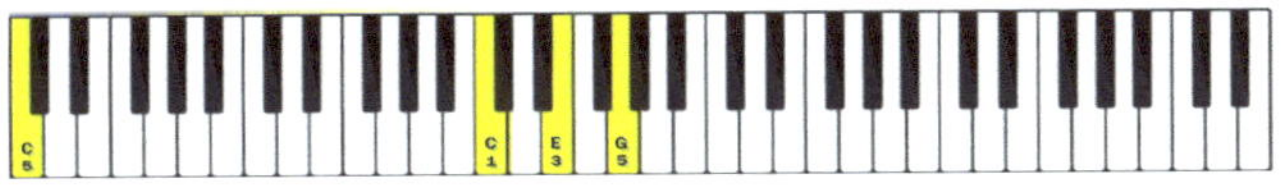

Chorus *grace so*

free washes

over

me, You have

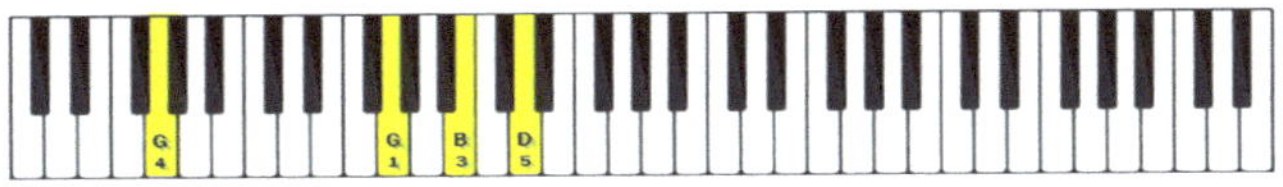

made me new now

You! Its Your

love pouring

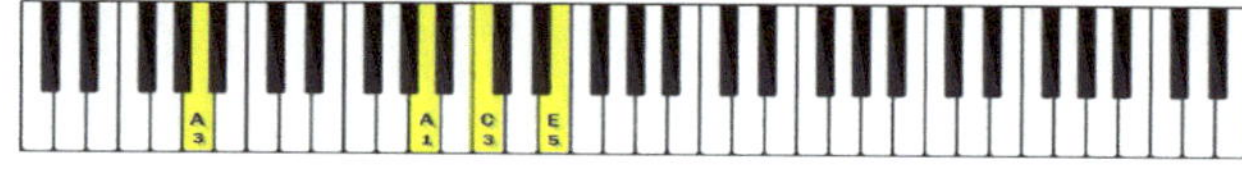

us, You have

life begins with

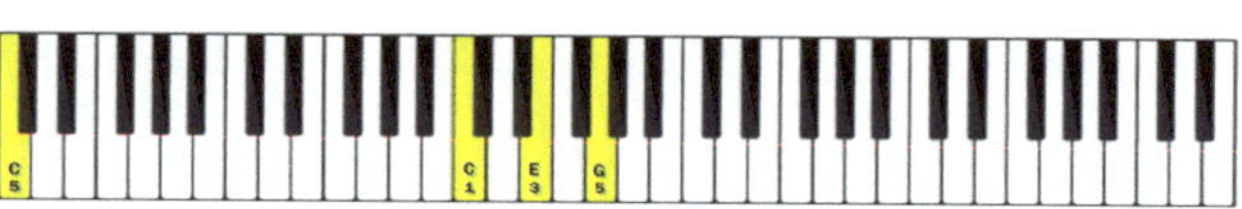

Bridge   *Free! Free*

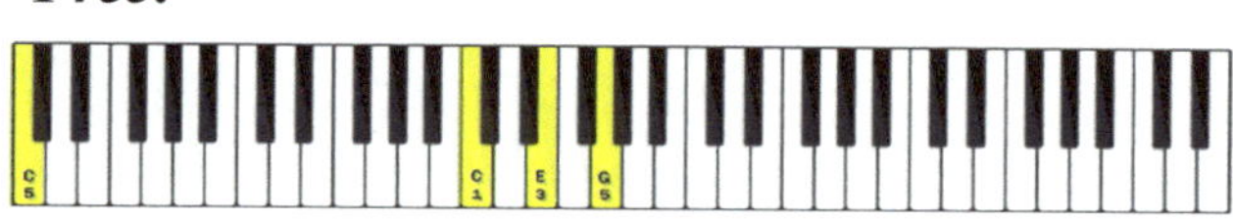

Free!

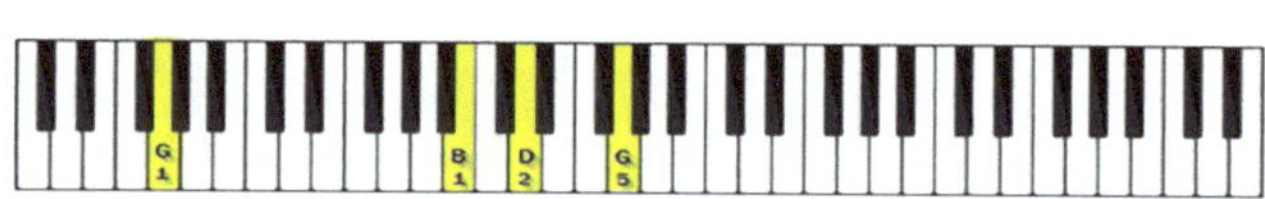

all the

life begins with

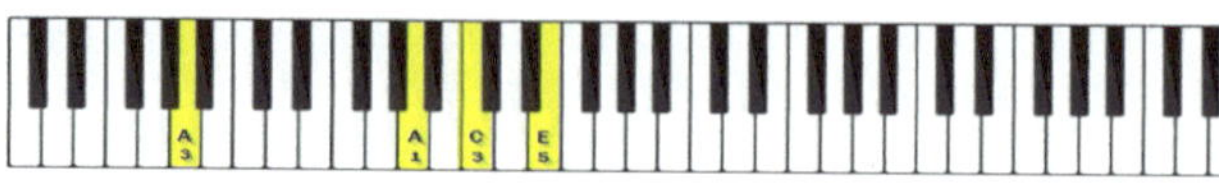

endless

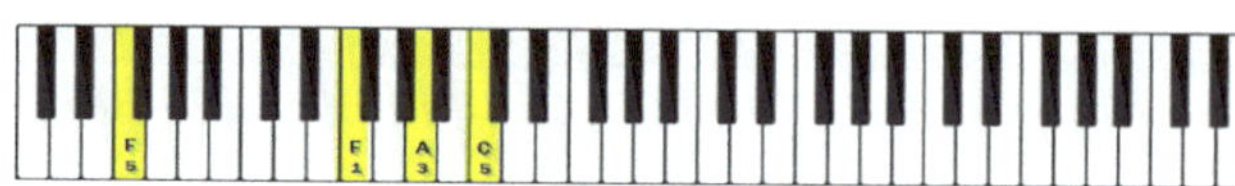

down on

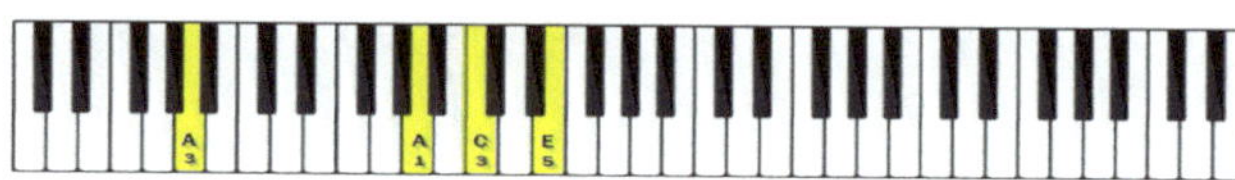

made us new now

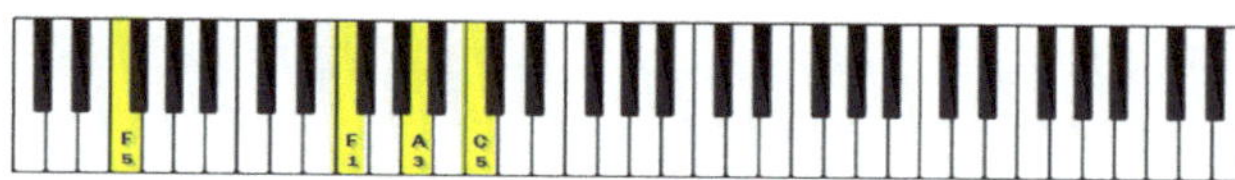

You! Yes we're

Forever we're

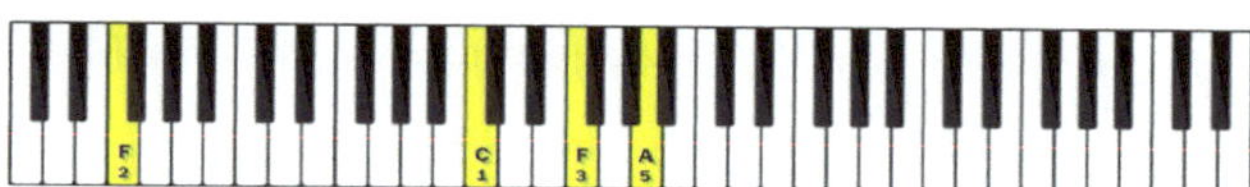

Come join the song of

redeemed! Yes we're

Free! Free!

en! When

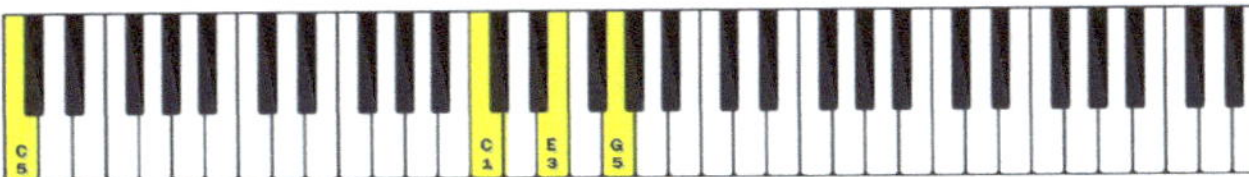

my life be-

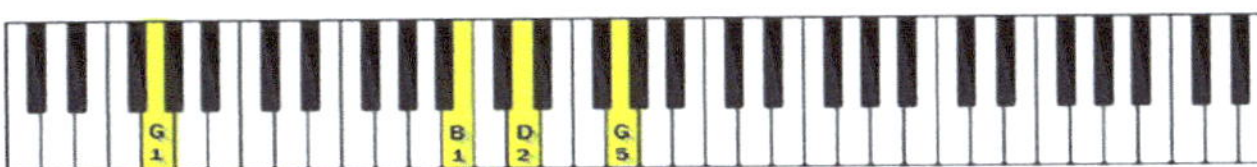

death was arrested and

gan!

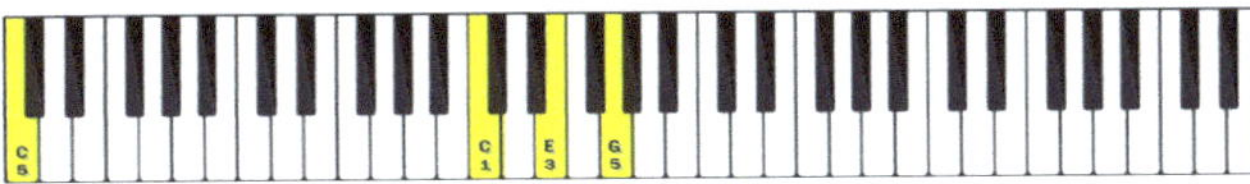

Forever am-

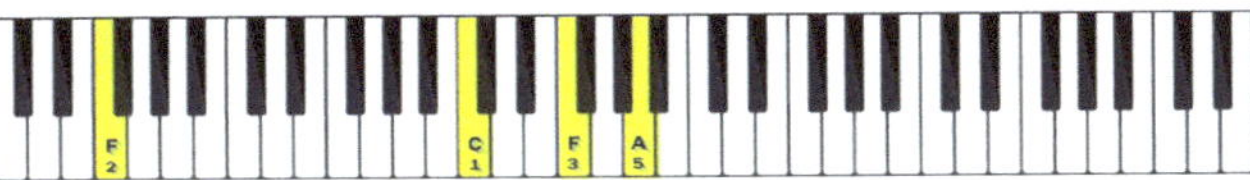

death was arrested and

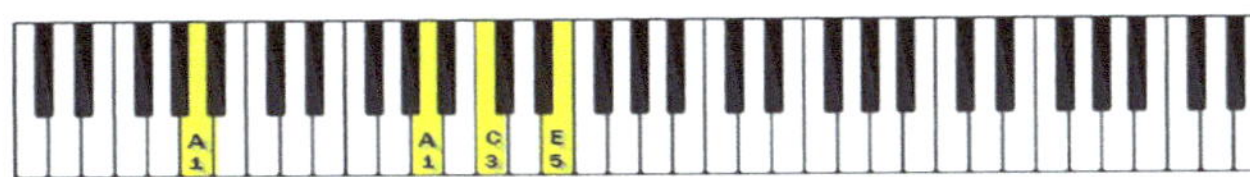

gan! When

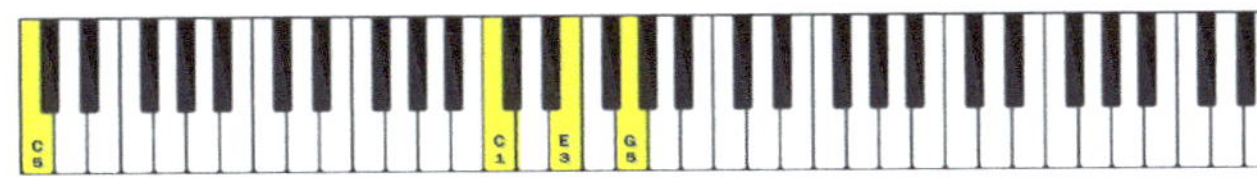

my life be-

Time=6

[Intro]
C Csus C5 (x2)

[Verse 1]
```
C               Csus        C5
Oh, I've heard a thousand stories
   C          Csus         C5
Of what they think You're like
   C              Csus  C5
But, I've heard the tender whisper
   C           Csus   C5
Of love in the dead of night
        F2(no3)C/E
And You tell me that You're pleased
        Dm        Gsus
And that I'm never alone
```

[Chorus]
```
                        F2
You're a Good, Good Father
                C
It's who You are
                Dm
It's who You are
                Gsus
It's who you are
                F2
And I'm loved by You
                C
It's who I am
                Dm
It's who I am
                Gsus
It's who I am
```

[Verse 2]
```
C               Csus        C5
Oh, and I've seen many searching
        C        Csus   C5
For answers far and wide
        C        Csus      C5
But I know we're all searching
        C            Csus C5
For answers only You provide
              F2(no3)            C/E
Cause You know just what we need
        Dm        Gsus
Before we, say a word
```

[Chorus]

[Bridge] 2X
```
              F2              Am
'Cause You are perfect in all of your ways
        Dm            C
You are perfect in all of your ways
        F2              Am    Gsus
You are perfect in all of Your ways to us
        F2                Am
You are perfect in all of your ways
              Dm                C
Oh, You're perfect in all of your ways
        F2              Am    Gsus
You are perfect in all of Your ways to us
```

[Verse 3]
```
C       Csus C5
Love so un-deniable
C       Csus C5
I, I can hardly speak
C       Csus C5
Peace so un-explainable
```
N.C. (no chord)
```
I, I can hardly think
        Fs(no3) C/E
As You call me deeper still
              Dm              C
As You call me deeper still
              F2              C/E
As You call me deeper still
              Dm        Gsus
Into love, love, love
```

[Chorus] 2X

Play along!
https://
www.youtube.
com/

Good, Good Father

Chris Tomlin

Chords Used: C(I) Dm (ii) F(IV) G(V) Am (vi)

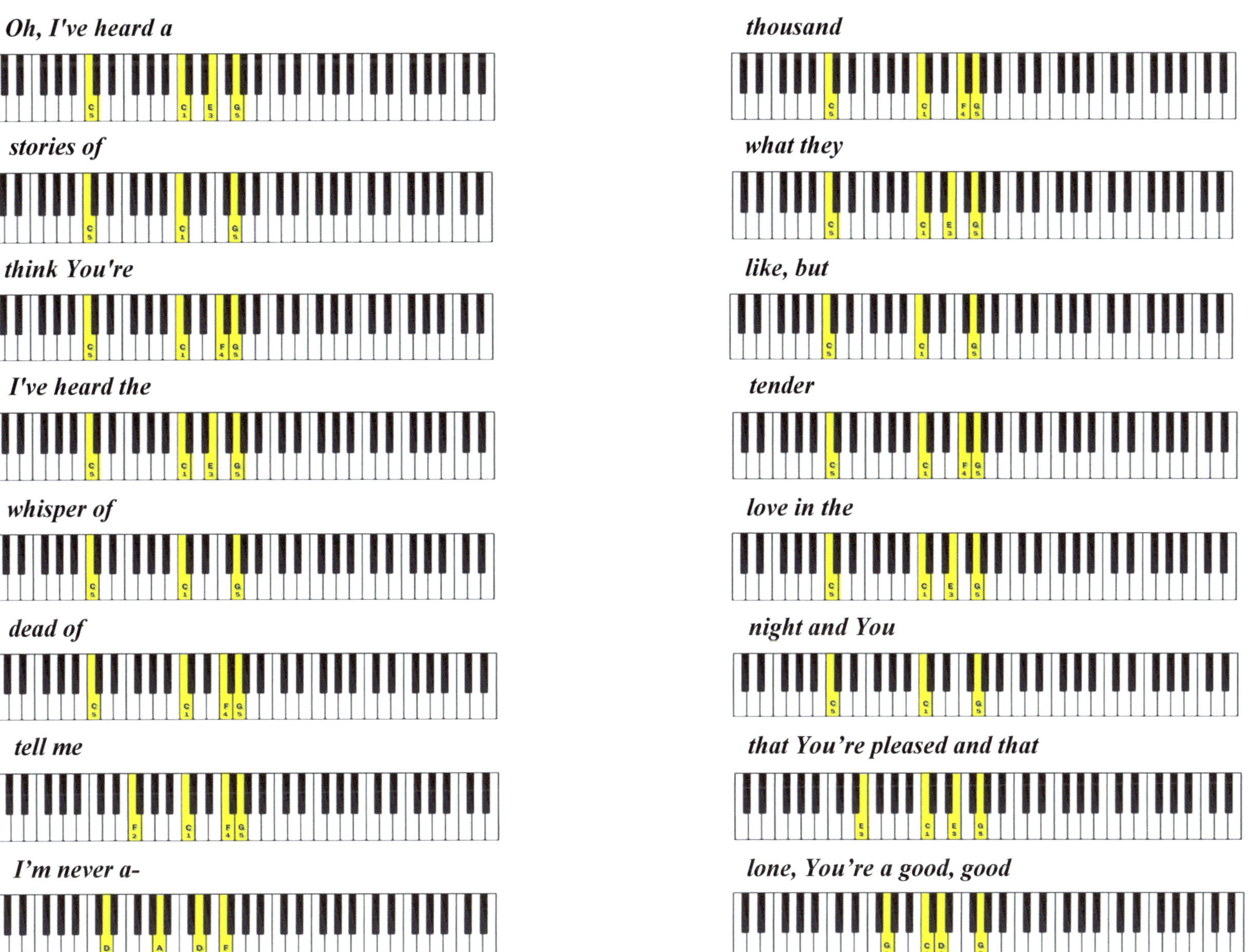

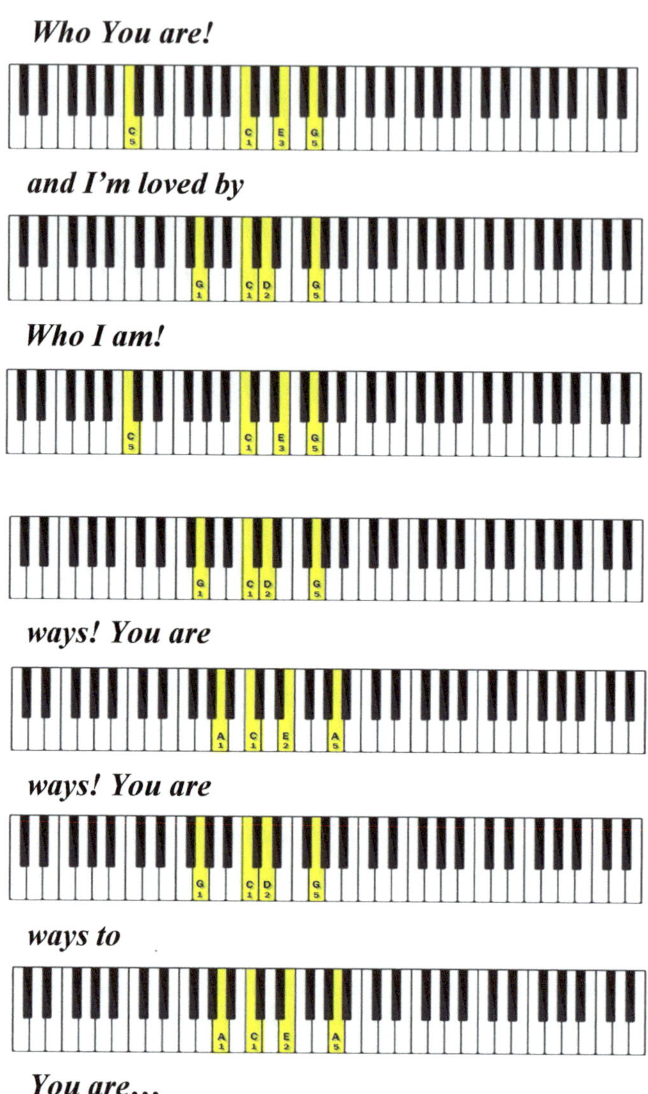

Chorus

Father! It's who you are!

Who You are

You its who I am!

Who I am!

Bridge

You are perfect in all of your

perfect in all of your

perfect in all of your

us!

Who You are!

and I'm loved by

Who I am!

ways! You are

ways! You are

ways to

You are…

Who You Say I Am

Hillsong Worship

Time=6

[Verse 1]
```
C                                  Am G     C
Who am I that the highest King would welcome me
C                                  Am  G   F
I was lost but He brought me in oh His love for me
        Am  G   F
oh His love for me
```

[Chorus 1]
```
        C                  G
Who the Son sets free oh is free indeed
     Am  G  F        C
I'm a child of God yes, I am
```

[Verse 2]
```
C                              Am  G    C
Free at last He has ransomed me His grace runs deep
C                              Am  G  F
While I was a slave to sin Jesus died for me
     Am   G  F
Yes He died for me
```

[Chorus 2]
```
        C                  G
Who the Son sets free Oh is free indeed
     Am  G  F        C
I'm a child of God Yes I am
        C                      G
In my Father's house there's a place for me
     Am   G  F        C
I'm a child of God Yes I am
```

[Bridge] (x2)
```
     Am         G/B
I am chosen not forsaken
   C                   F
I am who You say I am
            Am         G/B
You are for me not against me
   C               F
I am who You say I am
```

[Tag]
```
   Am         G/B       F
I am who You say I am
```

[Chorus 2]
```
        C                  G
Who the Son sets free oh is free indeed
     Am    G  F        C
I'm a child of God Yes I am
        C                      G
In my Father's house there's a place for me
     Am   G  F        C
I'm a child of God Yes I am
```

[Outro]
```
        C                      G
In my Father's house there's a place for me
     Am  G  F        C
I'm a child of God Yes I am
```

Who You Say I Am

Hillsong Worship

Chords Used: C(I) F(IV) G(V) Am(vi)

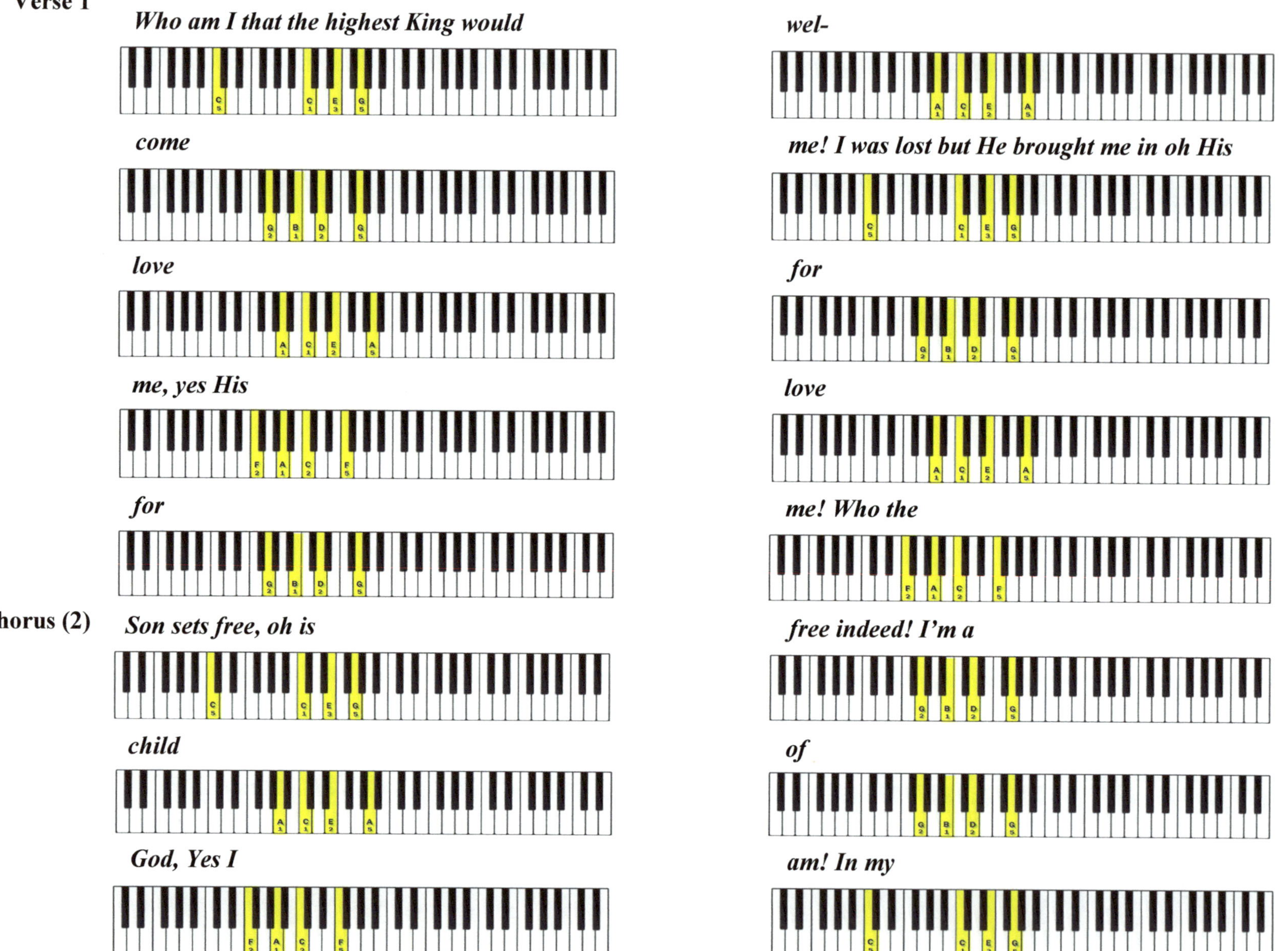

Father's house, there's a
place for me, I'm a
child
of
Bridge
God, yes I
am! I am
chosen, not for-
saken, I
am who You
say I am! You are
for me, not a-
gainst me, I
am who You say I
am! Oh I
Tag
Am who You
say I
am!

Time=6

[Intro]
| C | C | Am | Am
| G | G | F | F |

[Verse 1]
```
        C
All my words fall short
        Am
I got nothing new
           G
How could I express
          F
All my gratitude
```

[Verse 2]
```
        C
I could sing these songs
        Am
As I often do
             G
But every song must end
          F
And You never do
```

[Chorus]
```
        C
So I throw up my hands
                         G
And praise You again and again

'Cause all that I have is a
F          Am   G
Hallelujah, hallelujah
```

```
        C
And I know it's not much
                            G
But I've nothing else fit for a King

Except for a heart singing
F            Am  G  C
Hallelujah, hallelujah
```

[Verse 3]
```
        C
I've got one response
          Am
I've got just one move
            G
With my arms stretched wide
          F
I will worship You
```

[Chorus]
```
        C
So I throw up my hands
                         G
And praise You again and again

'Cause all that I have is a
   F      Am  G
Hallelujah, hallelujah
```

```
        C
And I know it's not much
                            G
But I've nothing else fit for a King

Except for a heart singing
F            Am  G  C
Hallelujah, hallelujah
```

[Bridge] 3X
```
   C
So come on my soul, oh, don't you get shy on me
G
Lift up your song, 'cause you've got a lion
F
inside of those lungs
                      C
Get up and praise the Lord!
```

Gratitude

Brandon Lake

Left hand octaves optional   **Chords Used: C(I) F(IV) G(V) Am(vi)**

Verse 1   *All my words fall short*

how could I express

Verse 2   *I could sing these songs*

but every song must end

Chorus   *So I throw up my hands and praise You again and*

hallelujah,

lujah! And I

King, except for a heart singing

I got nothing new

all my gratitude?

as I often do

and You never do

again 'cause all that I have is a

halle-

know it's not much, but I've got nothing else fit for

hallelujah, halle-

lu
Bridge 3X
So come on my soul, oh, don't you get shy on me
inside of those lungs get up and praise the
Chorus
So I throw up my hands and praise You again and
hallelujah,
lujah! And I
King, except for a heart singing
lu
jah!
lift up your song, 'cause you've got a lion
Lord!
again 'cause all that I have is a
halle-
know it's not much, but I've got nothing else fit for a
hallelujah, halle-
jah!

The Key of A Minor - The Relative Minor

Every major key has a ***RELATIVE MINOR*** which is always found 1 ½ steps (or three half-steps) below the root of the major key.

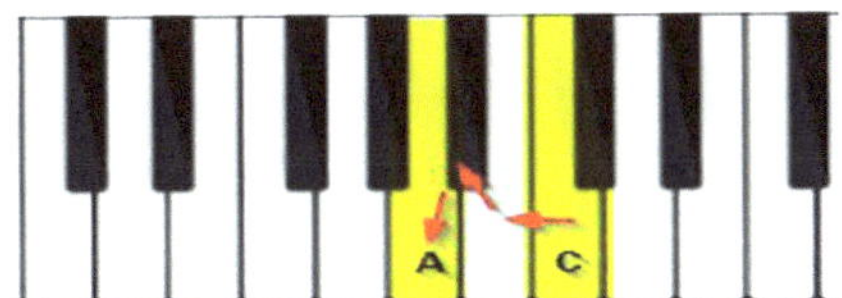

The reason the term relative minor is used is because they share the same keys on the keyboard. The key of C major is considered the simplest key on the keyboard because it uses none of the black keys. The key of ***A MINOR*** is the relative minor to the key of C major and also uses no black keys. The difference between C major and A minor is the ***TONAL CENTER***. Where in the key of C major, C is the root, in the key of A minor, **A is the root.** While most worship songs are written in major keys, worship songs in minor keys do exist, including many well-known Christmas carols. The quality of the chord changes due to the change in the tonal center.

<table>
<tr><td>

Major Key Triad Qualities

I Major
ii minor
iii minor
IV Major
V Major
vi minor
vii diminished

</td><td>

Minor Triad Qualities

i minor
ii diminished
III Major
iv minor
v minor
VI Major
VII Major

</td></tr>
</table>

VL-41

Triads in the Key of A Minor (Root Position)

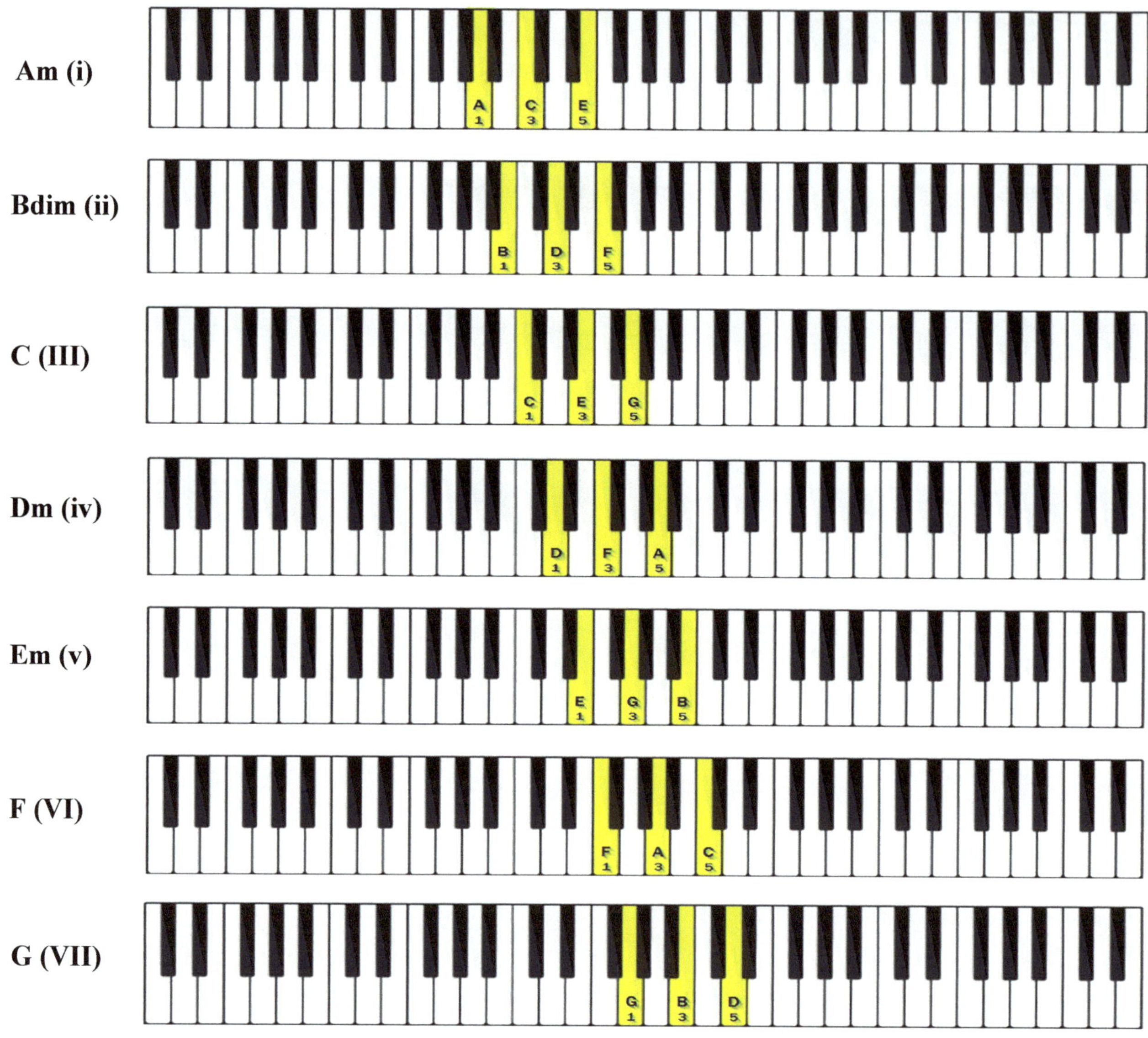

Hillsong Worship

While Oceans is publicly listed as being originally written in a major key, with the tonal center being that of the relative minor, I have included it in this section of the method. Many Christian songs are listed in the relative major key since it is more familiar to many players. The classical and jazz training that I have had puts this song in a minor key.

Time=4

[Intro]
Am G/B C G F

[Verse 1]
Am   G/B   C
You call me out upon the waters, the great
   G   F
unknown where feet may fail

Am   G/B   C
And there I find You in the mystery,
         G   F
in oceans deep my faith will stand

[Chorus]
F   C   G   F   C
And I will call upon Your name, and keep my eyes
         G   F
above the wave when oceans rise
             C   G   F   G   Am
My soul will rest in your embrace for I am Yours and You are mine

[Interlude]
Am G/B C G Dm

[Verse 2]
Am   G/B   C
Your grace abounds in deepest waters
                    G   F
Your sovereign hand will be my guide
Am   G/B   C
Where feet may fail and fear surrounds me,
              G   F
You've never failed and you won't start now

[Chorus]

[Instrumental]
Am G/B C G F

[Bridge] X3
Am   F
Spirit lead me where my trust is without borders
             C   G
Let me walk upon the waters wherever You would call me
Am   F
Take me deeper than my feet could ever wander
              C
And my faith will be made stronger,
G
in the presence of my Savior

[Chorus]

VL-42

Oceans

Hillsong Worship

Left hand octaves optional   **A Minor - Chords Used: Am(i) C(III) F (VI) G(VII)**

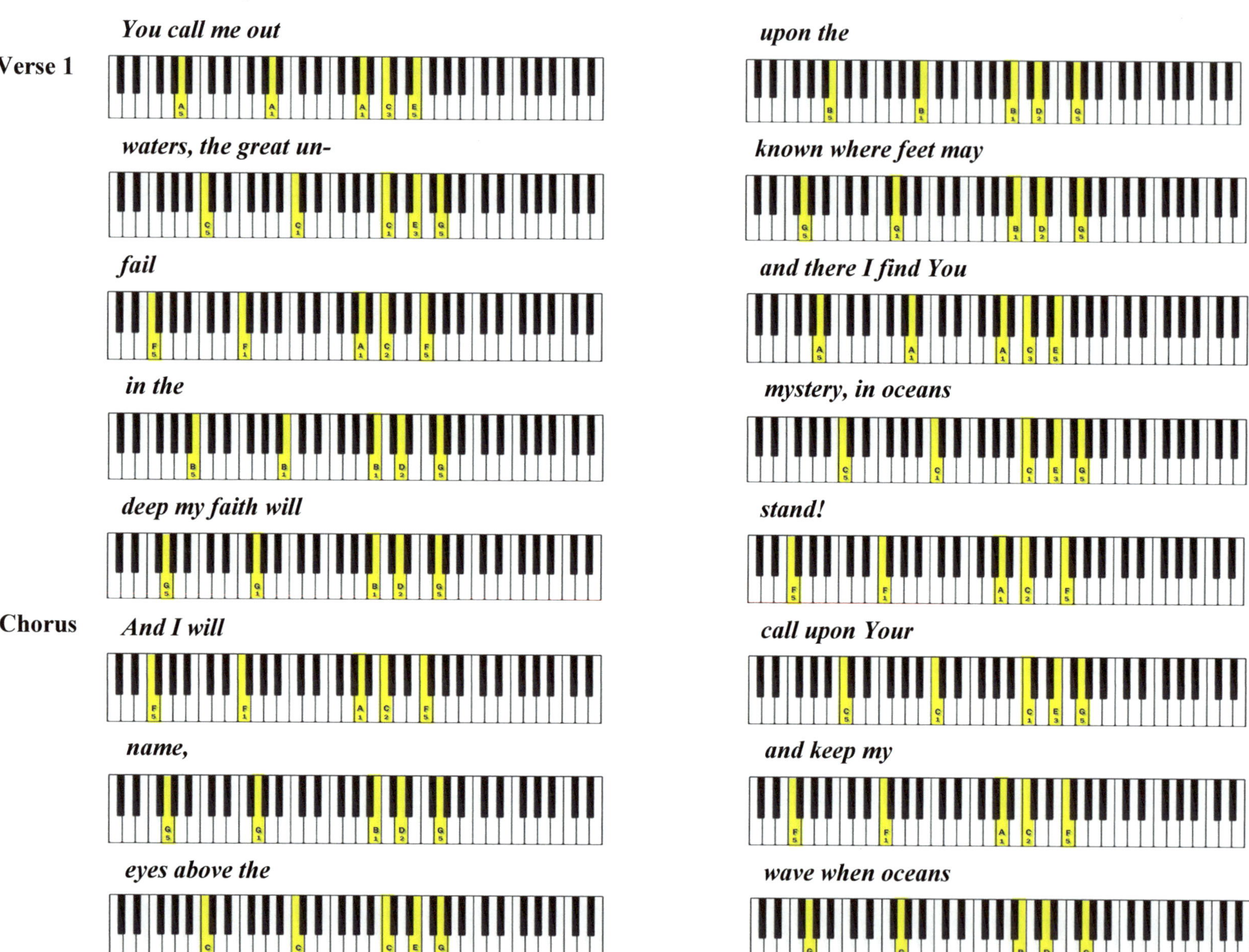

Verse 1

Chorus

rise my soul will
brace I am
You are
Instr.
rest in your em-
Yours and
mine!

Bridge

Spirit lead me where my

trust is without borders let me

walk upon the waters where-

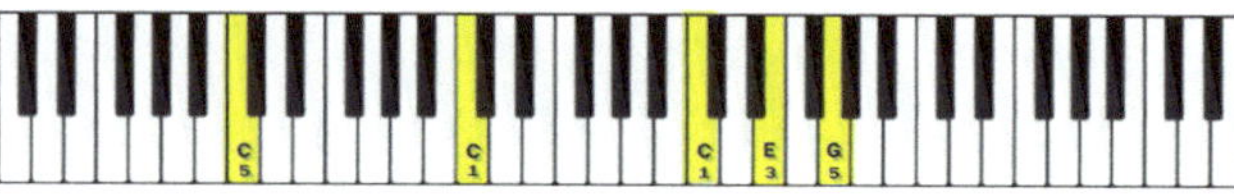

ever You would call me!

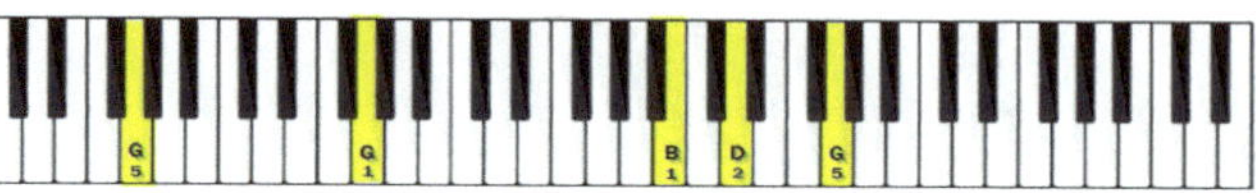

Take me deeper than my

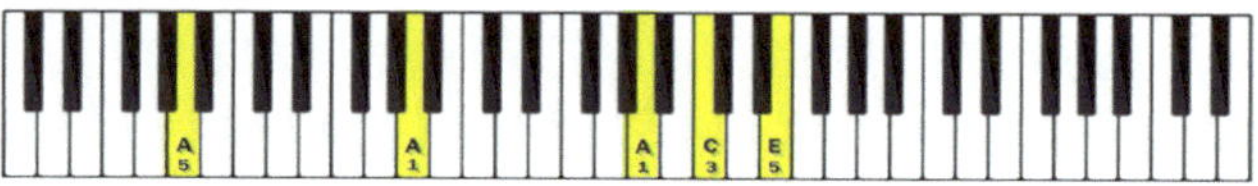

feet could ever wander and my

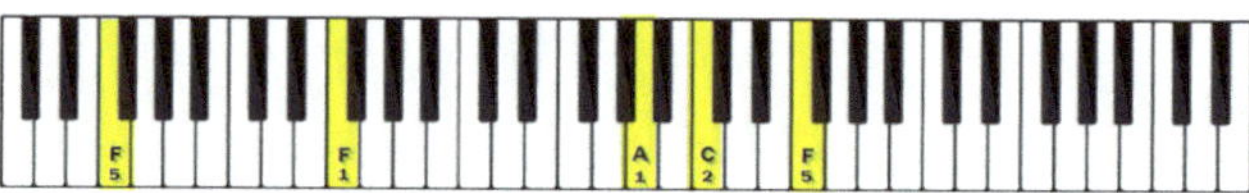

faith will be made stronger, in the

presence of my Savior!

Awesome God

Rich Mullins

Time=4

[Intro]
Am Dm G Am
Am Dm G Am

[Verse 1]
```
        Am
When He rolls up His sleeves He ain't just puttin' on the ritz
    Dm      G        Am
Our God is an awesome God
        Am
There is thunder in His footsteps and lightning in His fists
    Dm      G        Am
Our God is an awesome God
    F
The Lord wasn't joking when He kicked 'em out of Eden
  G                      C   G Am
It wasn't for no reason that He shed His blood
    F                              C
His return is very close and so you better be believin'
        Dm      G       Am
That our God is an awesome God
```

[Chorus]2X
```
    F       C
Our God is an awesome God
    G       Am
He reigns from Heaven above
      F          C
With wisdom, power and love
    Dm      G       Am
Our God is an awesome God!
```

[Verse 2]
```
            Am
And when the sky was starless in the void of the night
    Dm      G        Am
Our God is an awesome God
        Am
He spoke into the darkness and created the light
    Dm      G        Am
Our God is an awesome God
F                                  C
Judgment and wrath, He poured out on Sodom
G               C     G   Am
Mercy and grace He gave us at the cross
  F                          C
I hope that we have not too quickly forgotten
        Dm      G       Am
That our God is an awesome God!
```

[Chorus]3X
```
    F       C
Our God is an awesome God
    G       Am
He reigns from Heaven above
      F          C
With wisdom, power and love
    Dm      G       Am
Our God is an awesome God!
```

Rich Mullins

A Minor - Chords Used: Am(i) C(III) Dm (iv) F(VI) G(VII)

Verse 1

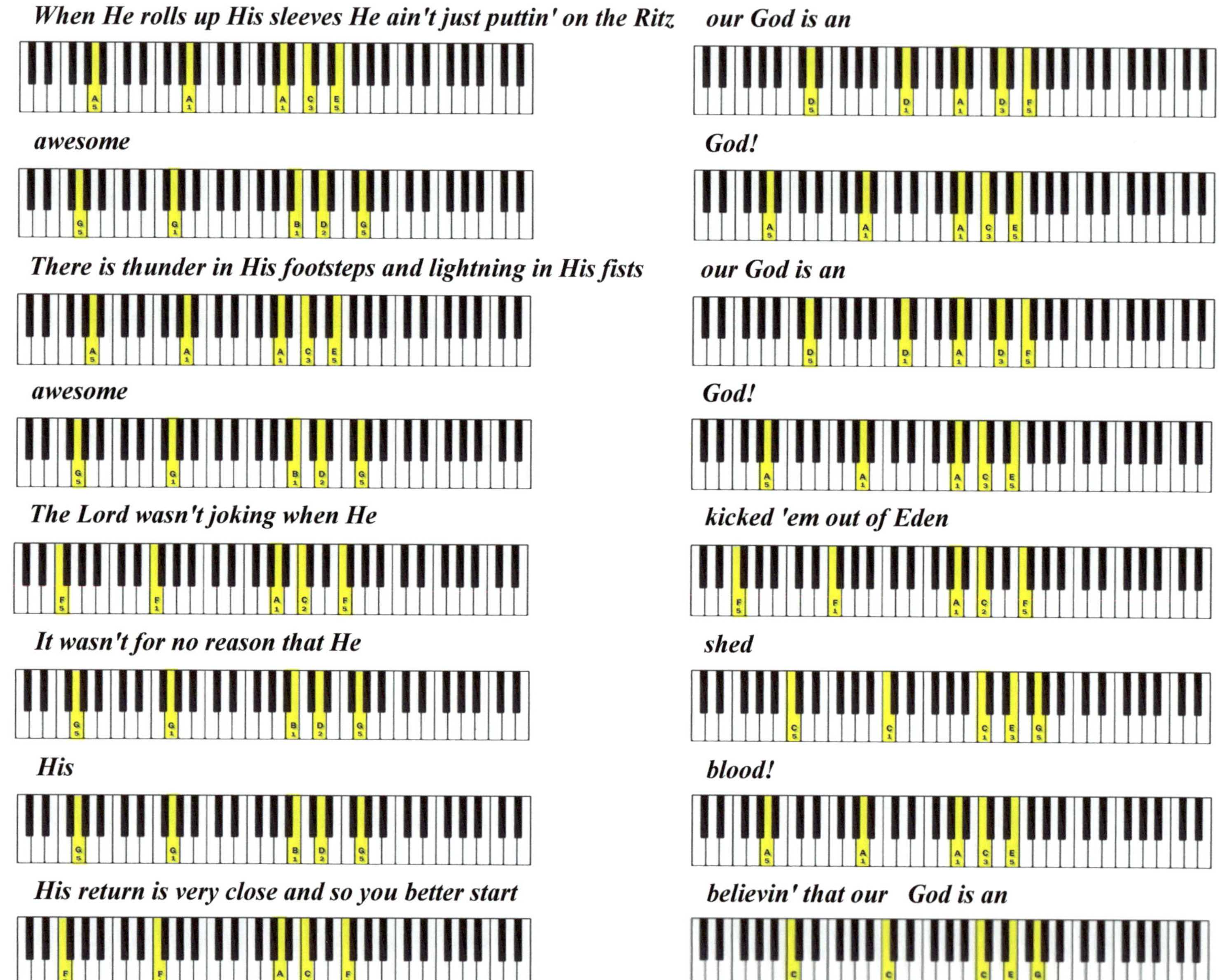

God is an

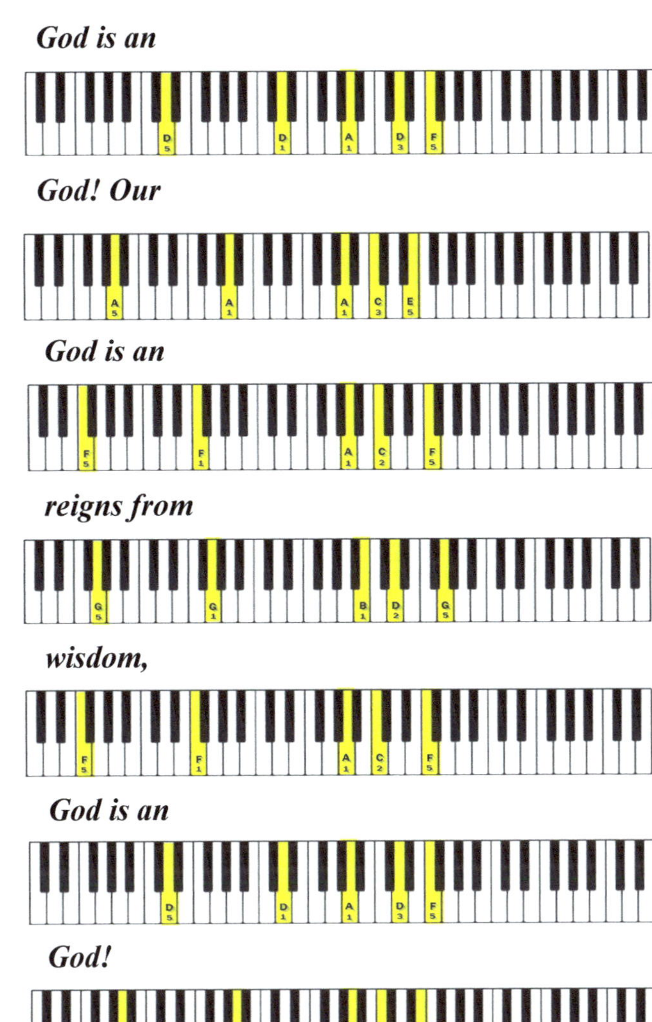

God! Our

Chorus

God is an

reigns from

wisdom,

God is an

God!

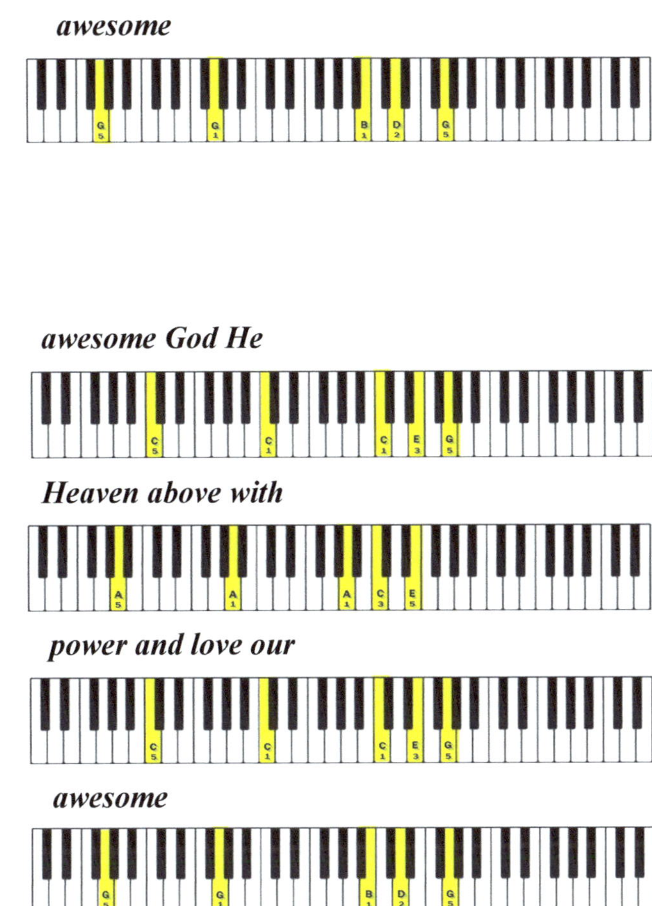

awesome

awesome God He

Heaven above with

power and love our

awesome

O Come, O Come Emmanuel

Traditional

Time=4

[Verse 1]

```
    Am          Dm    Am
O come, O come, Emmanuel
    Am          Dm Am
and ransom captive Israel
      F           G    Am
That mourns in lonely exile here
        Am    Dm  Am
until the Son of God appear
```

[Chorus]

```
   G    Am
Rejoice! Rejoice!
  Dm Em Am                Dm Am
Emmanuel shall come to thee O Israel
```

[Verse 2]

```
    Am              Dm        Am
O come Thou Dayspring come and cheer
    Am          Dm    Am
Our spirits by Thine advent here
      F         G       Am
Disperse the gloomy clouds of night
      Am            Dm   Am
And death's dark shadows put to flight
```

[Chorus]

```
   G    Am
Rejoice! Rejoice!
  Dm Em Am                Dm Am
Emmanuel shall come to thee O Israel
```

[Verse 3]

```
    Am          Dm    Am
O come Desire of nations bind
    Am          Dm    Am
In one the hearts of all mankind
      F           G       Am
Bid Thou our sad divisions cease
        Am        Dm     Am
And be Thyself our King of Peace
```

[Chorus]

```
   G      Am
Rejoice! Rejoice!
  Dm Em Am                Dm Am
Emmanuel shall come to thee O Israel
```

VL-44

O Come, O Come Emmanuel

Traditional

Verse

A Minor - Chords Used: Am(i) Dm (iv) Em(v) F(VI) G(VII)

Traditional
Lindsey Stirling Version

Time=6

[Verse 1]
```
  Am               F      Am      Dm
I wonder as I wander out under the sky,
  Am          Dm      Am
How Jesus the Savior did come for to die
                       F        Em
for poor ord'n'ry people like you and like I.
  Am        Em          Dm        Am
I wonder as I wander out under the sky.
```

[Verse 2]
```
  Am                  F       Am       Dm
When Mary birthed Jesus, 'twas in a cow's stall,
  Am            Dm        Am
With wise men and farmers and shepherds and all.
                        F        Em
But high from God's heaven a star's light did fall,
   Am           Em   Dm      Am
And the promise of ages it did then recall.
```

[Verse 3]
```
  Am               F      Am     Dm
If Jesus had wanted for any wee thing,
  Am          Dm      Am
A star in the sky, or a bird on the wing,
                     F        Em
Or all of God's angels in heav'n for to sing,
  Am          Em          Dm        Am
He surely could have it, 'cause he was the King.
```

VL-45

I Wonder as I Wander

Traditional

A Minor - Chords Used: Am(i) Dm (iv) Em(v) F(VI)

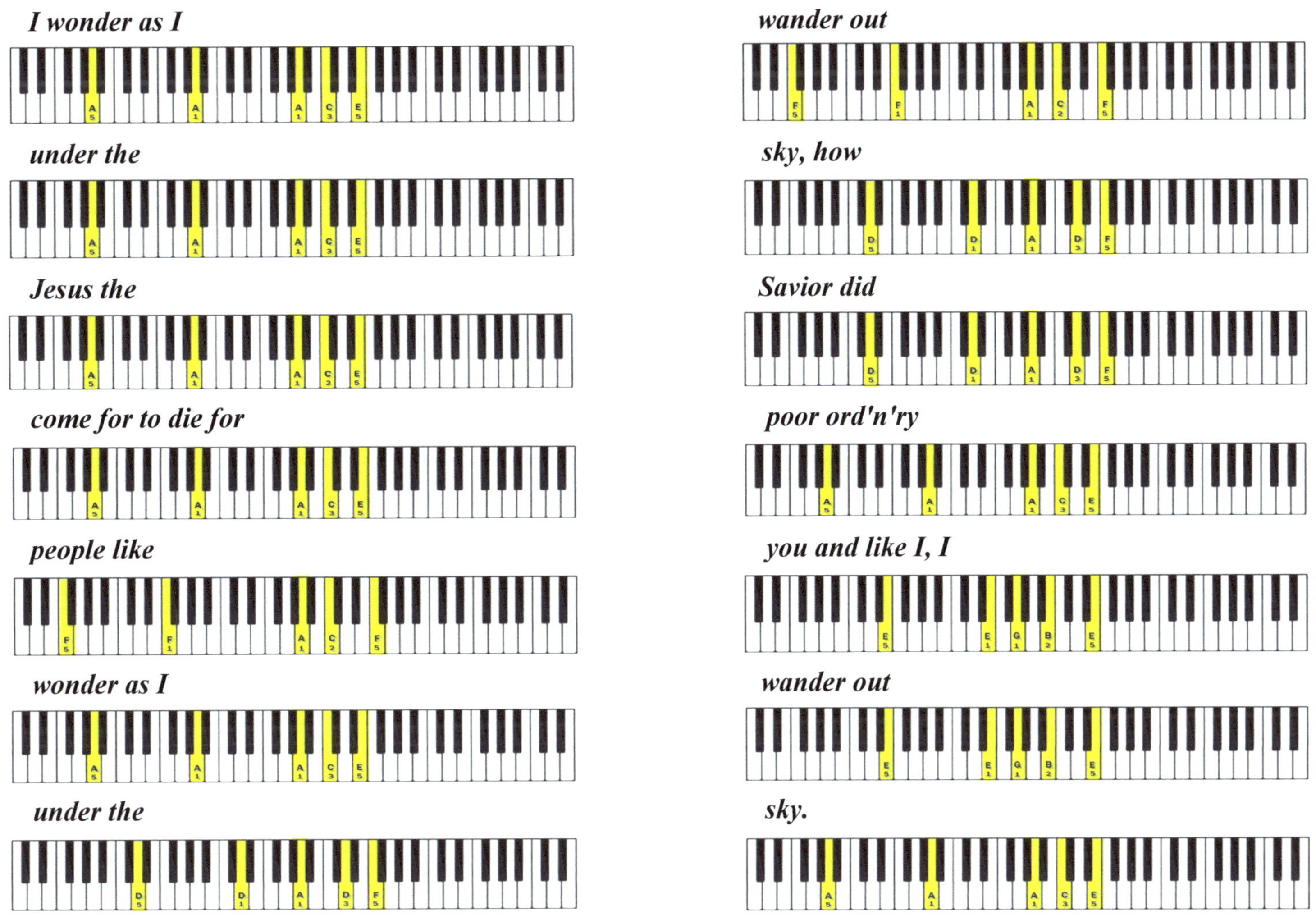

Adding the 7th

While most worship songs can be played using triads, there are songs that will use "***SEVENTH***" chords. So far in this method, we have used primarily triads. To create a seventh chord, the 7th key is added to the triad. Just as triads carry a quality, 7th chords have a quality as well which mirror those of the triads with one exception; the V chord which is ***dominant.*** A dominant chord possesses a strong sound that needs to resolve. The strong sound is generated by a specific span of notes called a ***TRITONE.*** A tritone is a distance of three whole steps between two keys. This specific sound at one time in history was named the "Tone of the Devil" due to its unsettling sound. Within the context of a dominant chord though, it creates a strong, powerful and beautiful sound.

Chord Qualities for Seventh Chords in the Key of C Major

I Major, ii Minor, iii Minor, IV Major, V, Dominant, vi, Minor vii, Diminished

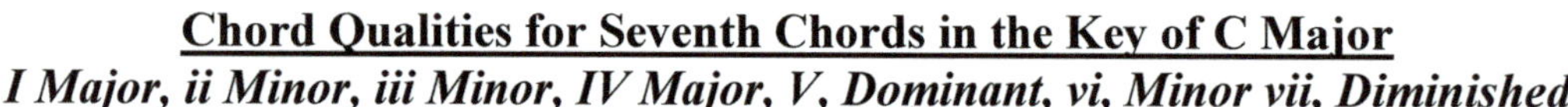

Note fingering for seventh chords

Cmaj7

Dm7

Em7

Fmaj7

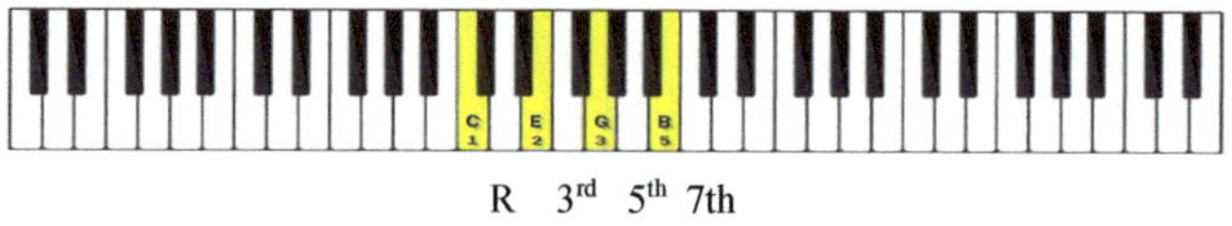

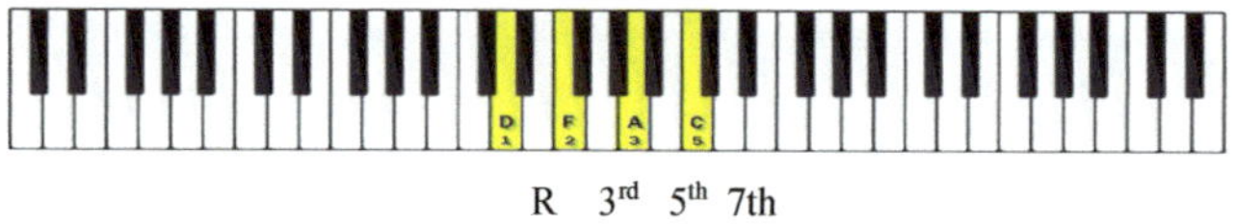

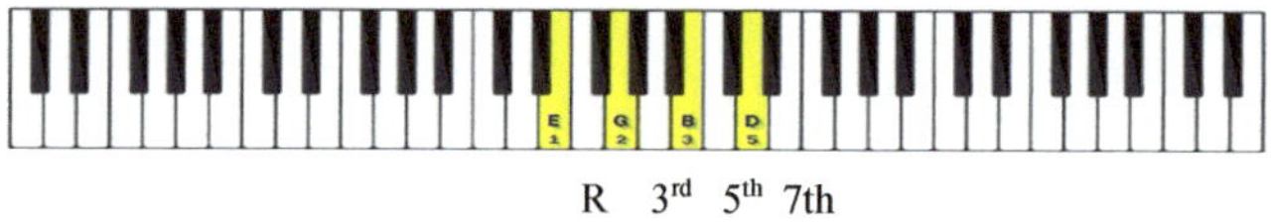

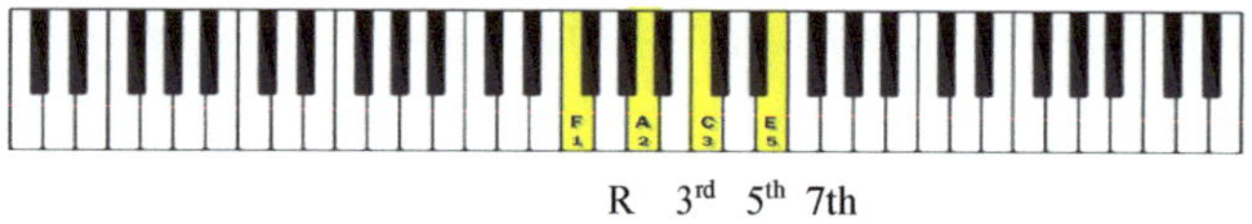

When only a 7 follows the letter, it is always a dominant 7 chord

G7

Am7

Bdim7

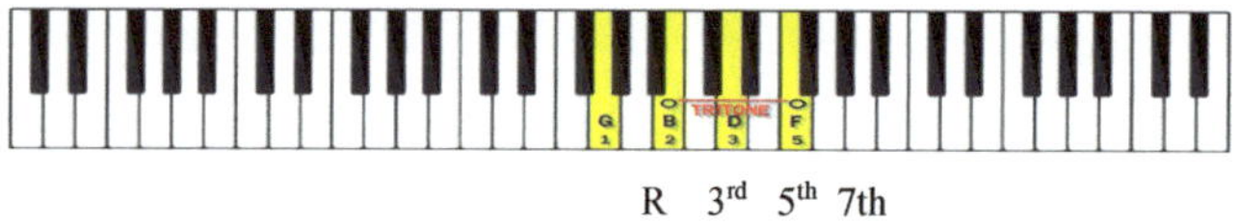

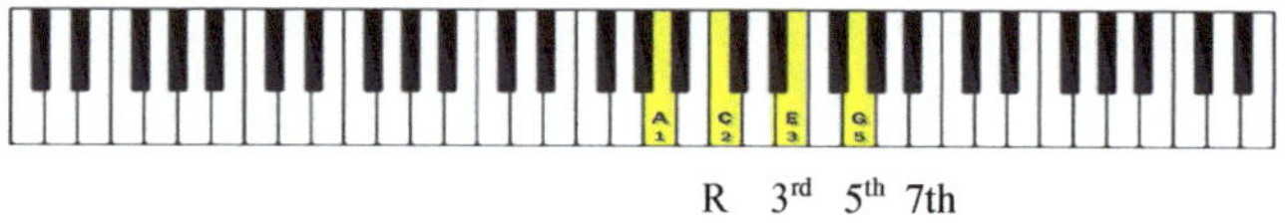

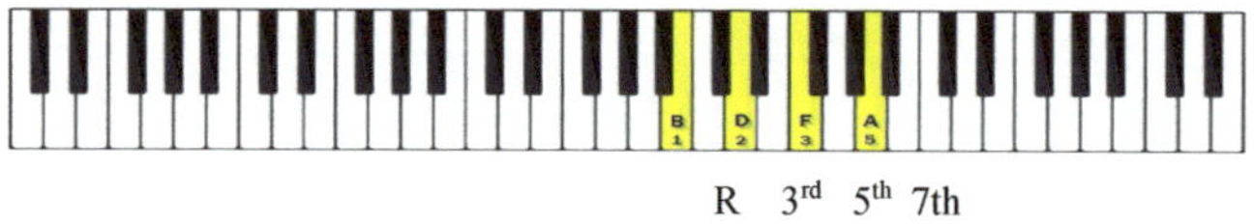

VL-46

Seventh chords also have inversions which should be included in the practice routine.

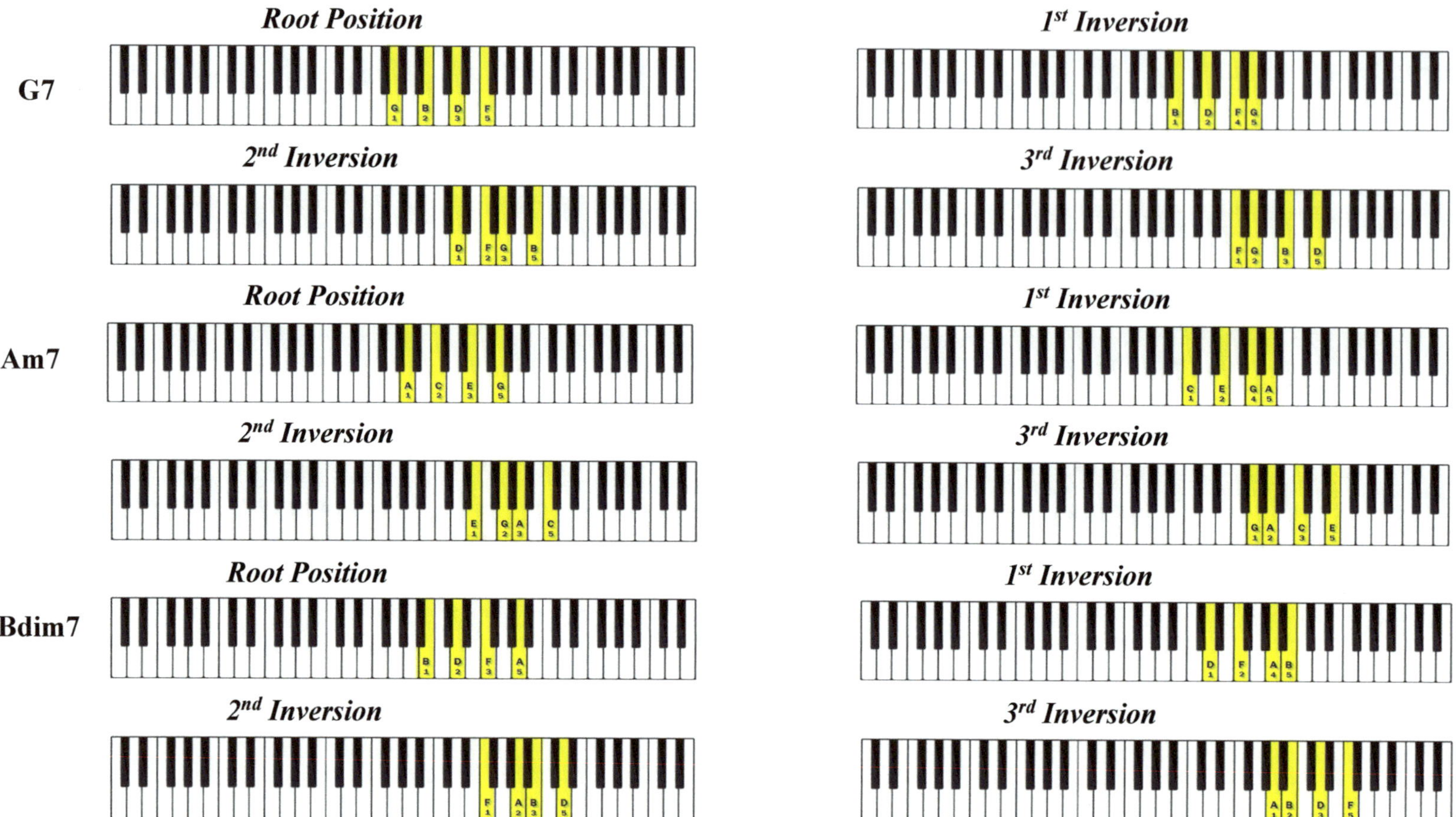

Root Position
1st Inversion
2nd Inversion
3rd Inversion
Root Position
1st Inversion
2nd Inversion
3rd Inversion
Root Position
1st Inversion
2nd Inversion
3rd Inversion
G7
Am7
Bdim7

Great Are You Lord

David Leonard, Jason Ingram, Leslie Jordan

Time=6

[Intro]

F Am7 G

[Verse] 2X

        F   Am7   Gsus

You give life, You are love, You bring light to the darkness

        F   Am7   Gsus   F

You give hope, You restore every heart that is broken

Am7   G   Gsus2 G

Great are You, Lord

[Chorus]

        F   Am7

It's Your breath in our lungs

        Gsus

So we pour out our praise, we pour out our praise

        F   Am7   Gsus

It's Your breath in our lungs, so we pour out our praise

to You only

[Instrumental]

C Csus2   F2   C

[Bridge] 3X

C

All the earth will shout Your praise

      Csus2

Our hearts will cry these bones will sing

F2   C

Great are You, Lord

[Chorus]

        F   Am7

It's Your breath in our lungs

        Gsus

So we pour out our praise, we pour out our praise

        F   Am7   Gsus

It's Your breath in our lungs, so we pour out our praise

 to You only

[Tag]

       F   Am7   G

We pour out our praise to You only

       F   Am7   G

We pour out our praise to You only

Great Are You Lord

David Leonard, Jason Ingram, Leslie Jordan

(C Major) Chords Used: C(I) F(IV) G(V) A(vi)

Verse

You give life,

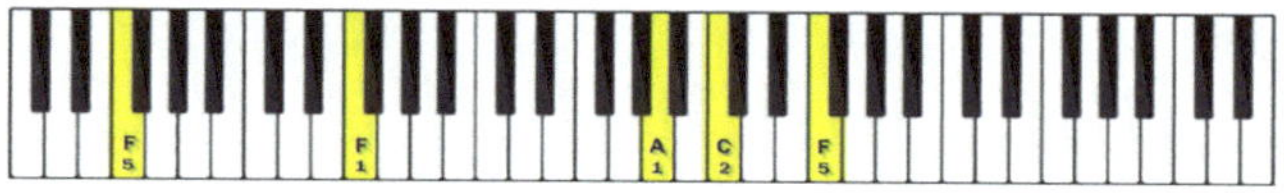

light to the darkness

store every

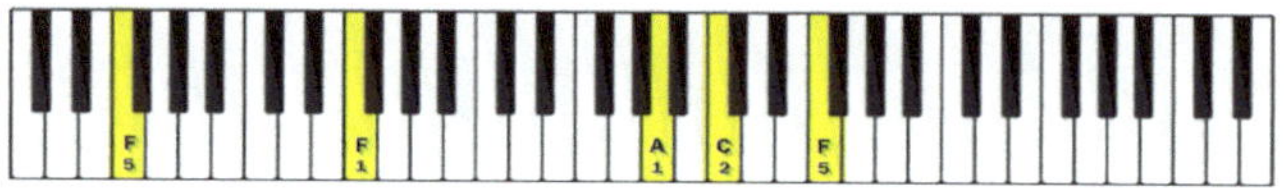

Lord!

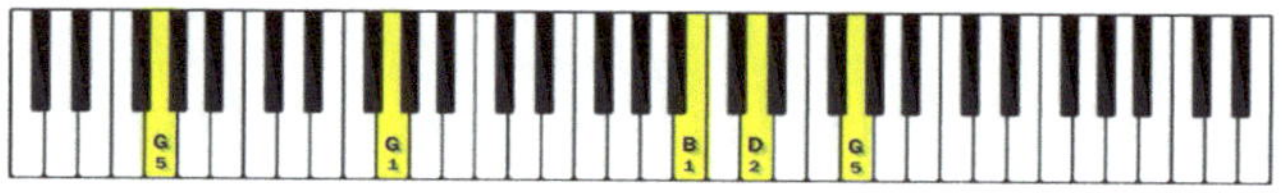

It's Your

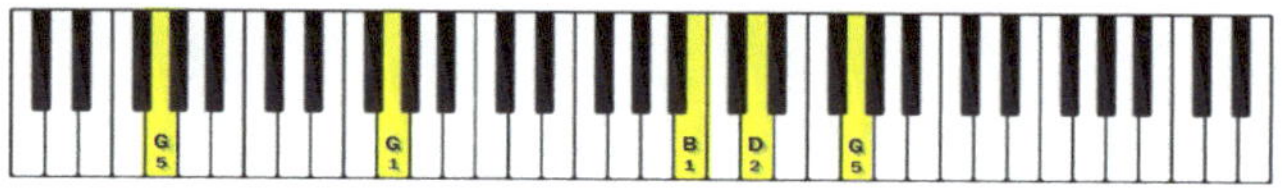

lungs, so we

breath in our

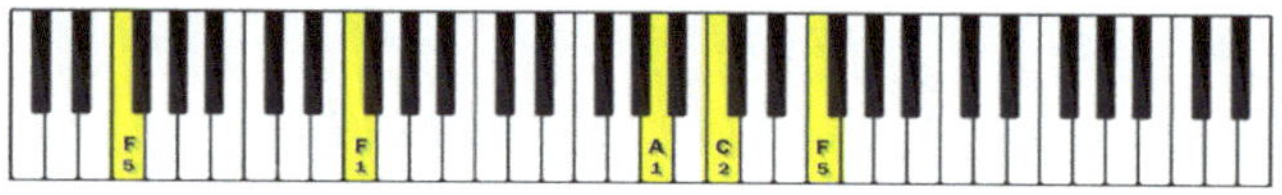

You are love, You bring

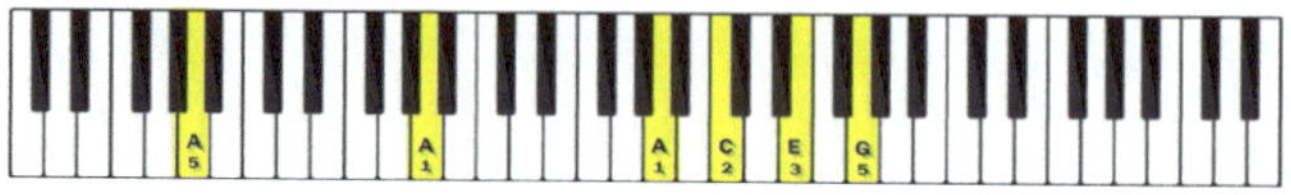

You give hope, You re-

heart that is broken

Great are You

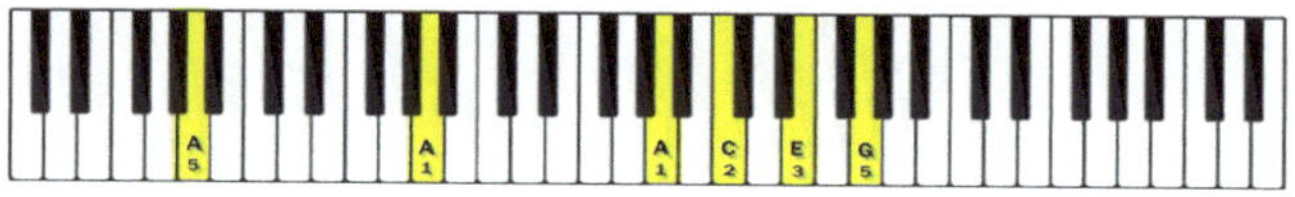

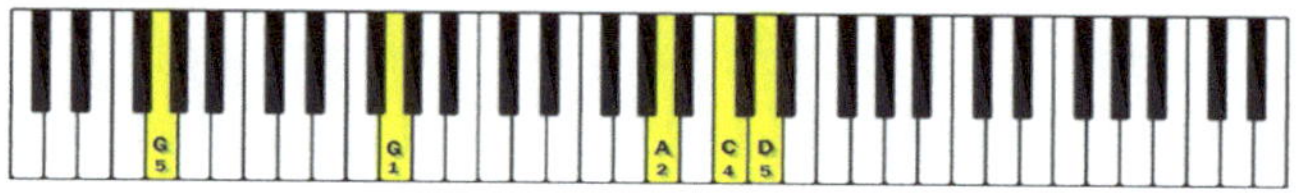

Chorus *breath in our*

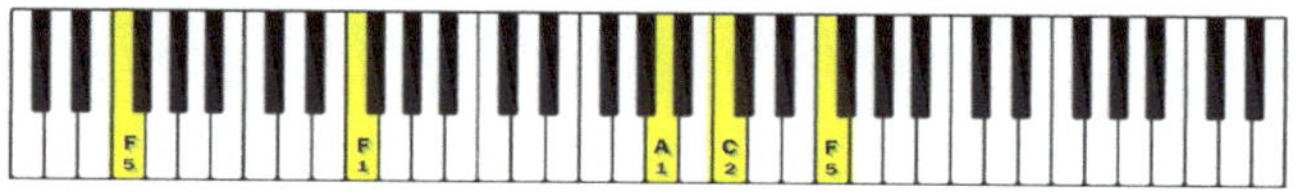

pour out our praise, we pour out our praise it's Your

lungs, so we

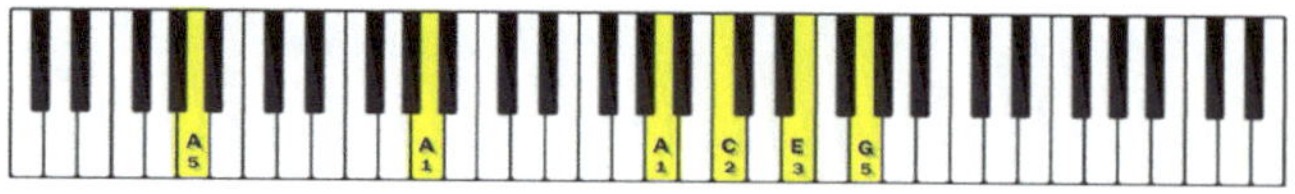

pour out our praise on you only!

hearts will cry these bones will sing

Lord!

hearts will cry these bones will sing

Lord!

hearts will cry these bones will sing

Lord!

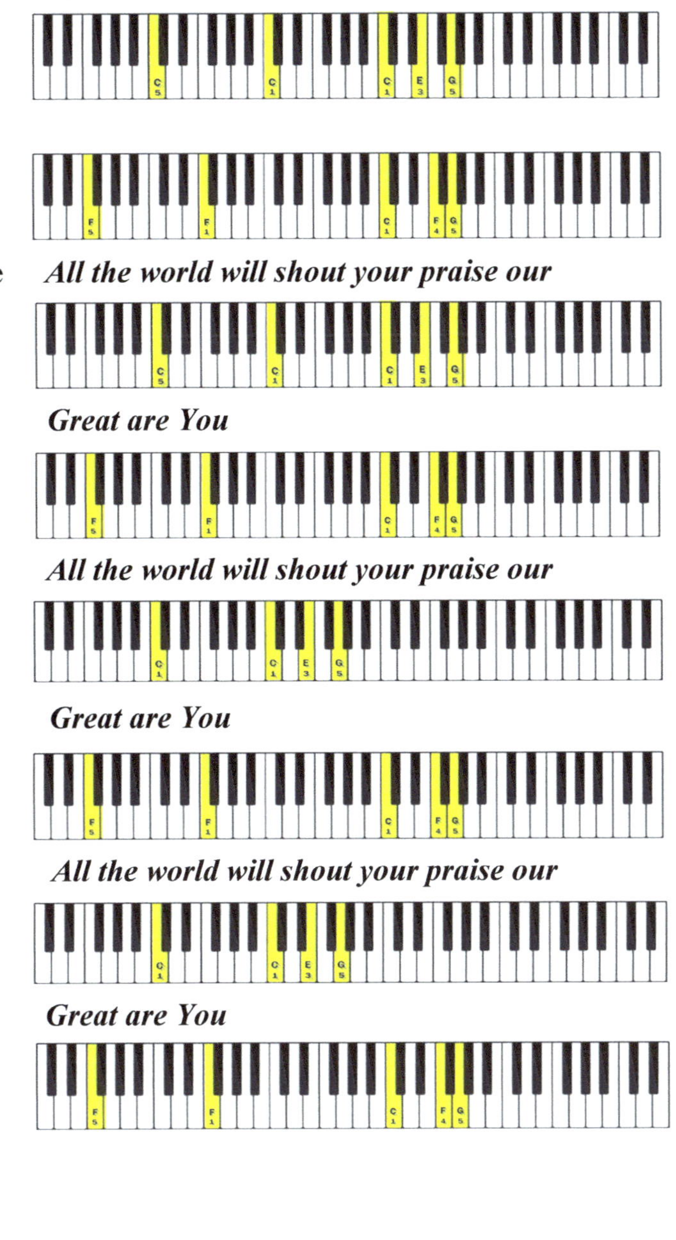

Instrumental

Bridge   *All the world will shout your praise our*

Great are You

All the world will shout your praise our

Great are You

All the world will shout your praise our

Great are You

Turn Your Eyes Upon Jesus

(Chorus)

Traditional

Time = 3 or 4 **Chords Used: C(I) Dm (ii) Em (iii)F(IV) G(V) A(vi)**

C Em/B Am C/G F Dm G7
Turn your eyes upon Jesus look full in His wonderful face
C Em/B Am F G G7 C
And the things of earth will grow strangely dim in the light of His glory and grace!

Turn your

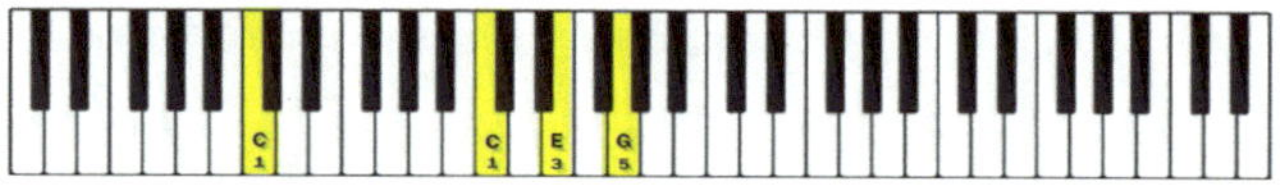

eyes upon

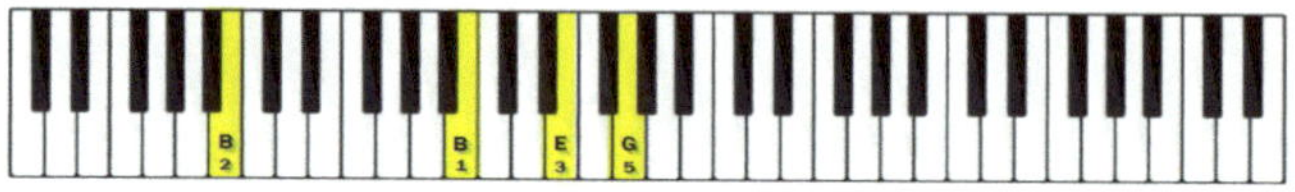

Je-

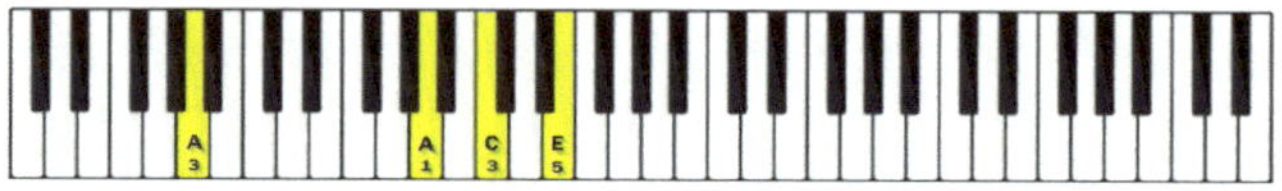

sus look

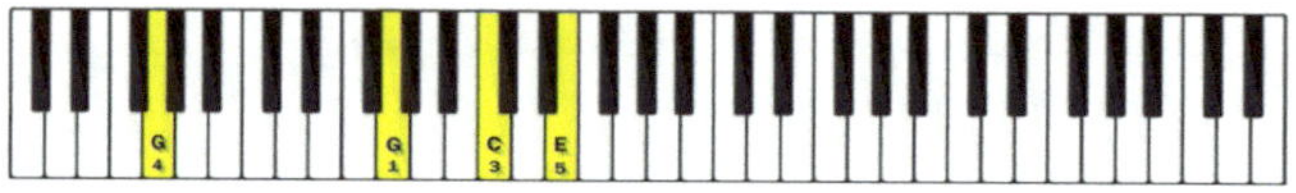

full in His

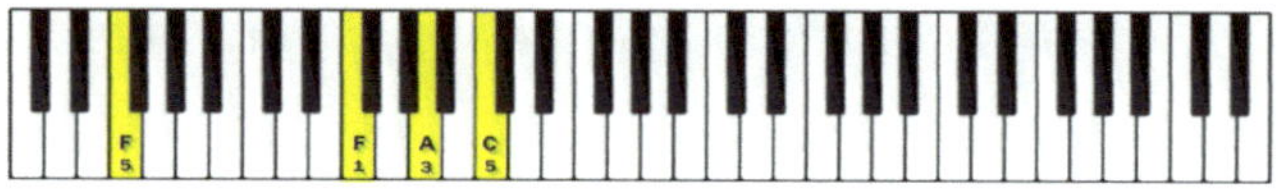

wonderful

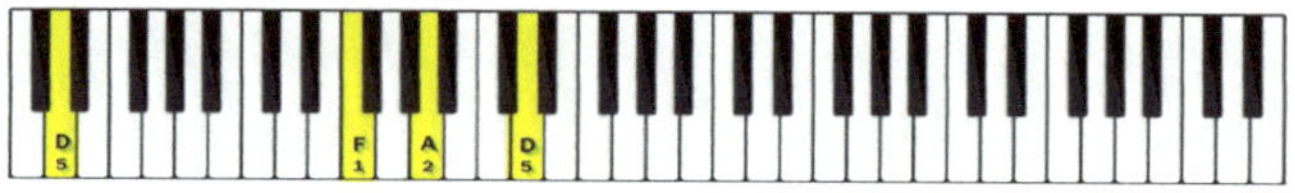

face! And the

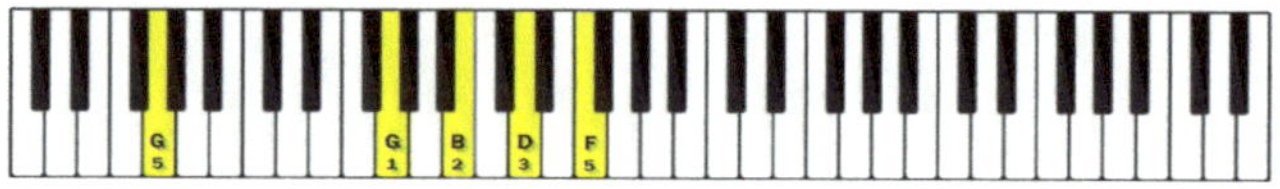

things of

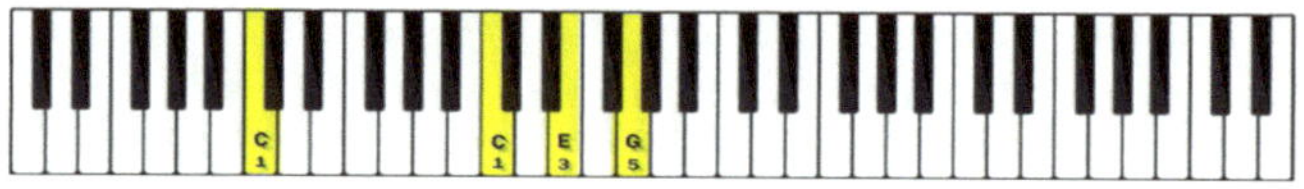

earth will grow

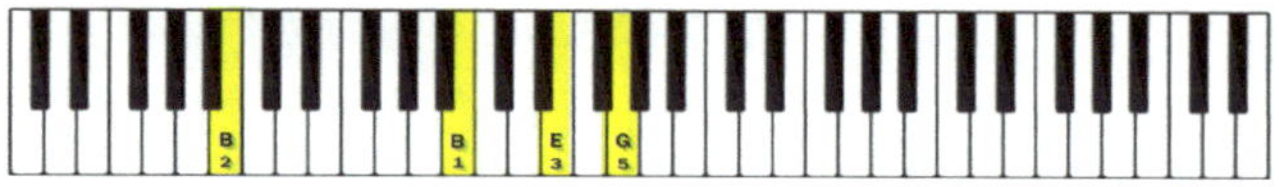

strangely

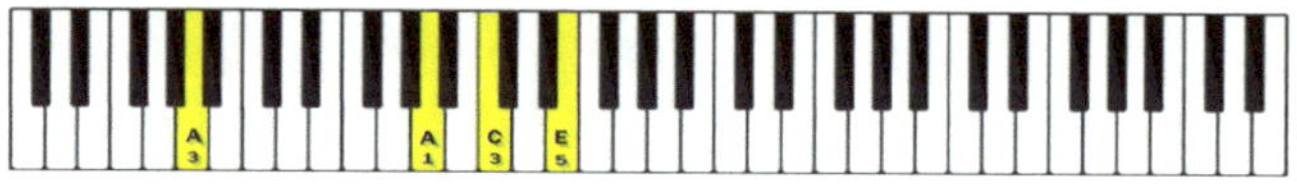

dim in the

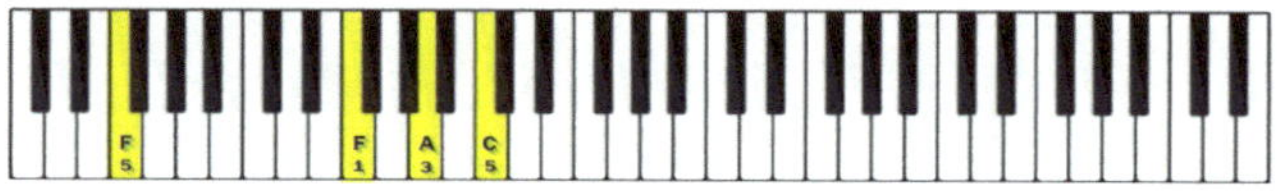

light of His

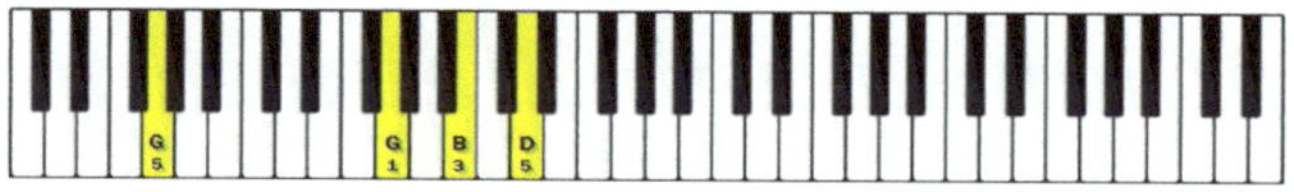

glory and

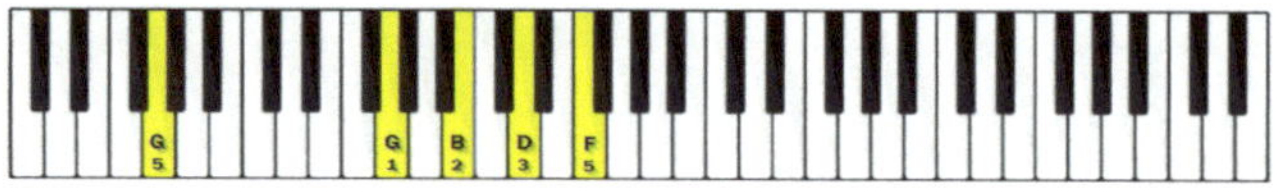

grace!

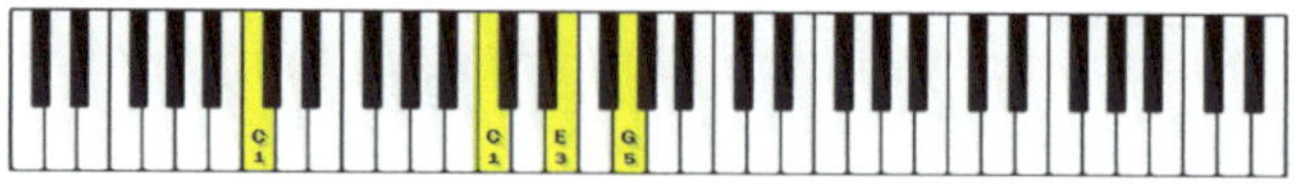

VL-48

Ear Training

The term "Ear Training" refers to exercises that musicians do to improve their ability to identify melodies and other musical patterns without having to see it written in musical notation. This is called "playing by ear". So far in this method, the focus has been strictly on chords. To play on a worship team, understanding chords is the essential skill to attain. However, if there is a desire to play melodic lines within the worship songs, practicing ear training exercises will help the learner to identify the melodies they wish to play. The first exercise in ear training in this section will be learning to recognize *INTERVALS*. An interval is the distance between to keys and the unique sound that is made when they are played either together or separately. The distance can be interpreted as the *number of steps BETWEEN the two keys.* The distances are referred to in the following ways:

1/2 steps	minor 2nd
1 step	major 2nd
1 1/2 steps	minor 3rd
2 steps	major 3rd
2 ½ steps	perfect 4th
3 steps	tritone
3 1/2 steps	perfect 5th
4 steps	minor 6th
4 ½ steps	major 6th
5 steps	minor 7th
5 ½ steps	major 7th
6 steps	perfect octave

Intervals in the Key of C Major

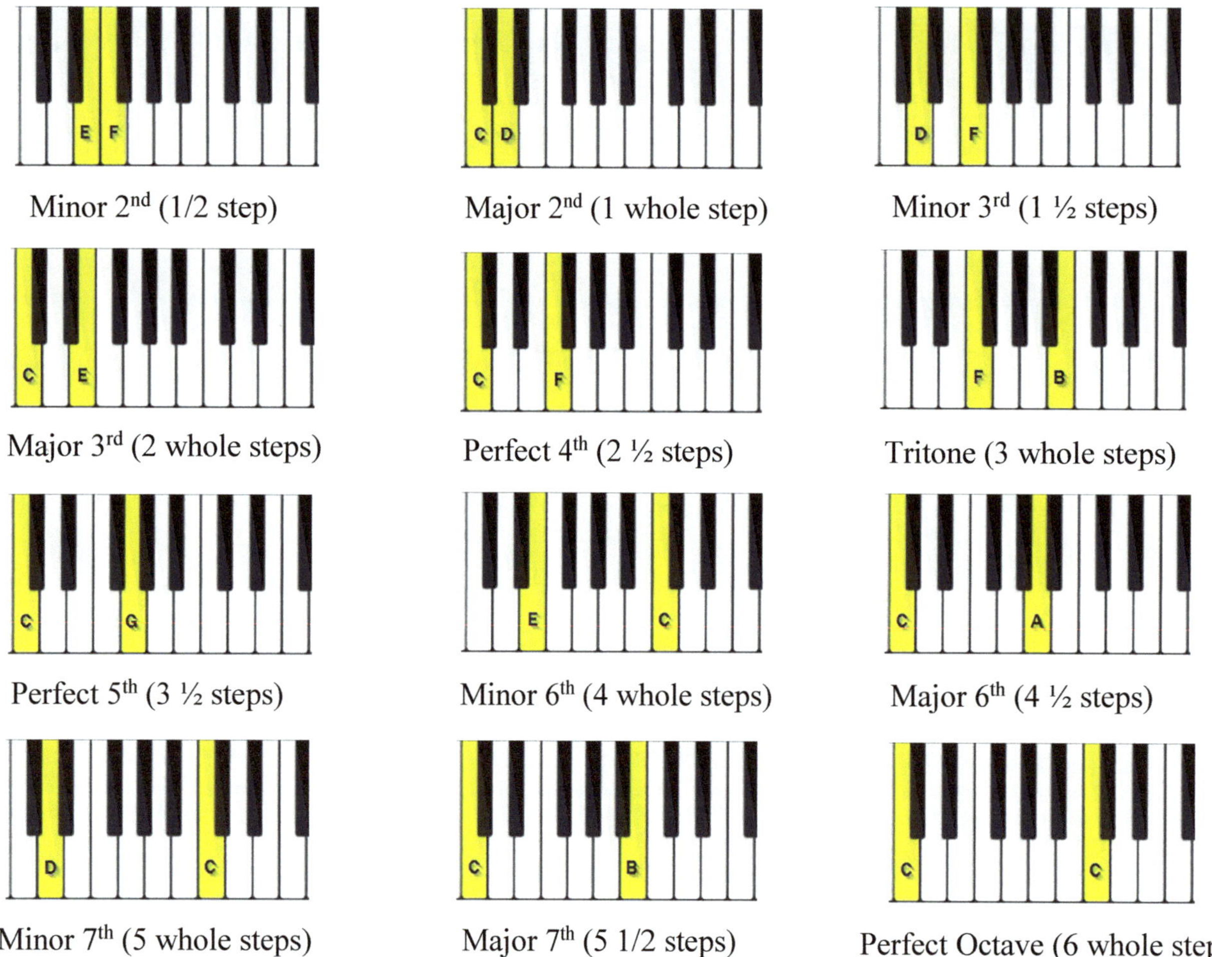

Intervals create melodic lines. Once you are able to identify intervals through ear training practice, identifying melodic lines will become simple and take very little time. To practice ear training with intervals, first select 2 or 3 specific intervals and familiarize yourself with their sound by playing them on your keyboard many times. Then play them with your eyes first open, then closed. Once you are able to recognize those sounds, then add another until you can identify all of them. One helpful tactic is to think of a song that begins with one of the intervals that you are working on. For example, the traditional wedding song "Here Comes the Bride" begins with a perfect fourth. If possible, have another person to play them for you to identify.

There are also many ear-training resources on YouTube. Below are a few that may be helpful.

https://youtu.be/Wzqa44N
-slU?si=riTCgBPd6easyej-

https://youtu.be/m3Sg68
XbngQ?si=HD1I6Ma4qXLi
oFyU

https://youtu.be/nl01K-
yCSY8?si=m8nieCpqmGFU-cEa

Chord Scales

A scale is simply a series of keys played in order. The term ***Chord Scales*** refers to the keys that are included with each type of chord that exists in a specific key. The keys in the chord scales are the keys that will always sound appropriate with a given chord. Knowing the chord scales will allow the player to embellish the chords played with melodic lines in an improvisational style. Chord scales should be included in the practice routine as another form of ear training.

The following scales are the chord scales for the key of C major

Note that the fingering for all of the chord scales in the key of C is the same. After the first three keys, the thumb tucks under close to the palm and plays the fourth key making fingers 2,3,4 and 5 available for the rest of the scale. When playing the scale going down, the third finger would cross over the thumb making fingers 2 and 1 available for the last two keys. Listed before the chord is the formal name for that particular chord scale. For ear-training purposes, the initial goal is to familiarize yourself with the unique sound of each chord scale.

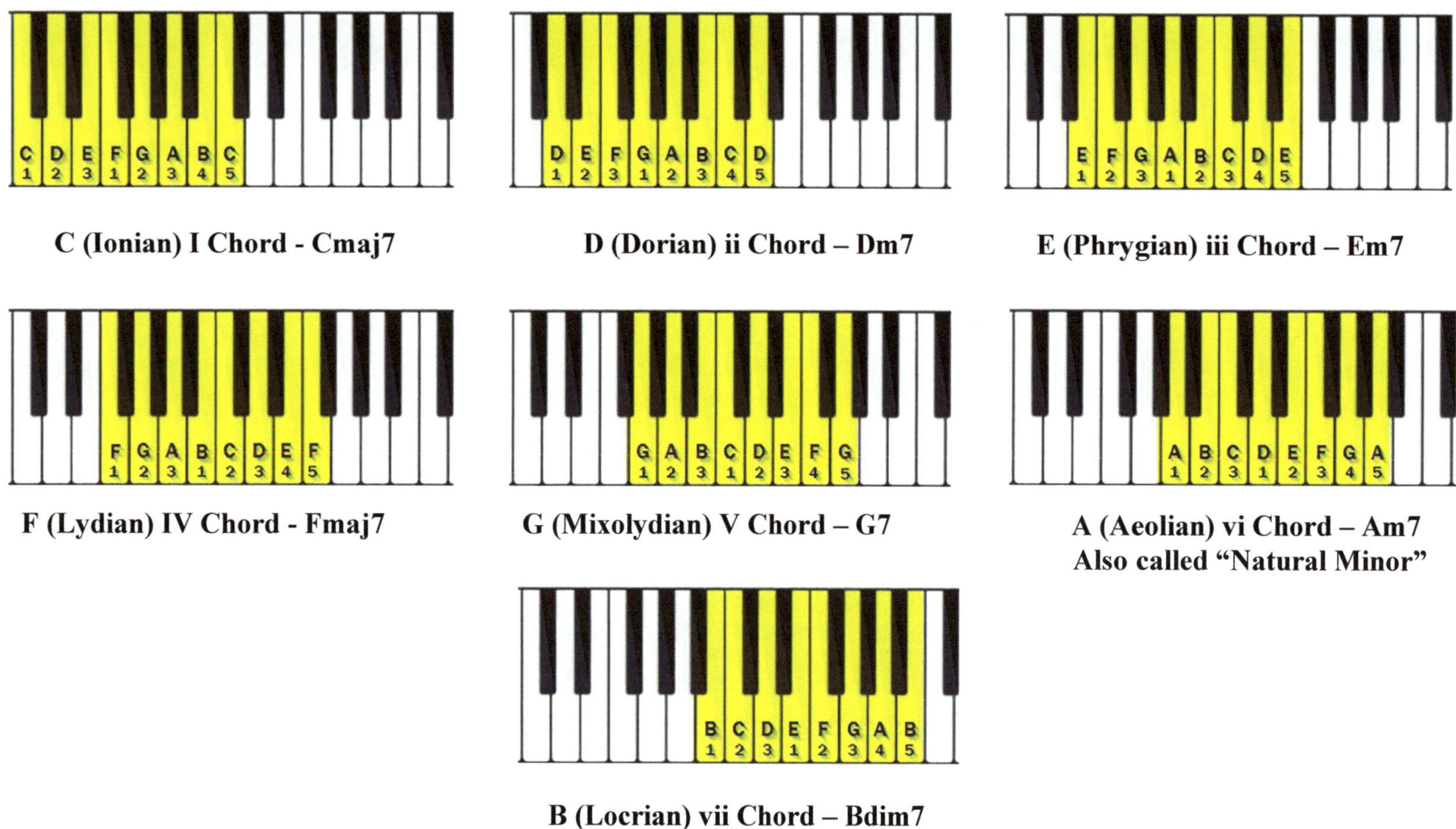

C (Ionian) I Chord - Cmaj7

D (Dorian) ii Chord – Dm7

E (Phrygian) iii Chord – Em7

F (Lydian) IV Chord - Fmaj7

G (Mixolydian) V Chord – G7

A (Aeolian) vi Chord – Am7
Also called "Natural Minor"

B (Locrian) vii Chord – Bdim7

Extended Triad Exercise Using Chord Progressions

One exercise that I highly recommend, is the extended triad exercise. With this exercise, standard chord progressions are rehearsed in all three triad positions. In the following example, the **I-IV-I-V-I** progression is shown.

A: The I chord is played in root position, the IV chord is played in the 2nd inversion, and the V chord is played the 1st inversion.

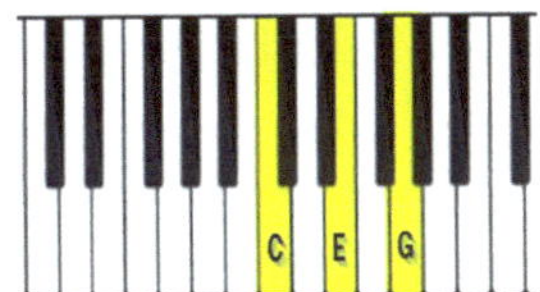 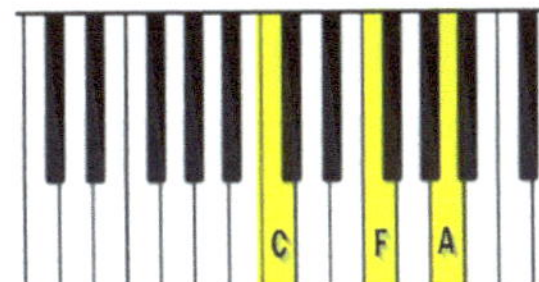 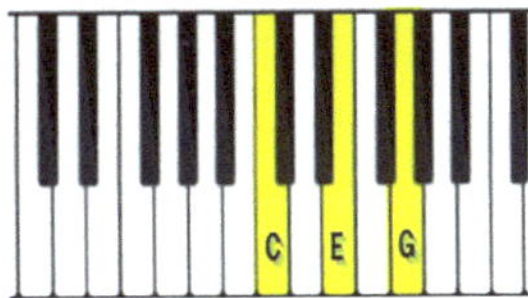 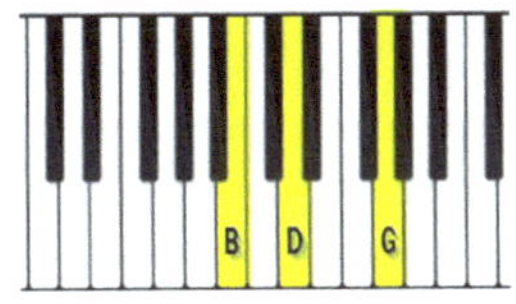 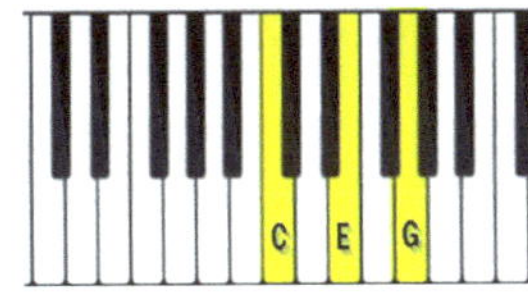

B: The I chord is played in the 1st inversion, the IV chord is played in root position, and the V chord is played the 2nd inversion.

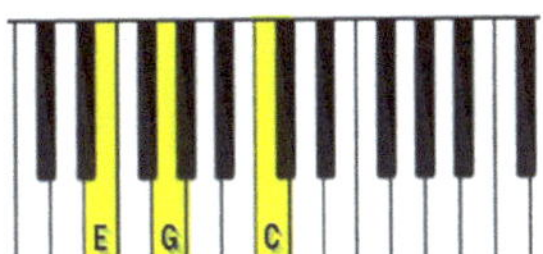 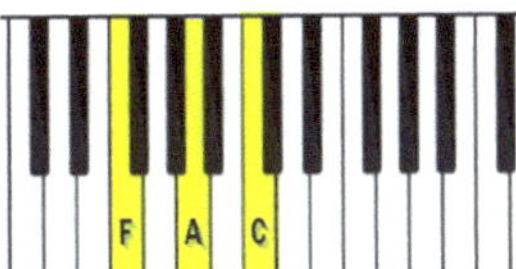 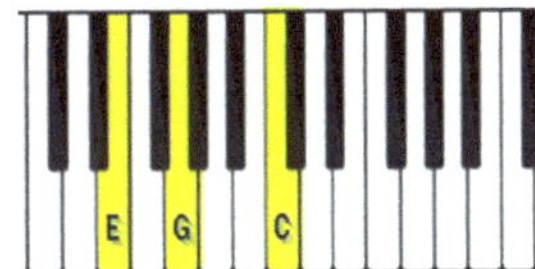 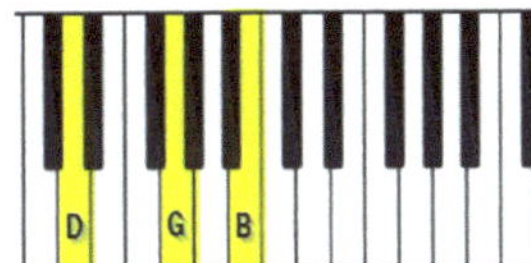 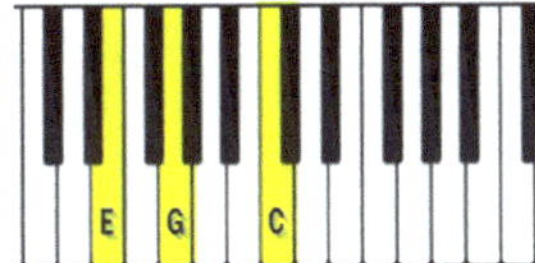

C: the I chord is played in the 2nd inversion, the IV chord is played in 1st inversion and the V chord is played in root position.

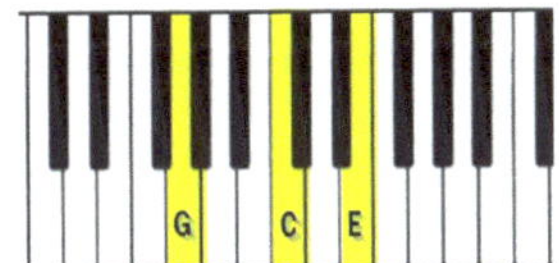 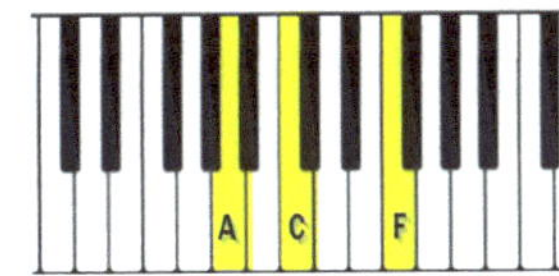 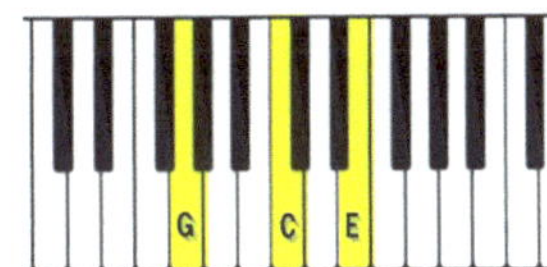 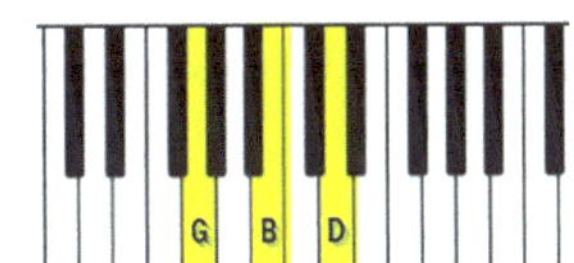 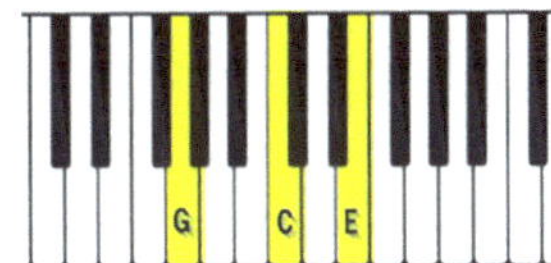

This type of practice will improve the ability to transition between chords smoothly and without hesitation.

"Numbers" – Right Hand Drill
Credit – Jerry Bergonzi, Boston, MA

Practicing "Numbers" will build musical vocabulary so particular melodic patterns will flow naturally when embellishing the accompaniment of a song. To practice numbers, use a chord chart of a song and play beginning with the root using fingers 1,2,3,5. For a C major chord, this would be C, D, E, G. For each chord change, begin with the root of that chords and follow the same pattern, moving through the songs playing the "*numbers*". Below are images of the keys used in a basic "Numbers" drill.

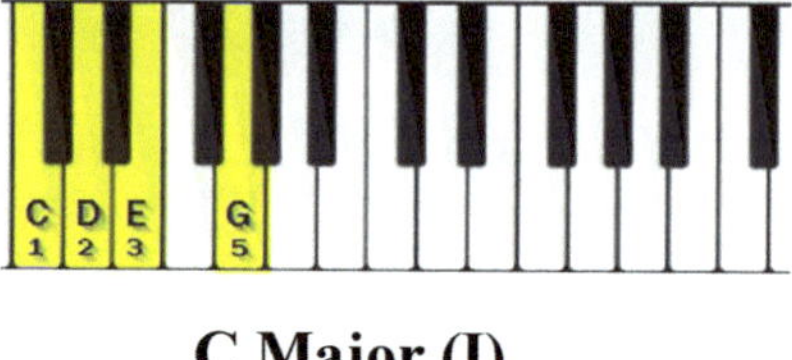

C Major (I)

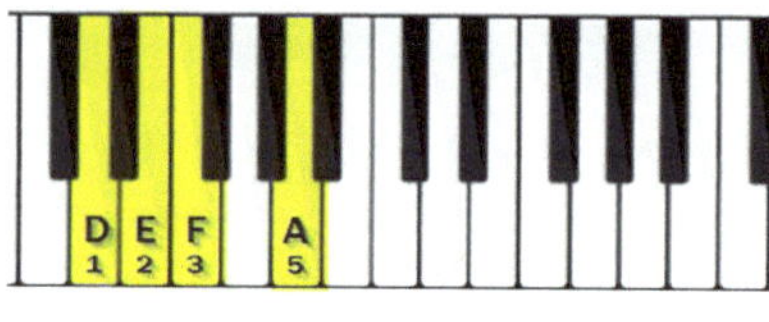

D Minor (ii)

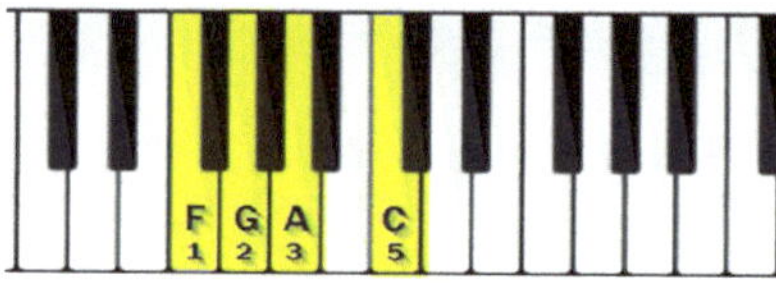

F Major (IV)

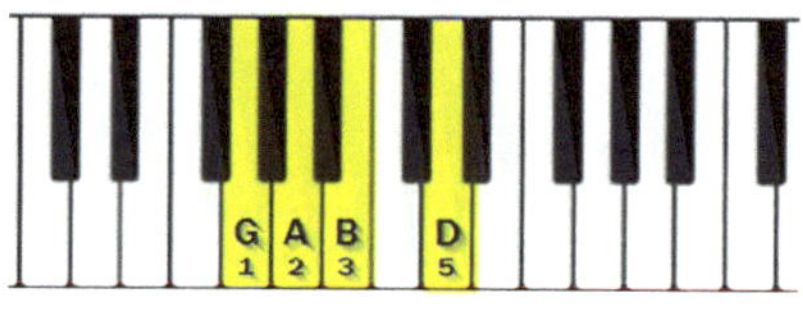

G Major (V)

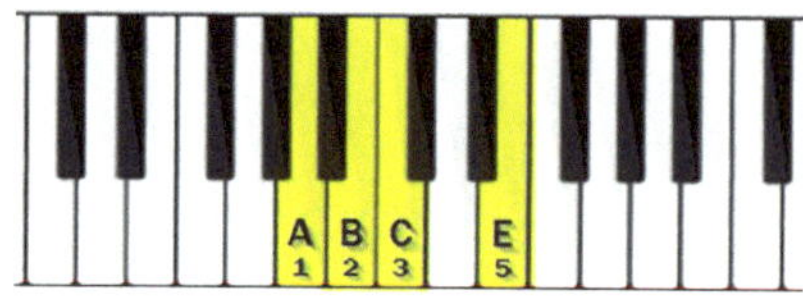

A Minor (vi)

Numbers should be initially played slowly and steadily using a metronome. As familiarity with the patterns develop and the player gains confidence, the tempo should increase. One or two sets per beat can be played depending on the skill of the player. This exercise is an introduction to playing chord scales.

Example: Not Afraid – Chorus

```
1235 1235 1235 1235 1235 1235 1235 1235
C
When I walk through the waters, I won't be overcome

1235 1235 1235 1235 1235 1235 1235 1235
Am
When I go through the rivers, I will not be drowned

1235 1235 1235 1235        1235 1235  1235 1235  1235 1235
F                          Am         G          C
My God will make a way, so I am        not afraid!
```

After mastery is reached with the 1235 pattern, use 5321

```
5321 5321 5321 5321 5321 5321 5321 5321
C
When I walk through the waters, I won't be overcome

5321 5321 5321 5321 5321 5321 53215 5321
Am
When I go through the rivers, I will not be drowned

5321 5321 5321 5321        5321 5321  5321 5321  5321 5321
F                          Am         G          C
My God will make a way, so I am not    afraid
```

Continue with this drill using the patterns of 1325 and 5231.

VL-52

Conclusion

Thank you for your interest in NoNotes Worship Method. My prayer is that NoNotes will provide those who have a passion for worship music, to gain the skills needed to be able to play keys for the purpose of glorifying God, whether that be on a church worship team, or simply at home. I personally feel indescribably close to God when I am experiencing worship music and that only intensifies when I am playing keys. Please feel free to share the PDF version of NoNotes with anybody who is interested in learning to play the piano keyboard who has little to no formal musical training. Book 1 of NoNotes only introduces the keys of C major and A minor. Subsequent books will include additional keys. If there is a need to begin playing quickly, there is a function on most keyboards called "Transpose" that allow the user to change the key so that the correct key is heard, but the player still plays the chords using the same keys as learned in this book. I would **never** recommend using this feature indefinitely as the goal is to be able to play in any key. However, this tool would allow a player to be able to perform earlier in their learning as the experience of playing worship keys is extremely valuable.

Special thanks to Yakie, Blanca, Nithin and Alina for working with me and the valuable feedback that was provided.

Special thanks to The Grace Worship team for modeling the love of Jesus through the support and kindness that they have shown me.

Thank you Ken, for your never-ending patience with me while working on this project.

Thank you Emily and Jessica, for helping me to become more involved with worship and missions. Because of your influences, I have grown closer to God.

Thank you Steve, for being the first person to teach me what "following chord changes" meant.

Renee, you taught me kills that I used to write this book. Thank you!

All profits made from the sale of this book will be donated to ministries within the Christian and Missionary Alliance (CMA).
©2024 by Susan London Hall

"...so that anyone can play."

All profits from the sale of NoNotes methods will be donated to various ministries within the Christian Missionary Alliance (CMA).